A

PENAL CODE

PREPARED BY

THE INDIAN LAW COMMISSIONERS,

AND

PUBLISHED BY COMMAND

OF

The Governor General of India in Council.

REPRINTED FROM THE CALCUTTA EDITION.

THE LAWBOOK EXCHANGE, LTD.
Clark, New Jersey

ISBN 978-1-58477-018-3

Lawbook Exchange edition 2002, 2020

The quality of this reprint is equivalent to the quality of the original work.

THE LAWBOOK EXCHANGE, LTD.
33 Terminal Avenue
Clark, New Jersey 07066-1321

*Please see our website for a selection of our other publications
and fine facsimile reprints of classic works of legal history:*
www.lawbookexchange.com

Library of Congress Cataloging-in-Publication Data

A penal code / prepared by the Indian Law Commissioners, and published
  by command of the Governor General of India in Council.
       p. cm.
    Originally published: London : Pelham Richardson, Cornhill, 1838.
    ISBN 1-58477-018-X
    1.   Criminal law—India. I. Indian Law Commission.
  KNS3794.31835.A52 1999
    345.54—dc21

                                                            99-16486
                                                                 CIP

Printed in the United States of America on acid-free paper

A

PENAL CODE

PREPARED BY

THE INDIAN LAW COMMISSIONERS,

AND

PUBLISHED BY COMMAND

OF

𝕿𝖍𝖊 𝕲𝖔𝖛𝖊𝖗𝖓𝖔𝖗 𝕲𝖊𝖓𝖊𝖗𝖆𝖑 𝖔𝖋 𝕴𝖓𝖉𝖎𝖆 𝖎𝖓 𝕮𝖔𝖚𝖓𝖈𝖎𝖑.

REPRINTED FROM THE CALCUTTA EDITION.

LONDON:

PELHAM RICHARDSON, CORNHILL.

1838.

TABLE OF CONTENTS.

TO THE

RIGHT HON'BLE GEORGE LORD AUCKLAND, C. G. C. B., GOVERNOR GENERAL OF INDIA IN COUNCIL.

My Lord,

The Penal Code which, according to the orders of Government of the 15th of June 1835, we had the honor to lay before your Lordship in Council on the 2d of May last, has now been printed under our superintendence, and has, as well as the Notes, been carefully revised and corrected by us, while in the Press.

The time which has been employed in framing this body of law will not be thought long by any person who is acquainted with the nature of the labour which such works require, and with the history of other works of the same kind. We should however have been able to lay it before your Lordship in Council many months earlier, but for a succession of unfortunate circumstances against which it was impossible to provide. During a great part of the year 1836, the Commission was rendered almost entirely inefficient by the ill-health of a majority of the Members: and we were altogether deprived of the valuable services of our colleague Mr. Cameron, at the very time when those services were most needed.

It is hardly necessary for us to intreat your Lordship in Council to examine with candour the work which we now submit to you. To the ignorant and inexperienced the task in which we have been engaged may appear easy and simple. But the members of the Indian Government are doubtless well aware that it is among the most difficult tasks in which the human mind can be employed; that persons placed in circumstances far more favourable than ours have attempted it with very doubtful success; that the best Codes extant, if malignantly criticised, will be found to furnish matter for censure in every page; that the most copious and precise of human languages furnish but a very imperfect machinery to the legislator; that, in a work so extensive and complicated as that on which we have been employed, there will inevitably be, in spite of the most anxious care, some omissions and some inconsistencies; and that we have done as much as could reasonably be expected from us if we have furnished the Government with that which may, by suggestions from experienced and judicious persons, be improved into a good Code.

Your Lordship in Council will be prepared to find in this performance those defects which must necessarily be found in the first portion of a Code. Such is the relation which exists between the different parts of the law, that no part can be brought to perfection while the other parts remain rude. The Penal Code cannot be clear and explicit while the substantive civil law and the law of procedure are dark and confused. While the rights of individuals and the powers of public functionaries are uncertain, it cannot always be certain whether those rights have been attacked, or those powers exceeded.

Your Lordship in Council will perceive that the system of penal law which we propose is not a digest of any existing system, and that no existing system has furnished us even with a ground work. We trust that your Lordship in Council will not hence infer that we have neglected to enquire, as we are commanded to do by Parliament, into the present state of that part of the law, or that in other parts of our labours we are likely to recommend unsparing innovation, and the entire sweeping away of ancient usages. We are perfectly aware of the value of that sanction which long prescription and national feeling give to institutions. We are perfectly aware that law-givers ought not to disregard even the unreasonable prejudices of those for whom they legislate. So sensible are we of the importance of these considerations, that, though there are not the same objections to innovation in penal legislation as to innovation affecting vested rights of property, yet, if we had found India in possession of a system of criminal law which the people regarded with partiality, we should have been inclined rather to ascertain it, to digest it, and moderately to correct it, than to propose a system fundamentally different.

But it appears to us that none of the systems of penal law established in British India has any claim to our attention, except what it may derive from its own intrinsic excellence. All those systems are foreign. All were introduced by conquerors differing in race, manners, language, and religion from the great mass of the people. The criminal

A

law of the Hindoos was long ago superseded, through the greater part of the Territories now subject to the Company, by that of the Mahomedans, and is certainly the last system of criminal law which an enlightened and humane Government would be disposed to revive. The Mahomedan criminal law has in its turn been superseded, to a great extent, by the British Regulations. Indeed, in the Territories subject to the Presidency of Bombay, the criminal law of the Mahomedans, as well as that of the Hindoos, has been altogether discarded, except in one particular class of cases; and even in such cases, it is not imperative on the Judge to pay any attention to it. The British Regulations, having been made by three different legislatures, contain, as might be expected, very different provisions. Thus in Bengal serious forgeries are punishable with imprisonment for a term double of the term fixed for perjury :* in the Bombay Presidency, on the contrary, perjury is punishable with imprisonment for a term double of the term fixed for the most aggravated forgeries:† in the Madras Presidency, the two offences are exactly on the same footing.‡ In the Bombay Presidency the escape of a convict is punished with imprisonment for a term double of the term assigned to that offence in the two other Presidencies,§ while a coiner is punished with little more than half the imprisonment assigned to his offence in the other two Presidencies. ‖ In Bengal the purchasing of Regimental necessaries from Soldiers is not punishable, except at Calcutta, and is there punishable with a fine of only fifty rupees.¶ In the Madras Presidency it is punishable with a fine of forty rupees.** In the Bombay Presidency it is punishable with imprisonment for four years.†† In Bengal the vending of Stamps without a license is punishable with a moderate fine; and the purchasing of Stamps from a person not licensed to sell them is not punished at all.‡‡ In the Madras Presidency the vendor is punished with a short imprisonment; but there also the purchaser is not punished at all.§§ In the Bombay Presidency, both the vendor and the purchaser are liable to imprisonment for five years, and to flogging.‖‖

Thus widely do the systems of penal law now established in British India differ from each other. Nor can we recommend any one of the three systems as furnishing even the rudiments of a good Code. The penal law of Bengal and of the Madras Presidency is in fact Mahomedan law, which has gradually been distorted to such an extent as to deprive it of all title to the religious veneration of Mahomedans, yet which retains enough of its original peculiarities to perplex and encumber the administration of justice. In substance it now differs at least as widely from the Mahomedan penal law as the penal law of England differs from the penal law of France. Yet technical terms and nice distinctions borrowed from the Mahomedan law are still retained. Nothing is more usual than for the Courts to ask the law officers what punishment the Mahomedan law prescribes in a hypothetical case, and then to inflict that punishment on a person who is not within that hypothetical case, and who by the Mahomedan law would be liable either to a different punishment, or to no punishment. We by no means presume to condemn the policy which led the British Government to retain, and gradually to modify, the system of criminal jurisprudence which it found established in these provinces. But it is evident that a body of law thus formed must, considered merely as a body of law, be defective and inconvenient.

The penal law of the Bombay Presidency is all contained in the Regulations; and is almost all to be found in one extensive Regulation.¶¶ The Government of that Presi-

---

* Bengal Regulation XVII of 1817, Section IX.
† Bombay Regulation XIV of 1827, Sections XVI. and XVII.
‡ Madras Regulation VI of 1811, Section III.
§ Bombay Regulation XIV of 1827, Section XXIV, and Regulation V of 1831, Section I. Bengal Regulation XII of 1818, Sec. V, Cl. 1. Madras Regulation VI of 1822, Sec. V, Cl. 2.
‖ Bombay Regulation XIV of 1827, Section XVIII. Bengal Regulation XVII of 1817, Section IX. Madras Regulation II of 1822, Section V.
¶ Calcutta Rule Ordinance and Regulation passed 21st August, Registered 13th Nov. 1821.
** Madras Regulation XIV of 1832, Section II, Cl. 1.
†† Bombay Regulation XXII of 1827, Section XIX.
‡‡ Bengal Regulation X of 1829, Section IX, Cl. 2.
§§ Madras Regulation XIII of 1816, Section X, Cl. 10.
‖‖ Bombay Regulation XVIII of 1827, Section IX, Cl. 1.
¶¶ Bombay Regulation XIV of 1827.

dency appears to have been fully sensible of the great advantage which much arise from placing the whole law in a written form before those who are to administer, and those who are to obey it ; and, whatever may be the imperfections of the execution, high praise is due to the design. The course which we recommend to the Government, and which some persons may perhaps consider as too daring, has already been tried at Bombay, and has not produced any of those effects which timid minds are disposed to anticipate even from the most reasonable and useful innovations. Throughout a large territory, inhabited to a great extent by a newly conquered population, all the ancient systems of penal law were at once superseded by a Code, and this without the smallest sign of discontent among the people.

It would have given us great pleasure to have found that Code such as we could with propriety have taken as the groundwork of a Code for all India. But we regret to say that the penal law of the Bombay Presidency has, over the penal law of the other Presidencies, no superiority, except that of being digested. In framing it, the principles according to which crimes ought to be classified, and punishments apportioned, have been less regarded than in the legislation of Bengal and Madras. The secret destroying of any property, though it may not be worth a single rupee, is punishable with imprisonment for five years.* Unlawful confinement, though it may last only for a quarter of an hour, is punishable with imprisonment for five years.† Every conspiracy to injure or impoverish any person is punishable with imprisonment for ten years;‡ so that a man who engages in a design as atrocious as the gunpowder plot, and one who is party to a scheme for putting off an unsound horse on a purchaser, are classed together, and are liable to exactly the same punishment. Under this law, if two men concert a petty theft, and afterwards repent of their purpose and abandon it, each of them is liable to twenty times the punishment of the actual theft.§ All assaults which cause a severe shock to the mental feelings of the sufferer are classed with the atrocious crime of rape, and are liable to the punishment of rape, that is, if the Courts shall think fit, to imprisonment for fourteen years.|| The breaking of the window of a house, the dashing to pieces a china cup within a house, the riding over a field of grain in hunting, are classed with the crime of arson, and are punishable, incredible as it may appear, with death. The following is the law on the subject: " Any person who shall wilfully and wrongfully set " fire to or otherwise damage or destroy any part of a dwelling house or building apper- " taining thereto, or property contained in a dwelling house, or building or enclosure " appertaining thereto, or crops standing or reaped in the field, shall be liable to any of " the punishments specified in Section III of this Regulation."¶ The Section to which reference is made contains a list of the punishments authorized by the Bombay Code, and at the head of that list stands death.

But these errors, the effects probably of inadvertence, are not, in our opinion, the most serious faults of the penal Code of Bombay. That Code contains enactments which it is impossible to excuse on the ground of inadvertence, enactments the language of which shews that when they were framed their whole effect was fully understood, and which appear to us to be directly opposed to the first principles of penal law. One of the first principles of penal law is this, that a person who merely conceals a crime after it has been committed ought not to be punished as if he had himself committed it. By the Bombay Code the concealment after the fact of murder is punishable as murder :—the concealment after the fact of gang-robbery is punishable as gang-robbery :**—and this, though the concealment after the fact of the most cruel mutilations, and of the most atrocious robberies committed by not more than four persons, is not punished at all.

If there be any distinction which more than any other it behoves the legislator to bear constantly in mind, it is the distinction between harm voluntarily caused and harm involuntarily caused. Negligence, indeed, often causes mischief, and often deserves punishment. But to punish a man whose negligence has produced some evil which he

---

* Regulation XIV of 1827, Section XLII. Clause 2.
† Regulation XIV of 1827, Section XXXIII. Clause 1.
‡ Regulation XVII of 1828.　　　　　§ Regulation XIV of 1837, Section XXXIX.
|| Regulation XIV of 1827, Section XXIX. Clause 1.
¶ Regulation XIV of 1827, Section XLII. Clause 1.
** Regulation XIV of 1827, Section I. Clause 1.

never contemplated as if he had produced the same evil knowingly, and with deliberate malice, is a course which, as far as we are aware, no jurist has ever recommended in theory, and which we are confident that no society would tolerate in practice. It is, however, provided by the Bombay Code that " the unintentional commission of any act " punishable by that Code shall be punished according to the Court's judgment of the " culpable disregard of injury to others evinced by the person committing the said act, " but the punishment for such unintentional commission shall not exceed that prescribed " for the offence committed."*

We have said enough to shew that it is owing, not at all to the law, but solely to the discretion and humanity of the Judges, that great cruelty and injustice is not daily perpetrated in the Criminal Courts of the Bombay Presidency.

Many important classes of offences are altogether unnoticed by the Bombay Code; and this omission appears to us to be very ill supplied by one sweeping clause, which arms the Courts with almost unlimited power to punish as they think fit offences against morality, or against the peace and good order of society, if those offences are penal by the religious law of the offender.† This clause does not apply to people who profess a religion with which a system of penal jurisprudence is not inseparably connected. And from this state of the law some singular consequences follow. For example, a Mahomedan is punishable for adultery: a Christian is at liberty to commit adultery with impunity.

Such is the state of the penal law in the Mofussil. In the meantime the population which lives within the local jurisdiction of the Courts established by the Royal Charters is subject to the English Criminal law, that is to say, to a very artificial and complicated system,—to a foreign system,—to a system which was framed without the smallest reference to India, - to a system which even in the country for which it was framed is generally considered as requiring extensive reform,—to a system finally which has just been pronounced by a commission composed of able and learned English lawyers to be so defective that it can be reformed only by being entirely taken to pieces and reconstructed.‡

Under these circumstances we have not thought it desirable to take as the groundwork of the Code any of the systems of law now in force in any part of India. We have, indeed, to the best of our ability, compared the Code with all those systems, and we have taken suggestions from all; but we have not adopted a single provision merely because it formed a part of any of those systems. We have also compared our work with the most celebrated systems of Western jurisprudence, as far as the very scanty means of information which were accessible to us in this country enabled us to do so. We have derived much valuable assistance from the French Code, and from the decisions of the French Courts of Justice on questions touching the construction of that Code. We have derived assistance still more valuable from the Code of Louisiana, prepared by the late Mr. Livingston. We are the more desirous to acknowledge our obligations to that eminent jurist, because we have found ourselves under the necessity of combatting his opinions on some important questions.

The reasons for those provisions which appear to us to require explanation or defence will be found appended to the Code in the form of Notes. Should your Lordship in Council wish for fuller information as to the considerations by which we have been guided in framing any part of the law, we shall be ready to afford it.

One peculiarity in the manner in which this Code is framed will immediately strike your Lordship in Council. We mean the copious use of illustrations. These illustrations will, we trust, greatly facilitate the understanding of the law, and will at the same time often serve as a defence of the law. In our definitions we have repeatedly found ourselves under the necessity of sacrificing neatness and perspicuity to precision, and of using harsh expressions because we could find no other expressions which would convey our whole meaning, and no more than our whole meaning. Such definitions standing by themselves might repel and perplex the reader, and would perhaps be fully comprehended only by a few students after long application. Yet such definitions are found,

* Regulation XIV of 1827, Section I, Clause 3.
† Regulation XIV of 1827, Section 1, Clause 1.
‡ Letter to Lord John Russell, from the Commissioners appointed to inquire into the state of the Criminal Law, dated 19th January 1837.

and must be found, in every system of law which aims at accuracy. A legislator may, if he thinks fit, avoid such definitions, and by avoiding them he will give a smoother and more attractive appearance to his workmanship : but in that case he flinches from a duty which he ought to perform, and which somebody must perform. If this necessary but most disagreeable work be not performed by the lawgiver once for all, it must be constantly performed in a rude and imperfect manner by every Judge in the Empire, and will probably be performed by no two Judges in the same way. We have, therefore, thought it right not to shrink from the task of framing these unpleasing but indispensable parts of a Code. And we hope that when each of these definitions is followed by a collection of cases falling under it, and of cases which, though at first sight they appear to fall under it, do not really fall under it, the definition and the reasons which led to the adoption of it will be readily understood. The illustrations will lead the mind of he student through the same steps by which the minds of those who framed the law proceeded, and may sometimes shew him that a phrase which may have struck him as uncouth, or a distinction which he may have thought idle, was deliberately adopted for the purpose of including or excluding a large class of important cases. In the study of geometry it is constantly found that a theorem which, read by itself, conveyed no distinct meaning to the mind, becomes perfectly clear as soon as the reader casts his eye over the statement of the individual case taken for the purpose of demonstration. Our illustration, we trust, will in a similar manner facilitate the study of the law.

There are two things which a legislator should always have in view while he is framing laws : the one is that they should be as far as possible precise ; the other that they should be easily understood. To unite precision and simplicity in definitions intended to include large classes of things, and to exclude others very similar to many of those which are included, will often be utterly impossible. Under such circumstances it is not easy to say what is the best course. That a law, and especially a penal law, should be drawn in words which convey no meaning to the people who are to obey it, is an evil. On the other hand, a loosely worded law is no law, and to whatever extent a legislature uses vague expressions, to that extent it abdicates its functions, and resigns the power of making law to the Courts of Justice.

On the whole, we are inclined to think that the best course is that which we have adopted. We have, in framing our definitions, thought principally of making them precise, and have not shrunk from rugged or intricate phraseology when such phraseology appeared to us to be necessary to precision. If it appeared to us that our language was likely to perplex an ordinary reader, we added as many illustrations as we thought necessary for the purpose of explaining it. The definitions and enacting clauses contain the whole law. The illustrations make nothing law which would not be law without them. They only exhibit the law in full action, and shew what its effects will be on the events of common life.

Thus the Code will be at once a statute book and a collection of decided cases. The decided cases in the Code will differ from the decided cases in the English law books in two most important points. In the first place, our illustrations are never intended to supply any omission in the written law, nor do they ever, in our opinion, put a strain on the written law. They are merely instances of the practical application of the written law to the affairs of mankind. Secondly, they are cases decided not by the judges but by the legislature, by those who make the law, and who must know more certainly than any judge can know what the law is which they mean to make.

The power of construing the law in cases in which there is any real reason to doubt what the law is amounts to the power of making the law. On this ground the Roman jurists maintained that the office of interpreting the law in doubtful matters necessarily belonged to the legislature. The contrary opinion was censured by them with great force of reason, though in language perhaps too bitter and sarcastic for the gravity of a Code. " Eorum vanam subtilitatem tam risimus quam corrigendam esse censuimus. Si " enim in præsenti leges condere soli imperatori concessum est, et leges interpretari solo " dignum imperio esse oportet. Quis legum ænigmata solvere et omnibus aperire ido- " neus esse videbitur nisi is cui legislatorem esse concessum est ? Explosis itaque his " ridiculosis ambiguitatibus tam conditor quam interpres legum solus imperator juste ex- " istimabitur."*

* Cod. Just. Lib. I. Tit. XIV. 12.

The decisions on particular cases which we have annexed to the provisions of the Code resemble the Imperial Rescripts in this, that they proceed from the same authority from which the provisions themselves proceed. They differ from the imperial rescripts in this most important circumstance, that they are not made *ex post facto*, that they cannot therefore be made to serve any particular turn, that the persons condemned or absolved by them are purely imaginary persons, and that, therefore, whatever may be thought of the wisdom of any judgment which we have passed there can be no doubt of its impartiality.

The publication of this collection of cases decided by legislative authority will, we hope, greatly limit the power which the Courts of Justice possess of putting their own sense on the laws. But we are sensible that neither this collection nor any other can be sufficiently extensive to settle every question which may be raised as to the construction of the Code. Such questions will certainly arise, and, unless proper precautions be taken, the decisions on such questions will accumulate till they form a body of law of far greater bulk than that which has been adopted by the legislature. Nor is this the worst. While the judicial system of British India continues to be what it now is, these decisions will render the law not only bulky, but uncertain and contradictory. There are at present eight chief courts subject to the legislative power of your Lordship in Council, four established by Royal Charter, and four which derive their authority from the Company. Every one of these tribunals is perfectly independent of the others. Every one of them is at liberty to put its own construction on the law : and it is not to be expected that they will always adopt the same construction. Under so inconvenient a system there will inevitably be, in the course of a few years, a large collection of decisions diametrically opposed to each other, and all of equal authority.

How the powers and mutual relation of these Courts may be placed on a better footing, and whether it be possible or desirable to have in India a single tribunal empowered to expound the Code in the last resort, are questions which must shortly engage the attention of the Law Commission. But whether the present judicial organization be retained or not, it is most desirable that measures should be taken to prevent the written law from being overlaid by an immense weight of comments and decisions. We conceive that it is proper for us, at the time at which we lay before your Lordship in Council the first part of the Indian Code, to offer such suggestions as have occurred to us on an important subject.

We do not think it desirable that the Indian legislature should, like the Roman Emperors, decide doubtful points of law which have actually been mooted in cases pending before the tribunals. In criminal cases, with which we are now more immediately concerned, we think that the accused party ought always to have the advantage of a doubt on a point of law, if that doubt be entertained after mature consideration by the highest judicial authority, as well as of a doubt on a matter of fact. In civil suits which are actually pending we think it on the whole desirable to leave to the Courts the office of deciding doubtful questions of law which have actually arisen in the course of litigation. But every case in which the construction put by a judge on any part of the Code is set aside by any of those tribunals from which at present there is no appeal in India, and every case in which there is a difference of opinion in a Court composed of several judges as to the construction of any part of the Code, ought to be forthwith reported to the legislature. Every judge of every rank whose duty it is to administer the law as contained in the Code should be enjoined to report to his official superiors every doubt which he may entertain as to any question of construction which may have arisen in his Court. Of these doubts all which are not obviously unreasonable ought to be periodically reported by the highest judicial authorities to the legislature. All the questions thus reported to the Government might with advantage be referred for examination to the Law Commission, if that Commission be a permanent body. In some cases it will be found that the law is already sufficiently clear, and that any misconstruction which may have taken place is to be attributed to weakness, carelessness, wrongheadedness, or corruption on the part of an individual, and is not likely to occur again. In such cases it will be unnecessary to make any change in the Code. Sometimes it will be found that a case has arisen respecting which the Code is silent. In such a case it will be proper to supply the omission. Sometimes it may be found that the Code is inconsistent with itself. If so the inconsistency ought to be removed. Sometimes it will be found that the words of the law are not sufficiently precise. In such a case it will be proper to substitute others. Sometimes it will be found that the language of the law, though it is as precise as the subject admits, is not so clear that a person of ordinary intelligence can see its whole meaning. In these cases it will generally be expedient to add illustrations such as may distinctly shew in what sense the legislature intends the law to be understood, and may render it impossible that the same question or any similar question should ever again occasion difference of opinion. In this manner every successive edition of the Code will solve all the important questions as to the construction of the Code which have arisen since the appearance of the edition immediately preceding. Important questions, particularly questions about which Courts of the highest rank have pronounced opposite decisions, ought to be settled without delay; and no point of law ought to continue to be a doubtful point more than three or four years after it has been mooted in a Court of Justice. An addition of a very few pages to the Code will stand in the place of several volumes of reports, and will be of far more value than such reports, inasmuch as the additions to the Code will proceed from the legislature, and will be of unquestionable authority, whereas the reports would only give the opinions of the Judges which other Judges might venture to set aside.

It appears to us highly desirable that, if the Code shall be adopted, all those penal laws which the Indian Legislature may from time to time find it necessary to pass should be framed in such a manner as to fit into the Code. Their language ought to be that of the Code. No word ought to be used in any other sense than that in which it is used in the Code. The very part of the Code in which the new law is to be inserted ought to be indicated. If the new law rescinds or modifies any provision of the Code that provision ought to be indicated. In fact the new law ought, from the day on which it is passed, to be part of the Code, and to affect all the other provisions of the Code, and to be affected by them as if it were actually a clause of the original Code. In the next edition of the Code the new law ought to appear in its proper place.

For reasons which have been fully stated to your Lordships in Council in another communication we have not inserted in the Code any clause declaring to what places and to what class of persons it shall apply.

Your Lordship in Council will see that we have not proposed to except from the operation of this Code any of the ancient Sovereign houses of India residing within the Company's territories. Whether any exception ought to be made is a question which, without a more accurate knowledge than we possess of existing treaties, of the sense in which those treaties have been understood, of the history of negotiations, of the temper, and of the power of particular families, and of the feeling of the body of the people towards those families, we could not venture to decide. We will only beg permission most respectfully to observe that every such exception is an evil;—that it is an evil that any man should be above the law;—that it is a still greater evil that the public should be taught to regard as a high and enviable distinction the privilege of being above the law;—that the longer such privileges are suffered to last the more difficult it is to take them away;— that there can scarcely ever be a fairer opportunity for taking them away than at the time when the Government promulgates a new Code binding alike on persons of different races and religions;—and that we greatly doubt whether any consideration, except that of public faith solemnly pledged, deserves to be weighed against the advantages of equal justice.

The peculiar state of public feelings in this country may render it advisable to frame the law of procedure in such a manner that families of high rank may be dispensed, as far as possible, from the necessity of performing acts which are here regarded, however unreasonably, as humiliating. But though it may be proper to make wide distinctions as respects form, there ought in our opinion to be, as respects substance, no distinctions except those which the Government is bound by express engagements to make. That a man of rank should be examined with particular ceremonies, or in a particular place, may in the present state of Indian society be highly expedient. But that a man of any rank should be allowed to commit crimes with impunity must in every state of society be most pernicious.

The provisions of the Code will be applicable to offences committed by soldiers, as well as to offences committed by other members of the community. But for those purely military offences which soldiers only can commit we have made no provision. It appears to us desirable that this part of the law should be taken up separately, and we have been given to understand that your Lordship in Council has determined that it shall be so taken up. But we have, as your Lordship in Council will perceive, made provision for punishing persons who, not being themselves subject to martial law, abet soldiers in the breach of Military discipline.

Your Lordship in Council will observe that in many parts of the Penal Code we have referred to the Code of Procedure which as yet is not in existence: and hence it may possibly be supposed to be our opinion that, till the Code of Procedure is framed, the Penal Code cannot come into operation. Such however is not our meaning. We conceive that almost the whole of the Penal Code such as we now lay it before your Lordship might be made law, at least in the Mofussil, without any considerable change in the existing rules of procedure. Should your Lordship in Council agree with us in this opinion, we shall be prepared to suggest those changes which it would be necessary immediately to make.

In conclusion we beg respectfully to suggest that, if your Lordship in Council is disposed to adopt the Code which we have framed, it is most desirable that the native population should, with as little delay as possible, be furnished with good versions of it in their own languages. Such versions, in our opinion, can be produced only by the combined labours of enlightened Europeans and natives: and it is not probable that men competent to execute all the translations which will be required will be found in any single province in India. We are sensible that the difficulty of procuring good translations will be great. But we believe that the means at the disposal of your Lordship in Council are sufficient to overcome every difficulty; and we are confident that your Lordship in Council will not grudge any thing that may be necessary for the purpose of enabling the people who are placed under your care to know what that law is according to which they are required to live.

We have the honor to be,

MY LORD,

Your Lordship's most obedient humble Servants,

T. B. MACAULAY.
J. M. MACLEOD.
G. W. ANDERSON.
F. MILLETT.

INDIAN LAW COMMISSION,
The 14th of October, 1837.

A

PENAL CODE,

ETC. ETC.

CHAPTER I.

GENERAL EXPLANATIONS.

1. Throughout this Code every definition of an offence, every penal provision, and every illustration of every such definition or penal provision, shall be understood subject to the exceptions contained in the Chapter entitled "General Exceptions," though these exceptions are not repeated in such definition, penal provision, or illustration.

Illustration.

Clause 294 contains the following definition of an offence. "Whoever does any act, or omits "what he is legally bound to do, with the intention of thereby causing, or with the knowledge "that he is likely thereby to cause the death of any person, and does by such act or omission cause "the death of any person, is said to commit the offence of voluntary culpable homicide." Here, it is not expressed that a child under seven years of age cannot commit voluntary culpable homicide; but the definition of voluntary culpable homicide is to be understood subject to the general exception contained in Clause 64, which provides that nothing shall be an offence which is done by a child under seven years of age.

2. Every expression which is explained in any part of this Code is used in every part of this Code in conformity with the explanation.

3. Wherever the causing of a certain effect with a certain intention, or with a knowledge of certain circumstances, is an offence, it is to be understood that if more persons than one jointly cause that effect, every one of them who has that intention, or that knowledge, commits that offence.

Illustrations.

(a) A digs a pit, intending or knowing it to be likely that he may thereby cause a person's death. B puts turf over the mouth of the pit, intending or knowing it to be likely that he may thereby cause a person's death. Here, if Z falls in and is killed, both A and B have committed voluntary culpable homicide.

(b) A and B are joint gaolers, and as such have the charge of Z, alternately, for six hours at a time. Each of them, during his time of attendance, illegally omits to furnish Z with food, intending or knowing it to be likely that he may thereby cause Z's death. Z dies of hunger. Both A and B have committed voluntary culpable homicide.

4. Wherever the causing of a certain effect by an act or by an omission is an offence, it is to be understood that the causing of that effect partly by an act and partly by an omission is the same offence.

Illustration.

A voluntarily causes Z's death, partly by illegally omitting to give Z food, and partly by beating Z. A has committed voluntary culpable homicide.

5. The pronoun "he" is used of any person whether male or female.

6. The word "man" denotes a male human being of any age: the word "woman" denotes a female human being of any age.

7. The word "party" denotes collections of persons, as well as persons.

Illustrations.

The Government of India, the Bank of Bengal, the Union Bank, the Asiatic Society are parties.

8. The word "King" denotes as well the Queen Regnant, as the King of the United Kingdom of Great Britain and Ireland.

B

9. The words " Government of India" denote the Executive Government of India, unless it be otherwise expressed.

10. The words " Government of a Presidency" denote the Governor in Council or Deputy Governor in Council of that Presidency, if there be a Council, but if there be no Council, then the Governor or Deputy Governor alone.

11. The word " Presidency" denotes all the territories subject to the Government of a Presidency.

12. The word " Judge" denotes not only every person who is officially designated as a judge, but also every person who is empowered by law to give in any legal proceeding, civil or criminal, a definitive judgment, or a judgment which if not appealed against would be definitive, or a judgment which if confirmed by some other authority would be definitive, or who is one of a body of persons which body of persons is empowered by law to give such a judgment.

Illustrations.

(a) A Collector sitting on a Summary Suit under Regulation VIII. of 1831, of the Bengal Presidency, is a Judge.

(b) A Magistrate sitting on a charge on which he has power to sentence to fine or imprisonment, with or without appeal, is a Judge.

(c) A landholder empowered by Regulation XV. of 1827 of the Bombay Presidency to try persons accused of certain offences, is a Judge.

13. The words " Court of Justice" denote a Judge who is empowered by law to act judicially alone, or a body of Judges which is empowered by law to act judicially as a body, when such Judge or body of Judges is acting judicially.

14. The words " public servant" denote a person falling under any of the descriptions hereinafter following: namely,

First, Every covenanted servant of the East India Company ;

Second, Every commissioned officer, Military or Naval, in the service of the East India Company ;

Third, Every commissioned officer of the King's army, while serving under the Government of India ;

Fourth, Every Judge ;

Fifth, Every Officer of a Court of Justice whose duty it is, as such officer, to investigate or report on any matter of law or fact, or to make, authenticate, or keep any document, or to take charge of any property, or to execute any judicial process, or to administer any oath, or to interpret, or to preserve order in the Court;

Sixth, Every Juryman ;

Seventh, Every Arbitrator to whom any cause has been referred by any Court of Justice ;

Eighth, Every person who holds any office by virtue of which he is empowered to place or keep any person in confinement;

Ninth, Every officer of Police whose duty it is, as such officer, to prevent offences, to give information of offences, to bring offenders to justice, or to protect the public heath, safety, or convenience ;

Tenth, Every officer whose duty it is, as such officer, to take, receive, keep, or expend any property, on behalf of the Government, or to make any survey, assessment, or contract, on behalf of the Government, or to execute any revenue process, or to investigate or to report on any matter affecting the pecuniary interests of the Government, or to make, authenticate, or keep any document relating to the pecuniary interests of the Government, or to prevent the infraction of any law for the protection of the pecuniary interests of the Government ;

Eleventh, Every officer whose duty it is, as such officer, to take, receive, keep, or expend any property for any secular common purpose of any village, town, or district, or to make, authenticate, or keep any document for the ascertaining of the rights of the people of any village, town, or district ;

Twelfth, Every person holding any situation the holders of which have been declared to be public servants by an order of the Government of India, or of the Government of the Presidency under which such situation is held.

Explanations. Persons falling under any of the above descriptions are public servants, whether appointed by the Government or not.

Wherever the words " public servant" occur, they shall be understood of every person who is in actual possession of the situation of a public servant, whatever legal defect there may be in his right to hold that situation.

15. " Wrongful gain" is the gain of property to which the party gaining is not legally entitled.

" Wrongful loss" is the loss of property to which the party losing it is legally entitled.

A party is said to gain wrongfully when such party retains wrongfully, as well as when such party acquires wrongfully. A party is said to lose wrongfully when such party is kept out of property wrongfully, as well as when such party is deprived of property wrongfully.

16. Whoever does any thing with the intention of causing wrongful gain to one party by means of wrongful loss or risk of wrongful loss to another party, is said to do that thing " fraudulently."

17. When property is put into the possession of a person's wife or servant, in trust for that person, it is put into that person's possession if it was not before in his possession, and continues in his possession if it was before in his possession.

18. Property in the possession of a child under twelve years of age, of a lunatic, or of an idiot, if such child, lunatic, or idiot be in the keeping of a guardian, or guardians, is in the possession of such guardian, or guardians.

19. Property is not said to be in the possession of any party other than a person.

Illustrations.

Property is not said to be in the possession of the Government of India, of the Government of Madras, of the Bank of Bengal, of the Agra Bank, of the Asiatic Society, but of the persons who are in trust for those parties.

20. A person is said to " counterfeit" who causes one thing to resemble another thing, intending to deceive by means of that resemblance.

Explanation. It is not essential to counterfeiting that the imitation should be exact.

Illustration.

If the embellishment of a coin be a wreath of forty leaves, and the inscription be KING WILLIAM, a person counterfeits that coin who, with the intention to deceive by means of a resemblance, makes a coin with a wreath of thirty-nine leaves, and the inscription KING WILLIAM.

21. The word " document" is not used to denote any matter except matter the whole, or part whereof is in hand writing, or is meant by the maker thereof to appear to be in hand writing. Therefore a printed hand bill, or a lithographed letter, no part of which was meant by the engraver to be taken for manuscript, is not a document. But a single word, or a single letter, or significant mark, if that word, letter, or mark be in hand writing, or be meant by the maker thereof so to appear, is a document, and is sufficient to make the whole of the matter connected therewith a document, and every part of that matter part of a document.

Illustration.

A promissory note the whole of which is in print, or copper plate, excepting the signature, which is in hand writing, is a document, and the part of the note which is in print or copper plate is part of a document.

22. The words " valuable security" denote a document which is, or purports to be a document whereby any legal right is created, extended, transferred, restricted, extinguished, or released, or whereby any party acknowledges that such party lies under legal liability, or has not a certain legal right.

23. A statement is said to be " made under a sanction which is tantamount to an oath" in each of the three cases hereinafter described ;

First, When it is made by one of the people called Quakers on affirmation received according to law instead of an oath ;

Secondly, When it is made under the sanction of a declaration made according to law by permission of an authority legally competent to require that an oath shall be taken to the same effect with such declaration ;

Thirdly, When it is made after an admonition to speak the truth, which admonition has been given according to law by an authority legally competent to require that an oath to speak the truth shall be taken by the person so admonished.

24. The words " to do a thing" denote omissions, as well as acts.

Illustration.

Clause 67 contains the following general exception :—" Nothing is an offence which a person " does in consequence of being mad or delirious at the time of doing it." A, a gaoler, goes mad, and in consequence of his madness, omits to supply his prisoners with food. The words " thing " done by a person" apply to A's omission, and he has committed no offence.

25. The word " act" denotes as well a series of acts as a single act: the word " omission" denotes as well a series of omissions as a single omission.

26. A person is said to cause an effect " voluntarily," when he causes it by means whereby he intended to cause it, or by means which, at the time of employing those means, he knew to be likely to cause it.

Illustration.

A sets fire, by night, to an inhabited house in a large town, for the purpose of facilitating a robbery, and thus causes the death of a person. Here, A may not have intended to cause death, and may even be sorry that death has been caused by his act: yet if he knew that he was likely to cause death he has caused death voluntarily.

27. The word " offence" denotes a thing made punishable by this Code.

28. The word " illegal" is applicable to every thing which is an offence, or which is contrary to any direction of the law, or which furnishes ground for a civil action : and a person is said to be " legally bound to do" whatever it is illegal in him to omit.

29. The word " injury" denotes any harm whatever illegally caused to any party in body, mind, reputation, or property.

30. The words " free consent" denote a consent given to a party who has not obtained that consent by directly or indirectly putting the consenting party in fear of injury.

31. The words " intelligent consent" denote a consent given by a person who is not, from youth, mental imbecility, derangement, intoxication, or passion, unable to understand the nature and consequences of that to which he gives his consent.

32. The words " a person of Asiatic blood" denote a person whose father, or mother, or grandfather, or grandmother was of Asiatic birth, and, as far as can be discovered, of pure Asiatic extraction.

33. The word " death" denotes the death of a human being, unless it be otherwise expressed.

34. The word " animal" denotes any living creature other than a human being.

35. The word " vessel" denotes any floating thing used for the conveyance by water of human beings, or of property.

36 Wherever the word " year" or the word " month" is used, it is to be understood that the year or the month is to be reckoned according to the British Calendar.

37. The word " Clause" denotes one of those portions of this Code which are distinguished by prefixed numeral figures.

38. The word " herein-before" and the word " herein-after" relate to matter contained within the same Clause in which these words occur.

39. Nothing which falls within any definition of an offence shall be construed as not being an offence, because it does not fall within the title of the Chapter containing that definition.

Illustration.

A illegally imports sugar from Bombay into Bengal. Here, A is within the definition of the offence of smuggling, though A's act may not affect the public Revenue, and though the Chapter by which the offence of smuggling is made punishable is entitled " Of offences relating to the Revenue."

CHAPTER II.*

OF PUNISHMENTS.†

40. The punishments to which offenders are liable under the provisions of this Code are,

First, Death:

Secondly, Transportation:

Thirdly, Imprisonment, which is of two descriptions, viz.

(1) Rigorous;

(2) Simple:

Fourthly, Banishment from the territories of the East India Company :

Fifthly, Forfeiture of property :

Sixthly, Fine.

41. In every case in which sentence of death has been passed, the Government of the Presidency within which the offender has been sentenced may, without the consent of the offender, commute the punishment for any other punishment provided by this Code.

42. In every case in which sentence of transportation for life has been passed, the Government of the Presidency within which the offender has been sentenced may, without the consent of the offender, commute the punishment for imprisonment of either description, or for banishment from the territories of the East India Company, which imprisonment or banishment may be for life, or for any term.

43. In every case in which sentence of imprisonment for a term of seven years, or upwards, has been passed on any offender who is not both of Asiatic birth and of Asiatic blood, it shall be lawful for the Government of the Presidency within which the offender has been sentenced, at any time within two years after the passing of such sentence, to commute the remaining imprisonment, without the consent of the offender, for transportation for a term not exceeding the unexpired term of imprisonment, to which may be added banishment for life, or for any term, from the territories of the East India Company.

44. In every case in which sentence of rigorous imprisonment for a term of one year or upwards, or of imprisonment of any description for a term of two years or upwards, has been passed on any person who is not both of Asiatic birth and of Asiatic blood, it shall be lawful for the Government of the Presidency within which the offender was sentenced, at any time before one third of the imprisonment has been suffered, to commute the remaining imprisonment, without the consent of the offender, for banishment from the territories of the East India Company, which banishment may be either for life or for any term.

45. In every case the Government of the Presidency within which an offender has been sentenced may, with the consent of the offender, commute the punishment for any other punishment provided by this Code, except death.

46. In every case the Government of the Presidency within which an offender has been sentenced may, at any time, remit the whole or any part of the punishment, without conditions, or on any conditions to which the offender has agreed.

47. In every case in which it is provided that an offender shall be punished with imprisonment of either description, it shall be competent to the Court which sentences such offender to direct in the sentence that such imprisonment shall be wholly rigorous, or that such imprisonment shall be wholly simple, or that any part of such imprisonment shall be rigorous and the rest simple.

48. In calculating fractions of terms of imprisonment, imprisonment for life shall be reckoned as equivalent to imprisonment for twenty-four years.

49. In every case in which an offender is sentenced to forfeiture of all property, the

---

* See Note A.

† The mode of inflicting, commuting, and remitting punishments belongs to the law of Procedure.

sentence renders that offender incapable of acquiring any property except for the benefit of the Government.

Illustration.

A, for waging war against the Government of India, is sentenced to forfeiture of all his property. After the sentence A's father dies, leaving an estate which, but for the sentence of forfeiture, would become the property of A. The estate becomes the property of Government.

50. Where no sum is expressed to which a fine may extend the amount of fine to which the offender is liable is unlimited.

51. In every case in which an offender is sentenced to a fine, unless he be also sentenced to death, to imprisonment for life, or to transportation for life, it shall be competent to the Court which sentences such offender to direct by the sentence that, in default of payment of the fine, the offender shall suffer imprisonment for a certain term, which imprisonment shall be in excess of any other imprisonment to which he may have been sentenced.

52. The term for which the Court directs the offender to be imprisoned, in default of payment of a fine, shall not exceed one fourth of the term of imprisonment which is the maximum fixed for the offence, if the offence be punishable with imprisonment as well as fine.

53. The imprisonment which the Court imposes in default of payment of a fine may be of any description to which the offender might have been sentenced for the offence.

54. If the offence be not punishable with imprisonment, as well as fine, the term for which the Court directs the offender to be imprisoned in default of payment of fine shall not exceed seven days, and the imprisonment shall be simple imprisonment.

55. The imprisonment which is imposed in default of payment of a fine shall terminate whenever that fine is either paid, or levied by process of law.

56. If, before the expiration of the term of imprisonment fixed in default of payment, such a proportion of the fine be paid or levied that the term of imprisonment suffered in default of payment is not less than proportional to the part of the fine still unpaid, the imprisonment shall terminate.

Illustration.

A is sentenced to a fine of one hundred rupees, and to four months imprisonment in default of payment. Here, if seventy-five rupees of the fine be paid or levied before the expiration of one month of the imprisonment, A will be discharged as soon as the first month has expired. If seventy-five rupees be paid or levied at the time of the expiration of the first month, or at any later time while A continues in imprisonment, A will be immediately discharged. If fifty rupees of the fine be paid or levied before the expiration of two months of the imprisonment, A will be discharged as soon as the two months are completed. If fifty rupees be paid or levied at the time of the expiration of those two months, or at any later time while A continues in imprisonment, A will be immediately discharged.

57. The fine, or any part thereof which remains unpaid, may be levied at any time within six years after the passing of the sentence, and if under the sentence the offender be liable to imprisonment for a longer period than six years, then at any time previous to the expiration of that period; and the death of the offender does not discharge from the liability any property which would, after his death, be legally liable for his debts.

58. Whenever any person, by doing any thing whereby he commits an offence falling under one penal provision of this Code, also commits an offence under another penal provision of this Code, the punishment shall not be cumulative, unless it be so expressly provided.

Illustration.

A strikes Z with violence, knowing it to be likely that he may thereby break Z's arm, and does break Z's arm. Here A commits an assault. He also by the same act commits the offence of voluntarily causing grievous hurt. But A is not liable to punishment both for assault, and for voluntarily causing grievous hurt.

59. Where it is provided that punishment shall be cumulative, that provision does not authorize the combining in any case of the punishments provided by more than two penal provisions of this Code.

60. Where any thing which is an offence is made up of parts, any of which parts is itself an offence, the offender shall not be punished with the punishment of more than one of such his offences, unless it be so expressly provided.

Illustrations.

(a) A gives Z fifty strokes with a stick. Here, A may have committed the offence of voluntarily causing hurt to Z by the whole beating, and also by each of the blows which make up the whole beating. If A were liable to punishment for every blow, he might be imprisoned for fifty years, one for each blow. But he is liable only to one punishment for the whole beating, that is to say, to imprisonment for a term not exceeding one year, if the hurt which he has voluntarily caused is not grievous, and for a term not exceeding ten years, nor less than six months, if the hurt which he has voluntarily caused is grievous.

(b) But if, while A is beating Z, Y interferes, and A strikes Y, here, as the blow given to Y is no part of the act whereby A voluntarily causes hurt to Z, A is liable to one punishment for voluntarily causing hurt to Z, and to another for the blow given to Y.

61. In all cases in which judgment is given in the manner prescribed in the law of procedure that a person is guilty of an offence, but that it is doubtful under which of certain penal provisions of this Code he is punishable, the offender shall be liable to be punished with whatever punishment is common to the penal provisions between which the doubt lies, and if imprisonment is common to the penal provisions between which the doubt lies, and any one of those provisions admits of simple imprisonment, the offender may be sentenced to simple imprisonment.

Illustrations.

(a) Judgment is given in the manner prescribed in the law of procedure that A is guilty either of murdering Z, or of previously abetting by aid the murder of Z. The punishment of murder, and that of previously abetting murder by aid, are the same. A is therefore liable to that punishment.

(b) Judgment is given in the manner prescribed in the law of procedure that A has committed an offence, but that it is doubtful whether that offence be theft or criminal breach of trust. Theft is punishable with rigorous imprisonment for three years, or fine, or both; criminal breach of trust is punishable with imprisonment of either description for the same term, or fine, or both. A is therefore liable to fine, which is common to both the penal provisions, and to rigorous imprisonment for three years, which is common to both the penal provisions. But he may be sentenced to simple imprisonment because one of the penal provisions admits of simple imprisonment.

(c) Judgment is given in the manner prescribed in the law of procedure that A has committed either theft, or criminal misappropriation of property not in possession. Here, as the punishment of fine is common to theft and to criminal misappropriation of property not in possession, A is liable to fine. Theft is punishable with imprisonment for a term which may extend to three years; criminal misappropriation of property not in possession is punishable with imprisonment for a term which may extend to two years. Imprisonment for two years is therefore common to both, and A may be punished with imprisonment for a term not exceeding two years. The imprisonment in both cases may be rigorous. A's imprisonment may therefore be rigorous. But the imprisonment for criminal misappropriation of property not in possession may be simple. Therefore A is liable to imprisonment of either description.

CHAPTER III.*

GENERAL EXCEPTIONS.

62. Nothing is an offence which is done by a person who is or in good faith believes himself to be commanded by law to do it.

Illustrations.

(a) A, a Soldier, fires on a mob, by the order of his superior Officer, in conformity with the commands of the law. A has committed no offence.

(b) A, an officer of a Court of Justice, being ordered by that Court to arrest Y, and being led into a belief that Z is Y, arrests Z, believing in good faith that in arresting Z he is obeying an order which he is commanded by law to obey. Here A may, under certain circumstances, be liable to a civil action, but he has committed no offence.

63. Nothing is an offence which is done by a person in the exercise, to the best of his judgment exerted in good faith, of any power given to him by law.

Illustration.

A sees Z commit what appears to A to be a murder. A in the exercise, to the best of his judgment exerted in good faith, of the power which the law gives to all persons of apprehending murderers in the fact, seizes Z, in order to bring Z before the proper authorities. A has committed no offence.

* See Note B.

64. Nothing is an offence which is done by a child under seven years of age.

65. Nothing is an offence which is done by a child above seven years of age and under twelve, who has not attained sufficient maturity of understanding to judge of the nature and consequences of his conduct on that occasion.

66. Nothing is an offence which is done by a person in a state of idiotcy.

67. Nothing is an offence which a person does in consequence of being mad or delirious at the time of doing it.

68. Nothing is an offence which a person does in consequence of being, at the time of doing it, in a state of intoxication, provided that either the substance which intoxicated him was administered to him without his knowledge, or against his will, or that he was ignorant that it possessed any intoxicating quality.

69. Nothing which is not intended to cause death, and which is not known by the doer to be likely to cause death, is an offence by reason of any harm which it may cause, or be intended by the doer to cause, or be known by the doer to be likely to cause to any person above twelve years of age who has given a free and intelligent consent, whether express or implied, to suffer that harm, or to take the risk of that harm, such consent not having been obtained by wilful misrepresentation on the part of the person who does the thing.

Illustrations.

(*a*) A, a dentist, offers Z, a person of ripe age and sound mind, a price for Z's teeth, and without any wilful misrepresentation, obtains Z's consent to the drawing of Z's teeth. A draws Z's teeth. Here, though A's act falls under the definition of the offence of voluntarily causing hurt, A has committed no offence.

(*b*) A converts Z, a person of ripe age and sound mind, to the Mahomedan religion, and, without any wilful misrepresentation, obtains Z's consent to be circumcised. A circumcises Z. A has committed no offence.

(*c*) A and Z agree to fence with each other for amusement. If this agreement implies the consent of each to suffer any harm which, in the course of such fencing, may be caused without foul play, then if A, while playing fairly, hurts Z, A has committed no offence.

(*d*) A, a friend of Z, calls at Z's house, in Z's absence, and writes and seals several letters there with Z's paper and wax, without asking any person's permission. Here, if the acquaintance between A and Z be such that, according to the usages of society, the consent of Z to such use of his property must be implied thence, A has committed no offence.

70. Nothing which is not intended to cause death is an offence by reason of any harm which it may cause, or be intended by the doer to cause, or be known by the doer to be likely to cause to any person for whose benefit it is done, in good faith, and who has given a free and intelligent consent, whether express or implied, to suffer that harm, or to take the risk of that harm, such consent not having been obtained by wilful misrepresentation on the part of the person who does the thing.

Illustration.

A, a surgeon, knowing that a particular operation is likely to cause the death of Z, who suffers under a painful complaint, but not intending to cause Z's death, and intending in good faith Z's benefit, performs that operation on Z, by Z's free and intelligent consent, not having obtained that consent by misrepresentation. A has committed no offence.

71. Nothing which is done in good faith for the benefit of a person who is under twelve years of age, or of unsound mind, by that person's lawful guardian or guardians, or by the authority of such lawful guardian or guardians, is an offence by reason of any harm which it may cause to that person:

Provided,

First, That this exception shall not extend to the intentional causing of death, or to the attempting to cause death ;

Secondly, That this exception shall not extend to the doing of any thing which the person doing it knows to be likely to cause death, for any purpose other than the preventing of death or grievous hurt;

Thirdly, That this exception shall not extend to the voluntary causing of grievous hurt, or to the attempting to cause grievous hurt, unless it be for the purpose of preventing death or grievous hurt, or in the performance of the rite of circumcision ;

Fourthly, That this exception shall not extend to rape, or to the gratification of unnatural lust, or to the attempting to commit rape or to gratify unnatural lust;

Fifthly, That this exception shall not extend to the abetment, either previous or subsequent, of any offence, to the committing of which offence it would not extend.

Illustrations.

(*a*) A, a parent, whips his child moderately, for the child's benefit. A has committed no offence.

(*b*) A confines his child, for the child's benefit. A has committed no offence.

(*c*) A, in good faith, for his daughter's benefit, intentionally kills her to prevent her from falling into the hands of Pindarries. A is not within the exception.

(*d*) A, in good faith, for his child's benefit, without his child's consent, has his child cut for the stone, knowing it to be likely that the operation will cause the child's death, but not intending to cause the child's death. A has committed no offence, inasmuch as his object was the preventing of death or grievous hurt to the child.

(*e*) A, in good faith, for his child's pecuniary benefit, emasculates his child. Here, inasmuch as A has caused grievous hurt to the child for a purpose other than the preventing of death or grievous hurt to the child, A is not within the exception.

(*f*) A, intending in good faith the pecuniary benefit of Z, his daughter, a child under twelve years of age, abets a rape committed by B on Z. Neither A nor B is within the exception.

72. Nothing is an offence by reason of any harm which it may cause to a person for whose benefit it is done in good faith, even without that person's consent, if the circumstances are such that it is impossible for that person to signify consent, or if that person is in such a state of mind as to be incapable of intelligent consent,* and has no legal guardian to whom it is possible to apply for authority :

Provided,

First, That this exception shall not extend to the intentional causing of death, or to the attempting to cause death ;

Secondly, That this exception shall not extend to the doing of any thing which the person doing it knows to be likely to cause death, for any purpose other than the preventing of death or grievous hurt ;

Thirdly, That this exception shall not extend to the voluntary causing of hurt, or to the attempting to cause hurt for any purpose other than the preventing of death or hurt ;

Fourthly, That this exception shall not extend to rape, or to the gratification of unnatural lust, or to the attempting to commit rape or to gratify unnatural lust ;

Fifthly, That this exception shall not extend to the abetment, either previous or subsequent, of any offence to the committing of which offence it would not extend.

Illustrations.

(*a*) Z is thrown from his horse, and is insensible. A, a surgeon, finds that Z requires to be trepanned. A, not intending Z's death, but in good faith, for Z's benefit, performs the trepan before Z recovers his power of judging for himself. A has committed no offence.

(*b*) Z is carried off by a tiger. A fires at the tiger, knowing it to be likely that the shot may kill Z, but not intending to kill Z, and in good faith intending Z's benefit. The tiger drops Z. It appears that A's ball has given Z a mortal wound. Nevertheless, A has committed no offence.

(*c*) A, a surgeon, sees a child suffer an accident, which is likely to prove fatal unless an operation be immediately performed. There is not time to apply to the child's legal guardians. A performs the operation, in spite of the entreaties of the child, intending in good faith the child's benefit. A has committed no offence.

(*d*) A is in a house which is on fire, with Z, a child. People below hold out a blanket. A drops the child from the house-top, knowing it to be likely that the fall may kill the child, but not intending to kill the child, and intending in good faith the child's benefit. Here, even if the child is killed by the fall, A has committed no offence.

73. Nothing is an offence by reason that it causes, or that it is intended to cause, or that it is known to be likely to cause any harm, if that harm is so slight that no person of ordinary sense and temper would complain of such harm.

Illustrations.

(*a*) A gets into a public carriage in which Z is sitting, and in seating himself slightly hurts Z by pressing him against the side of the carriage. Here, though A's act falls within the definition in Clause 316, yet if the whole harm caused was so slight that no man of ordinary sense and temper would complain of such harm, A has committed no offence.

(*b*) A, a servant in Z's house, having occasion to write a letter, dips a pen in ink, the property of Z. Here, though the act of A may fall under the definition of theft, A has committed no offence.

OF THE RIGHT OF PRIVATE DEFENCE.

74. Every person has a right, subject to the restrictions contained in the next following Clause, to defend,

First, His own body, and the body of every other person against every assault;

---

* For the definition of intelligent consent see Clause 31.

C

Secondly, His own property, and the property of every other person against every act which is an offence falling under the definition of theft, robbery, mischief, or criminal trespass, or which is an attempt to commit theft, robbery, mischief, or criminal trespass.

75. There is no right of private defence against an act done by a public servant who is legally competent, as such public servant, to do that act, though that act may be an offence in that public servant, or against an act done by the direction of a public servant, or body of public servants, legally competent, as such public servant, or as such body, to direct that act to be done, though the directing that act to be done may be an offence.

There is no right of private defence in cases in which there is time to have recourse to the protection of the public authorities, in the manner indicated in the Code of Criminal Procedure.

The right of private defence in no case extends to the inflicting of more harm than it is necessary to inflict for the purpose of defence.

Illustrations.

(a) Z, a public servant legally competent to arrest persons as being suspected of certain offences, arrests A maliciously, not having any ground to suspect A of any such offence. Here Z commits an offence. But as Z is legally competent to arrest A, A has no right of private defence against Z.

(b) A, a powerful man, well armed, finds Z, an unarmed boy, breaking into his house at night. A knows that he can defend his property against Z without killing Z. A kills Z. A has exceeded the right of private defence.

76. The right of private defence of the body extends, under the restrictions mentioned in the Clause last preceding, to the voluntary causing of death or of any other harm to the assailant, if the assault which occasions the exercise of the right be of any of the descriptions hereinafter enumerated; namely,

First, Such an assault as may reasonably cause the apprehension that death will otherwise be the consequence of such assault;

Secondly, Such an assault as may reasonably cause the apprehension that grievous hurt will otherwise be the consequence of such assault;

Thirdly, An assault with the intention of committing rape;

Fourthly, An assault with the intention of gratifying unnatural lust;

Fifthly, An assault with the intention of kidnapping;

Sixthly, An assault with the intention of wrongfully confining any person, under circumstances which may reasonably cause it to be apprehended that the wrongful confinement will be such as is punishable by this Code with imprisonment for a term exceeding one year.

77. If the assault be not of any of the descriptions enumerated in the clause last preceding, the right of private defence of the body does not extend to the voluntary causing of death to the assailant, but does extend, under the restrictions mentioned in Clause 75, to the voluntary causing to the assailant of any harm other than death.

78. The right of private defence of the body commences as soon as the danger to the body commences, though no assault may yet have been committed, and continues as long as the danger to the body continues.

79. The right of private defence of property extends, under the restrictions mentioned in Clause 75, to the voluntary causing of death or of any other harm to the wrongdoer, if the offence, the committing of which, or the attempting to commit which, occasions the exercise of the right, be an offence of any of the descriptions hereinafter enumerated; namely,

First, Robbery;

Secondly, House-breaking by night;

Thirdly, Mischief by fire committed on any building, tent, or vessel, which building, tent, or vessel is used as a human dwelling;

Fourthly, Theft, mischief, or house-trespass under such circumstances as may reasonably cause apprehension that death or grievous hurt would otherwise be the consequence of such theft, mischief, or house-trespass.

80. If the offence the committing of which, or the attempting to commit which, occasions the exercise of the right of private defence, be theft, mischief, or criminal trespass, not of any of the descriptions enumerated in the Clause last preceding, that right does not extend to the voluntary causing of death, but does extend, subject to the restrictions

mentioned in Clause 75, to the voluntary causing to the wrong doer of any harm other than death.

81. The right of private defence of property commences when the danger to the property commences.

The right of private defence of property against theft or robbery continues till either the offender has effected his retreat with the property, or the property has been recovered.

The right of private defence of property against criminal trespass or mischief continues as long as the offender continues in the commission of criminal trespass or mischief.

The right of private defence of property against house-breaking by night continues as long as the house-trespass which has been begun by such house-breaking continues.

82. When an act which would otherwise be a certain offence is not that offence by reason of the youth, the idiotcy, the madness, the delirium, or the intoxication of the person doing that act, or by reason of any misconception on the part of that person, every person has the same right of private defence against that act which he would have if that act were that offence.

Illustrations.

(a) Z, under the influence of madness, attempts to kill A. Z is guilty of no offence. But A has the same right of private defence which he would have if Z were sane.

(b) A enters by night a house which he is legally entitled to enter. Z, in good faith taking A for a house breaker, attacks A. Here Z, by attacking A under this misconception, commits no offence. But A has the same right of private defence against Z which he would have if Z were acting under no misconception.

83. In cases in which there is a right of private defence extending to the voluntary causing of death to the person whose act renders defence necessary, if the defender be so situated that he cannot effectually exercise that right without risk of harm to an innocent person, his right of private defence extends to the running of that risk.

Illustration.

A is attacked by a mob who attempt to murder him. He cannot effectually exercise his right of private defence without firing upon the mob, and he cannot fire without risk of harming young children who are mingled with the mob. A has a right to fire.

84. Nothing is an offence which is an exercise of the right of private defence, or which would be an exercise of the right of private defence if the circumstances under which it is done were such as the person who does it believes in good faith that they are.

Illustration.

Z, intending to frighten A by way of jest, stops A in the highway, and demands his money. A, believing in good faith that Z is a robber, and not knowing that he may save himself from being robbed without killing Z, kills Z. A has committed no offence.

CHAPTER IV.

OF ABETMENT.

85. Abetment is of two kinds, previous abetment, and subsequent abetment.

86. A person is said previously to abet the doing of a thing who,

First, Instigates any person to do that thing; or,

Secondly, Engages in any conspiracy for the doing of that thing; or,

Thirdly, Aids by any act or by any illegal omission the doing of that thing; or,

Fourthly, Conceals by any act or by any illegal omission the existence of a design to do that thing, intending or knowing it to be likely that he may, by such concealment, facilitate the doing of that thing.

Explanation. A person may previously abet the doing of a thing in any one of the four ways hereinbefore mentioned, though the thing abetted be not done.

87. A person is said previously to abet an offence, who previously abets the doing of a thing which is an offence, not being under any misconception such that if a person

being under that misconception did that thing, the doing of that thing would not be an offence.

A aids B to take a horse out of Z's possession. Here if B took the horse fraudulently B is guilty of theft. But if A aided B, believing that B had a right to take the horse, A is not said to have abetted the theft committed by B, though he has abetted the taking of the horse.

88. Whoever previously abets any offence by instigating any person to commit that offence shall, if that offence is committed by that person in consequence of that instigation, be punished with the punishment provided for that offence.

Explanation. Such instigation as is hereinbefore described being an offence, the successful instigating to such instigation is also an offence punishable in the same manner.

A instigates B to instigate C to commit a theft. C commits the theft in consequence of the instigation. A and B are liable to the punishment of theft.

89. If any person by doing any thing whereby he commits an offence under the last preceding Clause, also commits an offence under any Clause contained in any other Chapter of this Code, the punishment shall be cumulative.

A by putting B in fear of death, induces B to burn a stack of corn belonging to Z. Here, A is liable both to the punishment provided for burning such a stack of corn, and to the punishment of criminally putting B in fear of death.

90. Whoever, by instigation attended with the actual delivery of a bribe, previously abets any offence punishable with imprisonment, shall be punished with imprisonment of any description provided for that offence, for a term which may extend to one fourth part of the longest term provided for that offence, or such fine as is provided for that offence, or both.

A causes money to be paid to B, in order to induce B to give false evidence. Here, whether B gives the false evidence or not, A has committed the offence defined in this Clause.

91. Whoever, by instigation attended with the threat of causing any injury, previously abets any offence punishable with imprisonment, shall be punished with imprisonment of any description provided for that offence, for a term which may extend to one fourth part of the longest term provided for that offence, or such fine as is provided for that offence, or both.

92. If any person by doing any thing whereby he commits an offence under the last preceding Clause, also commits an offence under any Clause contained in any other Chapter of this Code, the punishment shall be cumulative.

93. Whoever, being present while any offence punishable with rigorous imprisonment for a term of one year or upwards is committed, previously abets that offence by instigating the offender to persist in the commission of that offence, shall be punished with imprisonment of either description for a term which may extend to one fourth part of the longest term provided for that offence, or fine, or both.

94. Whoever previously abets any offence by instigating the public generally, or any number or class of persons exceeding ten, to the commission of that offence, shall be punished with imprisonment of either description for a term which may extend to three years, or fine, or both.

(*a*) A affixes in a public place a placard, exhorting the members of a sect to meet at a certain time and place, for the purpose of attacking the members of an adverse sect, while engaged in a procession. A has committed the offence defined in this Clause.

(*b*) A inserts in a newspaper an article advising soldiers to shoot every Commanding Officer who uses them harshly. A has committed the offence defined in this Clause.

95. Whoever previously abets any offence, by engaging in any conspiracy for the commission of that offence, shall, if that offence is committed in pursuance of that conspiracy, be punished with the punishment provided for that offence.

Explanation. It is not necessary to bring a person within this Clause that he should have concerted the offence with the person who has committed the offence. It is sufficient that he was engaged in the conspiracy in pursuance of which the offence has been committed.

Illustration.

B concerts with C a plan for poisoning Z. It is agreed that C shall administer the poison. B then explains the plan to A without mentioning C's name. A agrees to procure the poison. C administers the poison. Z dies in consequence. Here though A and C have not conspired together, yet A has been engaged in the conspiracy in pursuance of which Z has been murdered. A has therefore committed the offence defined in this Clause, and is liable to the punishment of murder.

96. Whoever previously abets any offence punishable with imprisonment, by engaging in a conspiracy to commit that offence, shall, if any act or any illegal omission takes place in pursuance of that conspiracy, and in order to the committing of that offence, be punished with imprisonment of any description provided for that offence, for a term which may extend to one fourth part of the longest term provided for that offence, or such fine as is provided for that offence, or both.

Illustration.

A and B conspire to poison Z. A in pursuance of this conspiracy, and in order to the poisoning of Z, buys poison. Here, both A and B have committed the offence defined in this Clause. If they had murdered Z, and had been sentenced to imprisonment for doing so, the imprisonment would have been rigorous, and for life. Therefore, under Clause 48, each of them is liable to. rigorous imprisonment for a term which may extend to six years.

97. Whoever previously abets any offence by doing any act, or omitting what he is legally bound to do, with the intention of aiding the commission of that offence, shall, if that offence is committed, be punished with the punishment provided for that offence.

Illustrations.

(a) A keeps watch in the street, with the intention of securing B from interruption while B breaks into a house by night. A has committed the offence defined in this Clause.

(b) A, a servant hired to take charge of his master's plate, illegally omits to lock the plate up, with the intention of thereby rendering it easier for B to steal the plate. B steals the plate. A has committed the offence defined in this Clause.

(c) A, a police officer, directed by law to prevent the commission of robberies, sees B committing a robbery, and passing by without interfering, intending to facilitate the robbery by thus illegally omitting to perform his duty. A has committed the offence defined in this Clause.

98. Wherever in an attempt to commit an offence, or in the commission of an offence, or in consequence of the commission of an offence, a different offence is committed, then whoever by instigation, conspiracy, or aid, was a previous abettor of the first mentioned offence shall be liable to the punishment of the last mentioned offence, if the last mentioned offence were such as the said abettor knew to be likely to be committed in the attempt to commit the first mentioned offence, or in the commission of the first mentioned offence, or in consequence of the commission of the first mentioned offence ; and if both offences be actually committed, and the person who has committed them be liable to cumulative punishment, the abettor shall also be liable to cumulative punishment.

Illustrations.

(a) B, with arms, breaks into an inhabited house at midnight, for the purpose of robbery. A watches at the door. B being resisted by Z, one of the inmates, murders Z. Here, if A considered murder as likely to be committed by B in the attempt to rob the house, or in the robbing of the house, or in consequence of the robbing of the house, A is liable to the punishment provided for murder.

(b) A instigates B to resist a distress. B, in consequence, resists that distress. In offering the resistance B voluntarily causes grievous hurt to the officer executing the distress. As B has committed both the offence of resisting legal process and the offence of voluntarily causing grievous hurt, B is liable to cumulative punishment for these offences ; and if A knew that B was likely voluntarily to cause grievous hurt in resisting the distress, A will also be liable to cumulative punishment.

99. Whoever, by instigation, conspiracy, or aid, previously abets an offence, if in consequence of that instigation, or in pursuance of that conspiracy, or with that aid, an offence is committed which would be a different offence but for some misconception on the part of the doer from which misconception the abettor is free, or but for some intention or knowledge on the part of the doer, which intention or knowledge the abettor does not know that the doer has, shall be liable to the same punishment to which he would have been liable if no such misconception, intention, or knowledge had existed on the part of the doer.

Illustrations.

(a) A makes preparations for the burning of Z, a Hindoo widow, believing that she has given a free consent to be burned. Here, A previously abets by aid the offence of voluntary culpable homicide by consent. If the preparations which A has made are subsequently used, without A's knowledge, for the purpose of putting Z to death without her consent, those who so use them are guilty of murder. But A is liable only to the punishment to which he would have been liable if voluntary culpable homicide by consent had been committed.

(b) A instigates B to commit mischief on certain property which B believes to be worth less than five rupees, but which A knows to be worth more than one hundred rupees. Here, B is liable only to fine which may extend to an amount equal to ten times the loss caused. But A is punishable with imprisonment for a term which may extend to two years, and with unlimited fine.

100. Whoever by instigation, conspiracy, or aid, previously abets the doing of a thing which is done in consequence of that instigation, or in pursuance of that conspiracy, or with that aid, shall, if that thing would be a certain offence but for the youth, the idiotcy, the madness, the delirium, or the intoxication of the person doing that thing, or but for some misconception on the part of that person from which misconception the abettor is free, be punished with the punishment provided for that offence.

Illustrations.

(a) A instigates B, a child of four years old, to take property in a way which in a grown up person would be the offence of theft. B takes the property in consequence. B has committed no offence, but A is liable to the punishment of theft.

(b) A instigates B, a madman, to set fire to a dwelling house. B sets fire to the house in consequence. B has committed no offence. But A is liable to the punishment of setting fire to a dwelling house.

(c) A tells B, a Police officer, that Z is Y, knowing that B is charged to arrest Y, and meaning to cause Z to be illegally confined. B in consequence arrests Z, believing in good faith that he is commanded by law to do it. Here, B has committed no offence. But A is liable to be punished as if he had himself illegally confined Z.

(d) A instigates B to take property out of Z's possession, and in order to such instigation induces B to believe that the property belongs to A. B takes the property out of Z's possession intending thereby to cause loss to Z and gain to A, but believing that loss and gain to be rightful loss and rightful gain. B, acting under this misconception, does not take fraudulently, and therefore does not commit theft. But A is liable to the punishment to which he would have been liable if B had committed theft.

101. Whoever, being a public servant, conceals by any act or illegal omission the existence of a design to commit any offence the commission of which offence it is his duty as such public servant to prevent, and thereby previously abets that offence, shall, if that offence be committed, be punished with imprisonment of either description for a term which may extend to one half of the longest term of imprisonment provided for that offence, or fine, or both.

Illustration.

A, an officer of Police, being legally bound to give information of all designs to commit Dacoity which may come to his knowledge, and knowing that B designs to commit Dacoity, omits to give such information, knowing it to be likely that this omission will facilitate the commission of the Dacoity. Here, A has, by an illegal omission, concealed the existence of B's design, and has thus previously abetted Dacoity. If the Dacoity be actually committed, A has committed the offence defined in this Clause, and is liable to imprisonment of either description for a term which may extend, under Clause 48, to twelve years.

102. Whoever conceals by any act or illegal omission the existence of a design to commit any offence punishable with rigorous imprisonment for a term of one year or upwards, and thereby previously abets that offence, shall, if that offence be committed, be punished with imprisonment of either description for a term which may extend to one fourth part of the longest term of imprisonment provided for that offence, or fine, or both.

Illustration.

A, knowing that a widow is about to be burned with the corpse of her husband, tells the Magistrate that the family are determined that she shall not be burned. A thus misinforms the Magistrate, knowing it to be likely that the burning of the widow will thereby be facilitated. Here, A has by an act concealed the existence of a design to commit voluntary culpable homicide, and has thus previously abetted voluntary culpable homicide. If, therefore, voluntary culpable homicide be committed, A has committed the offence defined in this Clause.

103. A person is said subsequently to abet the doing of a thing who, knowing that thing to have been done, assists or attempts to assist, by any act or illegal omission, the doer of that thing to avoid any evil consequence of doing that thing, or to derive from the doing of that thing any advantage, with a view to which advantage that thing was done.

104. A person is said subsequently to abet an offence who subsequently abets what he knows to be an offence, or what he would know to be an offence but for his ignorance of the law.

Illustrations.

(*a*) A subsequently abets B in sitting Dhurna at Z's door, not knowing that B, by sitting Dhurna, has committed what is by law an offence, but knowing that B sat Dhurna with the intention of causing it to be believed that by so sitting he rendered Z an object of divine displeasure. Here, A but for his ignorance of the law would know B's act to be an offence, (See Clause 283). Here, therefore, A is said to have subsequently abetted the offence which B has committed.

(*b*) A subsequently abets the taking of property by B out of Z's possession. B has taken the property fraudulently; and has therefore been guilty of theft. But if A does not know the taking to be fraudulent, then as A, even if he knows the law, cannot know that B has been guilty of theft, A, though he has subsequently abetted the taking, is not said to have subsequently abetted B's offence.

105. Whoever, knowing that an offence has been committed, and knowing himself to be directed by law to give information in any quarter of that offence, subsequently abets that offence by intentionally omitting to give such information, shall be punished with imprisonment of either description for a term which may extend to six months, or fine, or both.

106. Whoever, knowing that an offence has been committed which is punishable with rigorous imprisonment for a term of one year or upwards, subsequently abets that offence by causing any marks of the commission of that offence to disappear, shall be punished with imprisonment of either description for a term which may extend to one twelfth part of the longest term of imprisonment provided for that offence, or fine, or both.

Illustration.

A, knowing that B has murdered Z, assists B to hide the body. A is liable to imprisonment of either description for one twelfth part of the term of imprisonment provided for murder, that is to say, to two years of imprisonment. (See Clause 48.)

107. Whoever, except as hereinafter excepted, subsequently abets any offence punishable with imprisonment for seven years or upwards, by harbouring the offender with the intention of screening such offender from legal punishment, shall be punished with imprisonment of either description for a term which may extend to six months, or fine which may extend to one thousand rupees, or both.

Exception. This provision does not extend to the case in which the harbour is given by the husband, or wife, or relation in the direct ascending or descending line, or brother, or sister of the person to whom the harbour is given.

108. Wherever a thing is done which is an offence by reason that it is fraudulently done, whoever subsequently abets that offence by assisting the offender to retain or dispose of any property acquired by that offence, shall be punished with imprisonment of either description for a term which may extend to one year, or fine, or both.

CHAPTER V.*

OF OFFENCES AGAINST THE STATE.

109. Whoever wages war against the Government of any part of the territories of the East India Company, or attempts to wage such war, or by instigation, conspiracy, or aid previously abets the waging of such war, shall be punished with death, or transportation for life, or imprisonment of either description for life, and shall forfeit all his property.

Illustrations.

(*a*) A joins an army of a foreign power which has invaded the territories of the East India Company, and serves in that army. A has committed the offence defined in this Clause.

(*b*) A conspires with other persons to cause an insurrection against the East India Company's Government in one of the Presidencies. A has committed the offence defined in this Clause.

(*c*) A instigates a native power to make war on the Government of India. A has committed the offence defined in this Clause.

* See Note C.

110. Whoever by any act, or by any illegal omission, conceals the existence of a design to wage war against the Government of any part of the territories of the East India Company, intending or knowing it to be likely that he may by such concealment facilitate the waging of such war, and thereby previously abets the waging of such war, shall be punished with imprisonment of either description for a term which may extend to fourteen years and must not be less than two years, and shall also be liable to fine.

111. Whoever, with the intention of inducing or compelling the Governor General of India, or the Governor or Deputy Governor of any Presidency, or any Member of the Council of India or of the Council of any Presidency, to exercise or refrain from exercising in any manner any of the lawful powers of such Governor General, Governor, Deputy Governor, or Member of Council, assaults or makes shew of assaulting, or wrongfully restrains or attempts wrongfully to restrain, or overawes by means of a riotous assembly, or attempts so to overawe such Governor General, Governor, Deputy Governor, or Member of Council, shall be punished with imprisonment of either description for a term which may extend to seven years and must not be less than one year, and shall also be liable to fine.

112. If any person, by doing any thing whereby he commits an offence under the last preceding Clause, also commits an offence under any other Clause of this Code, the punishment shall be cumulative.

113. Whoever, by words, either spoken or intended to be read, or by signs, or by visible representations, attempts to excite feelings of disaffection to the Government established by law in the territories of the East India Company, among any class of people who live under that Government, shall be punished with banishment for life or for any term from the territories of the East India Company, to which fine may be added, or with simple imprisonment for a term which may extend to three years, to which fine may be added, or with fine.

Explanation. Such a disapprobation of the measures of the Government as is compatible with a disposition to render obedience to the lawful authority of the Government, and to support the lawful authority of the Government against unlawful attempts to subvert or resist that authority, is not disaffection. Therefore the making of comments on the measures of the Government, with the intention of exciting only this species of disapprobation, is not an offence within this Clause.

114. Whoever wages war against the Government of any Asiatic power in alliance with the Government established by law in the territories of the East India Company, or attempts to wage such war, or by instigation, conspiracy, or aid previously abets the waging of such war, shall be punished with banishment from the territories of the East India Company, to which fine may be added, or with imprisonment of either description for a term which may extend to three years, to which fine may be added, or with fine.

115. Whoever uses any place within the territories of the East India Company for the purpose of making preparations to commit depredations on the territories of any power at peace with the Government of the said territories, or for the purpose of taking refuge after committing such depredations, shall be punished with imprisonment of either description for a term which may extend to fourteen years and must not be less than two years, and shall also be liable to fine, and to forfeiture of any specific property.

CHAPTER VI.*

OF OFFENCES RELATING TO THE ARMY AND NAVY.

116. Whoever by instigation, conspiracy, or aid, previously abets the committing of mutiny by a soldier or sailor in the service of the King, or of the East India Company, shall be punished with imprisonment of either description for a term which may extend to seven years and must not be less than one year, and shall also be liable to fine.

* See Note D.

117. Whoever by instigation, conspiracy, or aid, previously abets the committing of mutiny by a soldier or sailor in the service of the King, or of the East India Company, shall, if mutiny be committed in consequence of that instigation, in pursuance of that conspiracy, or with that aid, be punished with transportation for life, or imprisonment of either description for a term which may extend to life and must not be less than three years, and shall also be liable to fine.

118. Whoever by instigation, conspiracy, or aid, previously abets an assault by any soldier or sailor in the service of the King, or of the East India Company, on any superior officer of such soldier or sailor, shall be punished with imprisonment of either description for a term which may extend to three years and must not be less than six months, and shall also be liable to fine.

119. Whoever by instigation, conspiracy, or aid, previously abets an assault by any soldier or sailor in the service of the King, or of the East India Company, on any superior officer of such soldier or sailor, shall, if such assault be committed in consequence of that instigation, in pursuance of that conspiracy, or with that aid, be punished with imprisonment of either description for a term which may extend to seven years and must not be less than one year, and shall also be liable to fine.

120. Whoever by instigation, conspiracy, or aid, previously abets the desertion of any soldier or sailor in the service of the King, or of the East India Company, shall be punished with imprisonment of either description for a term which may extend to one year, or fine, or both.

121. Whoever by instigation, conspiracy, or aid, previously abets the desertion of any soldier or sailor in the service of the King, or of the East India Company, shall, if desertion be committed in consequence of that instigation, in pursuance of that conspiracy, or with that aid, be punished with imprisonment of either description for a term which may extend to three years, or fine, or both.

122. Whoever by instigation, conspiracy, or aid, previously abets the desertion of any soldier or sailor in the service of the King, or of the East India Company, to an enemy, shall be punished with imprisonment of either description for a term which may extend to seven years, and must not be less than one year, and shall also be liable to fine.

123. Whoever by instigation, conspiracy, or aid, previously abets the desertion of any soldier or sailor in the service of the King, or of the East India Company, to an enemy, shall, if desertion be committed in consequence of that instigation, in pursuance of that conspiracy, or with that aid, be punished with transportation for life, or imprisonment for a term which may extend to life, and shall also be liable to fine.

124. Whoever, except as hereinafter excepted, knowing that a soldier or sailor in the service of the King, or of the East India Company, has deserted, subsequently abets such desertion by harbouring such soldier or sailor, shall be punished with imprisonment of either description for a term which may extend to three months, or fine which may extend to five hundred rupees, or both.

Exception. This provision does not extend to the case in which the harbour is given by the husband, or wife, or relation in the direct ascending or descending line, or brother, or sister of the person to whom the harbour is given

125. Whoever by instigation, conspiracy, or aid, previously abets what he knows to be a breach of military or naval discipline by any soldier or sailor in the service of the King, or of the East India Company, shall, if such breach of discipline be committed in consequence of that instigation, in pursuance of that conspiracy, or with that aid, be punished with imprisonment of either description for a term which may extend to six months, or fine, or both.

Illustration.

B, a soldier, offers his military accoutrements for sale to A. A buys them, knowing that it is a breach of military discipline in B to part with those accoutrements. A has committed the offence defined in this Clause.

126. Whoever, not being a soldier in the service of the King, or of the East India Company, wears any garb or carries any token resembling any garb or token used by such a soldier, with the intention that it may be believed that he is such a soldier, shall be punished with imprisonment of either description for a term which may extend to three months, or fine which may extend to five hundred rupees, or both.

CHAPTER VII.

OF OFFENCES AGAINST THE PUBLIC TRANQUILLITY.

127. An assembly of twelve or more persons is designated as " a riotous assembly" if it is the object of that assembly to overawe the Legislative or Executive Government of India, or the Government of any Presidency, or any public servant, or any body of public servants in the exercise of the lawful powers of such public servants, or of such body; or to resist the execution of any law ; or to commit any assault, mischief, or criminal trespass ; or wrongfully to restrain any person ; or to put any person in fear of hurt, or of assault ; or wantonly to insult, or annoy any person ; or if that assembly is attended with circumstances which may reasonably excite apprehensions that its object is one of those aforesaid.

Explanation. An assembly which was not riotous when it assembled may subsequently become a riotous assembly.

128. Whoever, being aware of facts which render any assembly a riotous assembly, intentionally joins that assembly, or continues in it, is said to commit the offence of " rioting."

129. Whoever commits the offence of rioting shall be punished with imprisonment of either description for a term which may extend to six months, or fine, or both.

130. Whoever commits the offence of rioting by joining or continuing in a riotous assembly, knowing that such riotous assembly has been commanded to disperse in the manner prescribed in the Code of Procedure, shall be punished with imprisonment of either description for a term which may extend to two years, or fine, or both.

131. If any person commits the offence of rioting in such a manner that he commits an offence under the last preceding Clause, and also commits an offence under either of the two next following Clauses, the punishment shall be cumulative.

132. Whoever commits the offence of rioting, being armed with any weapon for shooting, stabbing, or cutting, or having made preparation for committing the offence of rioting by arming himself with any weapon whatever, shall be punished with imprisonment of either description for a term which may extend to two years, or fine, or both.

133. If murder be committed by any rioter, while committing the offence of rioting, every other person who, at the time of the committing of the murder, is committing the offence of rioting as a member of the same riotous assembly, shall be punished with imprisonment of either description for a term which may extend to five years, or fine, or both.

134. If any person, in committing the offence of rioting, commits an offence under any Clause contained in any other Chapter of this Code, the punishment shall be cumulative.

135. Whoever intentionally joins or continues in any assembly of twelve or more persons, knowing that such assembly has been commanded to disperse in the manner prescribed in the Code of Procedure, shall be punished with simple imprisonment for a term which may extend to one month, or fine, or both.

136. Whoever, malignantly and wantonly, or by doing any thing which is illegal, gives any provocation to any person, intending or knowing it to be likely that the effect of that provocation may be that the offence of rioting will be committed, shall, if the offence of rioting be committed in consequence of such provocation, be punished with imprisonment of either description for a term which may extend to one year, or fine, or both.

137. If any person, by doing any thing whereby he commits an offence under the last preceding Clause, also commits an offence under any other Clause of this Code, the punishment shall be cumulative.

Illustration.

A offers an insult to the religion of a class of persons, with the deliberate intention of wounding their feelings : he is punishable with imprisonment for a term not exceeding one year by Clause 282. But if he also knows it to be likely that he shall cause rioting, and does so cause rioting, he will be liable to punishment both under Clause 282 and under Clause 136 ; that is to say, he will be punishable with imprisonment for a term not exceeding two years.

CHAPTER VIII.*

OF THE ABUSE OF THE POWERS OF PUBLIC SERVANTS.

138. Whoever, being or expecting to be a public servant,† directly or indirectly accepts, obtains, or attempts to obtain from any party for himself, or for any other party, any gratification whatever, other than legal remuneration, as a motive or a reward for doing or forbearing to do any official act, or for shewing or forbearing to shew, in the exercise of his official functions, favor or disfavor to any party, or for rendering or attempting to render any service or disservice to any party with the Legislative or Executive Government of India, or with the Government of any Presidency, or with any public servant, as such, or with any body of public servants, as such, shall be punished with imprisonment of either description for a term which may extend to three years, or fine, or both.

Explanations. " Expecting to be a public servant." If a person not expecting to be in office obtains money by deceiving others into a belief that he is about to be in office, and that he will then serve them, he may be guilty of cheating, but he is not guilty of the offence defined in this Clause.

" Gratification." The word gratification is used to denote, not only pecuniary gratifications, and gratifications estimable in money, but also all gratifications of appetite, and all honorary distinctions.

" Legal remuneration." All remuneration is legal which is given to a public servant by the Government which he serves, or by any person thereunto authorised by that Government, or which a public servant is permitted to accept by the Government which he serves, or by any person thereunto authorised by that Government.

" A motive or a reward for doing." A person may receive a gratification as a motive for doing what he does not intend to do; or as a reward for doing what he has not done.

Illustrations.

(a) A, a public servant, obtains Z's consent that Z's sister shall live with A as A's mistress, as a motive to A for giving Z a place in A's gift A has committed the offence defined in this Clause.

(b) A, a public servant, obtains from Z, a banker, a situation in Z's bank for A's brother, as a reward to A for deciding a cause in favor of Z. A has committed the offence defined in this Clause.

(c) A, holding the office of Resident at the court of a subsidiary power, accepts a lac of rupees from the minister of that power. It does not appear that A accepted this sum as a motive or a reward for doing or forbearing to do any particular official act, or for rendering or attempting to render any particular service to that power with the British Government. But it does appear that A accepted the sum as a motive, or a reward for generally shewing favour in the exercise of his official functions to that power. A has committed the offence defined in this Clause.

(d) A, a public servant, induces Z erroneously to believe that A's influence with the Government has obtained a title for Z, and thus induces Z to give A money as a reward for this service. A has committed the offence defined in this Clause.

139. Whoever directly or indirectly accepts, obtains, or attempts to obtain from any party, for himself or for any other party, any gratification whatever, as a motive or a reward for inducing, by the exercise of personal influence, any public servant to do or to forbear to do any official act, or to shew in the exercise of the official functions of such public servant favor or disfavor to any party, or to render or attempt to render any service or disservice to any party with the Legislative or Executive Government of India, or with the Government of any Presidency, or with any public servant, as such, or with any body of public servants, as such, shall be punished with simple imprisonment for a term which may extend to six months, or fine, or both.

Illustrations.

An advocate who receives a fee for arguing a case before a Judge ; a person who receives pay for arranging and correcting a memorial addressed to Government setting forth the services and claims of the memorialist ; a paid agent for a condemned criminal who lays before the Government statements tending to shew that the condemnation was unjust ; are not within this Clause, inasmuch as they do not exercise personal influence.

---

* See Note E.
† For the definition of the words " public servant" see Clause 14.

140. Whoever, being a public servant, abets, either previously or subsequently, the offence defined in the last preceding Clause, when that offence is committed by means of real or pretended influence over himself, shall be punished with simple imprisonment for a term which may extend to three years, or fine, or both.

Illustration.

A is a public servant. B, A's mistress, receives a present as a motive for soliciting A to give an office to a particular person. A abets her doing so. B is punishable with imprisonment for a term not exceeding six months, or fine, or both. A is punishable with imprisonment for a term which may extend to three years, or fine, or both.

141. Whoever, being a Judge, directly or indirectly accepts, obtains, or attempts to obtain, for himself or for any other party, a gift of any valuable thing, other than refreshments according to the common usages of hospitality, from any party whom he knows to be plaintiff or defendant in any proceeding which is pending in the said Judge's Court, shall be punished with simple imprisonment for a term which may extend to two years, or fine, or both.

Explanation. By a gift is meant any thing which is in reality a gift, whatever color may be given to the transaction.

Illustrations.

(a) A, a Judge, hires a house of Z, who has a cause pending in A's Court. It is agreed that A shall pay fifty rupees a month, the house being such that, if the bargain were made in good faith, A would be required to pay two hundred rupees a month. A has obtained a gift of a valuable thing from Z.

(b) A, a Judge, buys of Z, who has a cause pending in A's Court, Government Promissory Notes at a discount, when they are selling in the market at a premium. A has obtained a gift of a valuable thing from Z.

(c) A, a Judge, sells to Z, who has a cause pending in A's Court, shares in a bank at a premium, when they are selling in the market at a discount. A has obtained a gift of a valuable thing from Z.

142. Whoever, being a Judge, pronounces on any question which comes before him in any stage of any judicial proceeding a decision which he knows to be unjust, shall be punished with simple imprisonment for a term which may extend to two years, or fine, or both.

143. Whoever, being a Judge, for any purpose of favor or disfavor to any party, disobeys any direction of the law of Procedure, shall be punished with simple imprisonment for a term which may extend to one year, or fine, or both.

144. Whoever, being in any office which gives him legal authority to commit persons to confinement, or to keep persons in confinement, commits any person to confinement, or keeps any person in confinement, in the exercise of that authority, knowing that in so doing he is acting unjustly, shall be punished with simple imprisonment for a term which may extend to two years, or fine, or both.

145. Whoever, being a public servant, knowingly disobeys any direction of the law as to the way in which he is to conduct himself as such public servant, intending or knowing it to be likely that he may by such disobedience cause injury to any party, or save any person from legal punishment, shall be punished with simple imprisonment for a term which may extend to one year, or fine, or both.

Illustrations.

(a) A, being an officer directed by law to take property in execution in order to satisfy a decree pronounced in Z's favour by a Court of Justice, knowingly disobeys that direction of law with the knowledge that he is likely thereby to cause injury to Z. A has committed the offence defined in this clause.

(b) A, being a magistrate in the Bengal Presidency, and being directed by law to commit an offender for trial before the Sessions Judge, knowingly disobeys that direction of law with the intention of thereby saving that offender from legal punishment. A has committed the offence defined in this Clause.

146. Whoever, being a public servant, and being, as such public servant, charged with the preparation of any document, frames that document in a manner which he knows to be incorrect, intending or knowing it to be likely that he may thereby cause injury to any party, or save any person from legal punishment, shall be punished with imprisonment of either description for a term which may extend to three years, or fine, or both.

147. Whoever, being a public servant, and being legally bound, as such public ser-

vant, not to engage in trade, engages in trade, shall be punished with simple imprisonment for a term which may extend to three months, or fine, or both.

148. Whoever, being a public servant, and being legally bound, as such public servant, not to purchase or bid for certain property, purchases or bids for that property, either directly or by means of an agent, shall be punished with simple imprisonment for a term which may extend to three months, or fine, or both.

149. Whoever, being a public servant, knowingly and without any reasonable excuse disobeys any lawful order issued by his official superior or superiors for his guidance in the discharge of his public functions, or offers any intentional insult to any of his official superiors, or knowingly and without any reasonable excuse neglects the discharge of his official duties, shall be punished with fine to an amount not exceeding his salary for three months, if he be paid by salary; but if he be paid by fees, not exceeding thrice the amount of legal fees received by him in some one month; and if he be paid in land, not exceeding one fourth of the clear annual value of such land.

150. Whoever, not belonging to a certain class of public servants, wears any garb or carries any token resembling any garb or token used by that class of public servants, with the intention that it may be believed or with the knowledge that it is likely to be believed that he belongs to that class of public servants, shall be punished with imprisonment of either description for a term which may extend to three months, or fine which may extend to five hundred rupees, or both.

151. If any person, in doing any thing whereby he commits an offence under any Clause in this Chapter, also commits an offence under any Clause contained in any other Chapter of this Code, the punishment shall be cumulative.

Illustration.

A, a public servant, threatens to assess Z's land unjustly high unless Z will give him money, and thus obtains money from Z. Here, A has committed the offence defined in Clause 138, inasmuch as he has obtained from Z a gratification as a motive for forbearing to shew disfavor to Z in the exercise of A's official functions. A has also committed extortion inasmuch as he has obtained property from Z by putting Z in fear of injury. Therefore A is liable to the punishment of extortion added to that provided by Clause 138.

CHAPTER IX.*

OF CONTEMPTS OF THE LAWFUL AUTHORITY OF PUBLIC SERVANTS.

152. Whoever absconds in order to avoid being served with a summons or notice proceeding from any public servant, or body of public servants, legally competent, as such public servant, or as such body, to issue such summons or notice, shall be punished with imprisonment of either description for a term which may extend to one month, or fine which may extend to five hundred rupees, or both.

153. Whoever in any manner intentionally prevents the serving on himself, or on any other, of any summons or notice proceeding from any public servant, or body of public servants, legally competent as such public servant, or as such body, to issue such summons or notice, or intentionally prevents the lawful affixing to any place of any such summons or notice, or intentionally removes any such summons or notice from any place to which it is lawfully affixed, or intentionally prevents the lawful making of any proclamation, under the authority of any public servant, or body of public servants, legally competent, as such public servant, or as such body, to direct such proclamation to be made, shall be punished with imprisonment of either description for a term which may extend to one month, or fine which may extend to five hundred rupees, or both.

154. If any person, by doing any thing whereby he commits an offence under the last

* See Note F.

preceding clause, also commits an offence under any clause contained in any other Chapter of this Code, the punishment shall be cumulative.

155. Whoever, being legally bound to attend in person or by an agent at a certain place and time, in obedience to an order proceeding from any public servant, or body of public servants, legally competent, as such public servant, or as such body, to issue such order, intentionally omits to attend at that place, or time, or departs from the place where he is bound to attend before the time at which it is lawful for him to depart, shall be punished with imprisonment of either description for a term which may extend to one month, or fine which may extend to five hundred rupees, or both.

Illustrations.

(a) A, being legally bound to appear before the Supreme Court at Calcutta in obedience to a subpoena issuing from that Court, intentionally omits to appear. A has committed the offence defined in this Clause.

(b) A, being legally bound to appear before a Zillah Judge, as a witness, in obedience to a summons issued by that Zillah Judge, intentionally omits to appear. A has committed the offence defined in this Clause.

(c) A, a proprietor of lands ordered to be sold, receives an order from the Collector to attend an Ameen in person, or by an agent, in the manner prescribed by Section 10, Regulation XLV of 1793, of the Bengal Presidency. A, being legally bound to obey this order, intentionally disobeys it. A has committed the offence defined in this Clause.

(d) A, a Ryot, is summoned by the Tehsildar to attend at the annual settlement of Revenue, in the manner prescribed by Section 5, Regulation III of 1831, of the Madras Presidency. A, being legally bound to attend, intentionally omits to do so. A has committed the offence defined in this Clause.

156. Whoever, being legally bound to produce or deliver up any document to any public servant, as such, or to any body of public servants, as such, intentionally omits so to produce or deliver up the same, shall be punished with imprisonment of either description for a term which may extend to one month, or fine which may extend to five hundred rupees, or both.

Illustrations.

(a) A, being legally bound to produce a document before a Zillah Court, intentionally omits to produce the same. A has committed the offence defined in this Clause.

(b) A, a Putwarree, is ordered by the Collector to attend with his accounts an officer deputed by the Collector, in the manner prescribed by Section 25, Regulation XII of 1817, of the Bengal Presidency. A, being legally bound to obey this order, intentionally disobeys it. A has committed the offence defined in this Clause.

(c) A has a Rowanna for salt, which Rowanna he is legally bound, under Clause 3, Section 46, Regulation X of 1819, of the Bengal Presidency, to deliver up to a Darogah of a Salt Chokee. A intentionally omits to deliver up the same. A has committed the offence defined in this Clause.

157. Whoever, being legally bound to give any notice or to furnish information on any subject to any public servant, as such, or to any body of public servants, as such, intentionally omits to give such notice, or to furnish such information in the manner and at the time required by law, shall be punished with imprisonment of either description for a term which may extend to one month, or fine which may extend to five hundred rupees, or both.

Illustrations.

(a) A is holder of Lakheraj lands, and as such is legally bound to furnish information to the Collector in the manner prescribed by Section 7, Regulation VIII of 1800, of the Bengal Presidency. A intentionally omits to do so. A has committed the offence defined in this Clause.

(b) A succeeds to a Malgoozaree estate, and is legally bound to notify such succession to the Collector, in the manner prescribed by Section 21, Regulation VIII of 1800, of the Bengal Presidency. A intentionally omits to do so. A has committed the offence defined in this Clause.

158. Whoever, being legally bound to furnish information on any subject to any public servant, as such, or to any body of public servants, as such, furnishes information on that subject which he knows to be false, shall be punished with imprisonment of either description for a term which may extend to six months, or fine which may extend to one thousand rupees, or both.

Illustration.

A is legally bound to furnish a true return of his assessable carriages and horses to the Assessor for Bombay, in the manner prescribed by Section 25, Regulation XIX of 1827, of the Bombay Presidency. A makes a return which he knows to be false. A has committed the offence defined in this Clause.

159. Whoever refuses to bind himself by an oath, or sanction tantamount to an oath,

to state the truth, when required so to bind himself by a public servant, or body of public servants, legally competent to require that he shall so bind himself, shall be punished with imprisonment of either description for a term which may extend to six months, or fine, or both.

160. Whoever, being legally bound by an oath, or sanction tantamount to an oath, to state the truth on any subject to any public servant, or body of public servants, refuses to answer any question demanded of him touching that subject by such public servant, or body, in the exercise of the legal powers of such public servant, or body, shall be punished with imprisonment of either description for a term which may extend to six months, or fine, or both.

161. Whoever refuses to sign any statement made by him when required to sign that statement by a public servant, or body of public servants, legally competent to require that he shall sign that statement, shall be punished with imprisonment of either description for a term which may extend to three months, or fine which may extend to one thousand rupees, or both.

162. Whoever, being legally bound by an oath, or sanction tantamount to an oath, to state the truth on any subject to any public servant, or body of public servants, states to such public servant or body as true that which he knows to be false touching that subject, shall be punished with imprisonment of either description for a term which may extend to three years and must not be less than six months, and shall also be liable to fine.*

163. Whoever gives to any public servant, or body of public servants, any information which he knows to be false, intending or knowing it to be likely that such false information may cause such public servant, or such body, to use the lawful power of such public servant, or of such body, to the loss or annoyance of any person, shall be punished with imprisonment of either description for a term which may extend to six months, or fine which may extend to one thousand rupees, or both.

Illustration.

A falsely informs a public servant that A knows Z to have contraband salt in a secret place, knowing that it is likely that the consequence of the information will be a search of Z's premises tended with annoyance to Z. A has committed the offence defined in this Clause.

164. In every case in which any public servant, as such, or any person authorized by any public servant, as such, or by any body of public servants, as such, is legally empowered to enter any place, or to remain in any place, or to make any search, or to examine any thing, or to put any mark upon any thing, whoever, either, by any act or by any illegal omission, intentionally prevents, or attempts to prevent such public servant or authorised person from exercising such lawful power, or intentionally causes annoyance to such public servant, or authorised persons in the exercise of such lawful power, shall be punished with imprisonment of either description for a term which may extend to three months, or fine which may extend to five hundred rupees, or both.

Explanation. " Examine any thing." The word "examine" extends to all operations whereby the quality or quantity of any thing is ascertained.

Illustrations.

(a) Gauging, measuring, surveying, weighing, are modes of examination.

(b) Z is an officer of a Court of Justice lawfully empowered to enter A's house for the purpose of making a search A, by fastening the door, attempts to prevent Z from entering. A has committed the offence defined in this Clause

(c) Z is a Revenue officer lawfully empowered to measure A's land, for the purpose of assessment. A intentionally prevents Z from measuring the land. A has committed the offence defined in this Clause.

(d) Z is a Custom house officer lawfully empowered to go on board of a ship on its arrival in port. A, the commander of the ship, refuses to admit Z on board. A has committed the offence defined in this Clause.

(e) Z is a Custom house officer lawfully empowered to stay on board of a ship in a port in Bengal, and entitled, during such stay, to be furnished by the commander of the ship with fresh water. (Act No. XVI of 1837.) A, the commander of the ship, illegally omits to furnish Z with fresh water, and by such his illegal omission intentionally causes annoyance to Z in the exercise of Z's lawful powers. A has committed the offence defined in this Clause.

165. If any person, by doing any thing whereby he commits an offence under the

---

* For cases in which the false statement amounts to false evidence, see Clause 190.

last preceding Clause, also commits an offence under any Clause contained in any other Chapter of this Code, the punishment shall be cumulative.

166. Whoever offers any resistance to the taking of any property by the lawful authority of any public servant, as such, or of any body of public servants, as such, shall be punished with imprisonment of either description for a term which may extend to six months, or fine, or both.

167. If any person, by doing any thing whereby he commits an offence under the last preceding Clause, also commits an offence under any Clause contained in any other Chapter of this Code, the punishment shall be cumulative.

168. Whoever intentionally obstructs any sale of property offered for sale by the lawful authority of any public servant, as such, or of any body of public servants, as such, shall be punished with imprisonment of either description for a term which may extend to one month, or fine which may extend to five hundred rupees, or both.

169. If any person, by doing any thing whereby he commits an offence under the last preceding Clause, also commits an offence under any Clause contained in any other Chapter of this Code, the punishment shall be cumulative.

170. Whoever bids for any property offered for sale by the lawful authority of any public servant, as such, or of any body of public servants, as such, on account of any person, whether himself or any other, whom he knows to be under any legal incapacity to purchase that property at that sale, or bids for such property not intending to perform the obligations under which he lays himself by such bidding, shall be punished with imprisonment of either description for a term which may extend to one month, or fine, or both.

171. Whoever offers any resistance to the taking into custody of himself, or of any other, under the lawful authority of any public servant, as such, or of any body of public servants, as such, shall be punished with imprisonment of either description for a term which may extend to six months, or fine, or both.

172. If any person, by doing any thing whereby he commits an offence under the last preceding Clause, also commits an offence under any Clause contained in any other Chapter of this Code, the punishment shall be cumulative.

173. Whoever intentionally rescues or attempts to rescue any person from any custody in which that person is detained under the lawful authority of any public servant, as such, or of any body of public servants, as such, shall be punished with imprisonment of either description for a term which may extend to six months, or fine, or both.

174. If any person, by doing any thing whereby he commits an offence under the last preceding Clause, also commits an offence under any Clause contained in any other Chapter of this Code, the punishment shall be cumulative.

175. Whoever escapes or attempts to escape from any custody in which he is detained under the lawful authority of any public servant, as such, or of any body of public servants, as such, shall be punished with imprisonment of either description for a term which may extend to three months, or fine, or both.

176. If any person, by doing any thing whereby he commits an offence under the last preceding Clause, also commits an offence under any Clause contained in any other Chapter of this Code, the punishment shall be cumulative.

177. Whoever, except as hereinafter excepted, knowing that a public servant or body of public servants has, in the exercise of the lawful powers of such public servant or body, directed a certain person to be taken into custody, harbours that person, with the intention of preventing that person from being so taken into custody, shall be punished with imprisonment of either description for a term which may extend to one month, or fine which may extend to two hundred rupees, or both.

Exception. This provision does not extend to the case in which the harbour is given by the husband, or wife, or relation in the direct ascending or descending line, or brother, or sister, of the person to whom the harbour is given.*

178. Whoever, except as hereinafter excepted, knowingly harbours any person who has escaped from custody in which he was detained by the lawful authority of some public servant, or body of public servants, shall be punished with imprisonment of

* For rescue, escape, and harbour after sentence, see Chapter X.

either description for a term which may extend to two months, or fine which may extend to five hundred rupees, or both.

Exception. This provision does not extend to the case in which the harbour is given by the husband, or wife, or relation in the direct ascending or descending line, or brother, or sister, of the person to whom the harbour is given.

179. Whoever intentionally offers any insult, or causes any interruption to any public servant, or body of public servants, while such public servant or body is in the discharge of the public functions of such public servant, or body, shall be punished with imprisonment of either description for a term which may extend to three months, or fine which may extend to five hundred rupees, or both.

180. If any person, by doing any thing whereby he commits an offence under the last preceding Clause, also commits an offence under any Clause contained in any other Chapter of this Code, the punishment shall be cumulative.

181. Whoever, knowing himself to be directed by law to give any assistance to any public servant, or body of public servants, in the execution of the public duty of such public servant or body, intentionally omits to give such assistance, shall be punished with imprisonment of either description for a term which may extend to one month, or fine which may extend to two hundred rupees, or both.

182. Whoever, knowing that by a local order promulgated by a public servant, or body of public servants, lawfully empowered to promulgate such order, he is directed to abstain from a certain act, or to take certain order with certain property in his possession, disobeys such direction, shall, if such his disobedience causes or tends to cause any danger to human life, health, or safety, or any obstruction or annoyance, or risk of such obstruction or annoyance to persons lawfully employed, or any rioting, or any risk of rioting, be punished with imprisonment for a term which may extend to one month, or fine which may extend to two hundred rupees, or both.

Explanation. It is not necessary that the offender should intend to produce harm, or contemplate his disobedience as likely to produce harm. It is sufficient that he knows of the order which he disobeys, and that his disobedience produces or is likely to produce harm.

Illustrations.

(a) An order is promulgated by a public servant lawfully empowered to promulgate such order, forbidding the celebration of a Hindoo festival accompanied with swinging in front of the houses of the English gentlemen at Chowringhee. A knowingly disobeys the order, and thereby causes annoyance or risk of annoyance to English families. A has committed the offence defined in this Clause.

(b) An order is promulgated in the manner aforesaid directing all persons to keep their dogs within doors for fear of hydrophobia. A knowingly disobeys the order. Here, if A's disobedience tends to cause danger to human life, health, or safety, A has committed the offence defined in this Clause.

(c) An order is promulgated in the manner aforesaid directing that a religious procession shall not pass down a certain street. A knowingly disobeys the order, and thereby causes danger of riot. A has committed the offence defined in this Clause.

183. If any person, by doing any thing whereby he commits an offence under the last preceding Clause, also commits an offence under any Clause contained in any other Chapter of this Code, the punishment shall be cumulative.

184. Whoever directly or indirectly holds out any threat of any injury to any public servant, or to any person in whom he believes that public servant to be interested, for the purpose of inducing that public servant to do any act, or to forbear or delay to do any act, connected with the exercise of the public functions of such public servant, shall be punished with imprisonment of either description for a term which may extend to one year, or fine, or both.

185. If any person, by doing any thing whereby he commits an offence under the last preceding Clause, also commits an offence under any Clause contained in any other Chapter of this Code, the punishment shall be cumulative.

186. Whoever directly or indirectly holds out any threat of any injury to any person for the purpose of inducing that person to refrain or desist from making any legal application for protection against any injury to any public servant, or body of public servants, legally empowered, as such, to give such protection, shall be punished with imprisonment of either description for a term which may extend to one year, or fine, or both.

187. If any person, by doing any thing whereby he commits an offence under the last preceding Clause, also commits an offence under any other Clause of this Code, the punishment shall be cumulative.

CHAPTER X.*

OF OFFENCES AGAINST PUBLIC JUSTICE.

188. Whoever, in any stage of any judicial proceeding, being bound by an oath, or by a sanction tantamount to an oath, to state the truth, states that to be true which he knows to be false touching any point material to the result of such proceeding, is said " to give false evidence."

Explanations. It is not necessary that the offender should intend to mislead the Judge as to the general merits of the question at issue. It is sufficient if he intends to mislead the Judge as to any point material to that question.

An interpreter bound by an oath, or by a sanction tantamount to an oath, to interpret truly to a Court of Justice, if he intentionally gives a false interpretation of any words which it is material that he should duly interpret, is guilty of giving false evidence.

A trial before a Court Martial is a Judicial Proceeding.

An investigation directed by law preliminary to a proceeding before a Court of Justice is a stage of a judicial proceeding, though that investigation may not take place before a Court of Justice.

An investigation directed by a Court of Justice according to law, and conducted under the authority of a Court of Justice, is a stage of a judicial proceeding, though that investigation may not take place before a Court of Justice.

Illustrations.

(*a*) A, in support of a just claim which B has against Z for one thousand rupees, falsely swears, on the trial, that he heard Z admit the justice of B's claim. A has given false evidence.

(*b*) A, in an inquiry before a Magistrate for the purpose of ascertaining whether Z ought to be committed for trial, makes on oath a false statement material to the question. As this inquiry is a stage of a judicial proceeding, A has given false evidence.

(*c*) A, in an inquiry before an officer deputed by a Court of Justice to ascertain, on the spot, the boundaries of land, makes on oath a false statement material to the question. As this inquiry is a stage of a judicial proceeding, A has given false evidence.

189. Whoever causes any circumstance to exist, intending that such circumstance may appear in evidence in some stage of a judicial proceeding, and that such circumstance so appearing in evidence may cause any person who in such judicial proceeding acts as a Judge, Magistrate, Juryman, or Arbitrator, or makes any investigation under the authority of a Court of Justice, to entertain an erroneous opinion touching any point material to the result of such proceeding, is said " to fabricate false evidence."

Illustrations.

(*a*) A puts jewels into a box belonging to Z, with the intention that they may be found in that box, and that this circumstance may cause Z to be convicted of theft. A has fabricated false evidence.

(*b*) A, with the intention of causing Z to be convicted of a criminal conspiracy, writes a letter in imitation of Z's handwriting, purporting to be addressed to an accomplice in such criminal conspiracy, and puts the letter in a place which he knows that the officers of the Police are likely to search. A has fabricated false evidence.

(*c*) A, having a just claim against Z for one thousand rupees, forges Z's signature to a bond for one thousand rupees, for the purpose of supporting that claim before a Court of Justice. A has fabricated false evidence.

190. Whoever gives or fabricates false evidence shall, except in the case hereinafter excepted, be punished with imprisonment of either description for a term which may extend to seven years and must not be less than one year, and shall also be liable to fine.

* See Note G.

Exception. A person who fabricates false evidence intending thereby to save himself from conviction for an offence, and not intending nor knowing it to be likely that the false evidence so fabricated may cause any injury to any other party, is not within the penal provision of this Clause.

Illustrations.

(*a*) A commits an offence. He then takes a horse and rides with great speed to a distant place, in order that he may, by appearing there in an incredibly short time after the commission of his offence, cause a Court of Justice to think him innocent. A is not liable to punishment as a fabricator of false evidence.

(*b*) A, after wounding a person with a knife, goes into the room where Z is sleeping, smears Z's clothes with blood, and lays the knife under Z's pillow, intending not only that suspicion may thereby be turned away from himself, but also that Z may be convicted of voluntarily causing grievous hurt. A is liable to punishment as a fabricator of false evidence.

191. Whoever gives or fabricates false evidence, intending or knowing it to be likely that he may thereby cause any person to be convicted of any offence which is capital by this Code, shall be punished with transportation for life, or with rigorous imprisonment for a term which may extend to life and must not be less than seven years, and shall also be liable to fine.*

192. Whoever gives or fabricates false evidence, intending or knowing it to be likely that he may thereby cause any person to be convicted of an offence which by this Code is not capital, but punishable with imprisonment for a term of more than seven years, shall be punished as a person convicted of that offence would be liable to be punished.†

Illustration.

A gives false evidence before a Court of Justice, intending thereby to cause Z to be convicted of a Dacoity. The punishment of Dacoity is transportation for life or rigorous imprisonment for a term which may extend to life and must not be less than three years, with or without fine. A, therefore, is liable to such transportation or imprisonment, and to fine.

193. Whoever removes, conceals, delivers to any party, or causes to be transferred to any party any property, intending thereby to prevent that property from being taken as a forfeiture, or in satisfaction of a fine, under a sentence which has been pronounced, or which he knows to be likely to be pronounced by a Court of Justice, or from being taken in execution of a decree which has been made, or which he knows to be likely to be made by a Court of Justice in a civil suit, shall be punished with imprisonment of either description for a term which may extend to one year, or fine, or both.

194. Whoever claims any property knowing that he has no rightful claim to such property, or practices any deception touching any right to any property, intending thereby to prevent that property from being taken as a forfeiture, or in satisfaction of a fine, under a sentence which has been pronounced, or which he knows to be likely to be pronounced by a Court of Justice, or from being taken in execution of a decree which has been made, or which he knows to be likely to be made by a Court of Justice in a civil suit, shall be punished with imprisonment of either description for a term which may extend to one year, or fine, or both.

195. Whoever, in any declaration made and subscribed by him, which declaration any Court of Justice is bound by law to receive as evidence of any fact, states as true what he knows to be false touching any point material to the effect of such declaration, shall be punished with imprisonment of either description for a term which may extend to two years, or fine, or both.

196. Whoever, fraudulently, or for the purpose of annoyance, institutes any civil suit knowing that he has no just ground to institute such suit, shall be punished with imprisonment of either description for a term which may extend to one year, or fine, or both.

Explanation. It is not necessary that the party to whom the offender intends to cause wrongful loss or annoyance should be the party against whom the suit is instituted.

---

* For the case in which death is voluntarily caused by false evidence, see the head of Voluntary Culpable Homicide.
† The subornation of false evidence falls under the head of Abetment.

Illustration.

A, intending fraudulently to deprive Z of property to which A knows that A has no right, institutes a suit against B for that property by collusion with B. A has committed the offence defined in this Clause.

197. Whoever intentionally offers any insult or causes any interruption to any public servant, or body of public servants, while such public servant or body is sitting as a Court of Justice, shall be punished with imprisonment of either description for a term which may extend to six months, or fine which may extend to one thousand rupees, or both.

198. If any person, by doing any thing whereby he commits an offence under the last preceding Clause, also commits an offence under any Clause contained in any other Chapter of this Code, the punishment shall be cumulative.

199. Whoever directly or indirectly holds out any threat of any injury to any person for the purpose of inducing that person to refrain or desist from instituting, prosecuting, or defending any civil suit, or from taking any legal step incident to or consequent upon such institution, prosecution, or defence, or from giving evidence in any stage of any judicial proceeding whatever, shall be punished with imprisonment of either description for a term which may extend to two years, or fine, or both.

200. If any person, by doing any thing whereby he commits an offence under the last preceding Clause, also commits an offence under any other Clause in this Code, the punishment shall be cumulative.

201. Whoever escapes or attempts to escape from any custody in which he is lawfully detained in pursuance of a sentence of a Court of Justice, or by virtue of a commutation of such sentence, shall be punished with imprisonment of either description for a term which may extend to two years, or fine, or both.

202. If any person, by doing any thing whereby he commits an offence under the last preceding Clause, also commits an offence under any other Clause contained in this Code, the punishment shall be cumulative.

203. Whoever, having been lawfully transported for a term not extending to life, returns from such transportation, the term of such transportation not having expired, and his punishment not having been remitted, shall be punished with transportation for life, and shall also be liable to fine.

204. Whoever, having been sentenced to a punishment which has been lawfully commuted for transportation for a term of years and subsequent banishment for life, returns from such transportation or banishment, his punishment not having been remitted, shall be punished with transportation for life, and shall also be liable to fine.

205. Whoever, having been lawfully banished, returns from such banishment, his term of banishment not having expired, and his punishment not having been remitted, shall be punished with transportation for a term which may extend to seven years, to which banishment for life shall always be added.

206. Whoever, except as hereinafter excepted, knowing that any person has escaped from any custody in which such person was lawfully detained in pursuance of the sentence of a Court of Justice, or by virtue of a commutation of such sentence, or has returned from lawful transportation or banishment, the term of such transportation or banishment not having expired, and the punishment of such person not having been remitted, gives harbour, assistance, or intelligence to such person, with the intention of saving such person from the legal consequences of such escape or return, shall be punished with simple imprisonment for a term which may extend to six months, or fine which may extend to one thousand rupees, or both.

Exception. This provision does not extend to the case in which the harbour, assistance, or intelligence is given by the husband, or wife, or relation in the direct ascending or descending line, or brother, or sister of the person to whom the harbour, assistance, or intelligence is given.

207. Whoever, having accepted any conditional remission of punishment in the manner described in the Code of Procedure, knowingly violates any condition on which such remission was granted, shall be punished with the punishment to which he was originally sentenced, if he has already suffered no part of that punishment, and if he has suffered any part of that punishment, then with so much of that punishment as he has not already suffered.

CHAPTER XI.*

OF OFFENCES RELATING TO THE REVENUE.

208. Whoever imports or attempts to import any property into the Territories of the East India Company, or exports or attempts to export any property from the said Territories, or conveys or attempts to convey any property from place to place within the said Territories, in contravention of any law by which such importation, exportation, or conveyance is prohibited or regulated, is said to commit the offence of " smuggling."

Illustrations.

(*a*) A imports goods by landing them at a place at which the landing of them is prohibited by law. A has committed the offence of smuggling.

(*b*) A conveys goods through the Territories of the East India Company without a permit, being forbidden by law so to convey them. A has committed the offence of smuggling.

(*c*) A exports goods without paying an export duty on them, being forbidden by law so to export them. A has committed the offence of smuggling.

209. Whoever commits the offence of smuggling shall be punished with imprisonment of either description for a term which may extend to three months, or with fine which may extend to an amount equal to five hundred rupees added to five times the market value of the property smuggled, or with both.

210. Whoever fraudulently receives smuggled goods knowing the same to have been smuggled, shall be punished with imprisonment of either description for a term which may extend to three months, or with fine which may extend to an amount equal to five hundred rupees added to five times the market value of the property smuggled, or with both.

211. Whoever, being in charge of any vessel, places that vessel in any situation in which he is forbidden to place it by any public servant, or body of public servants, employed in the collection of the revenue, and empowered by law, as such public servant, or body, to forbid the placing of such vessel in such situation, shall be punished with fine which may extend to one thousand rupees.

212. Whoever cultivates, collects, or manufactures any article in contravention of any law by which the cultivation, collection, or manufacture of that article is prohibited or regulated, shall be punished with simple imprisonment for a term which may extend to three months, or fine which may extend to five hundred rupees, or both.

Illustrations.

(*a*) A, contrary to law, cultivates the poppy. A has committed the offence defined in this Clause.

(*b*) A cultivates tobacco in a district in which such cultivation is prohibited by law. A has committed the offence defined in this Clause.

(*c*) A, contrary to law, collects opium from the poppy. A has committed the offence defined in this Clause.

(*d*) A, in the Bombay Presidency, contrary to law, collects toddy from the brab tree. A has committed the offence defined in this Clause.

213. Whoever makes or has in his possession any implement, material, or receptacle in order to the doing of any thing which is an offence under the last preceding Clause, shall be punished with simple imprisonment for a term which may extend to three months, or fine which may extend to five hundred rupees, or both.

Illustrations.

(*a*) A makes a saltpan for the purpose of collecting salt, contrary to law. A has committed the offence defined in this Clause.

(*b*) A has in his possession a still, for the purpose of distillation, contrary to law. A has committed the offence defined in this Clause.

214. Whoever sells or offers for sale any article in contravention of any law by which the selling or offering for sale of such article is prohibited or regulated, shall be punished with imprisonment of either description for a term which may extend to three months, or fine which may extend to five hundred rupees, or both.

See Note H.

215. Whoever has in his possession any article in contravention of any law by which the possession of that article is prohibited or regulated, shall be punished with fine which may extend to twice the value of that article.

216. Whoever, being bound by law to put any mark on any article in his possession, omits to put such mark on such article, shall be punished with fine which may extend to the value of such article.

217. Whoever performs any part of the process of counterfeiting any stamp from which the Government derives a revenue, shall be punished with imprisonment of either description for a term which may extend to seven years and must not be less than one year, and shall also be liable to fine.

218. Whoever has in his possession any implement or material, intending or knowing it to be likely that the same may be used for the purpose of counterfeiting any stamp from which the Government derives a revenue, shall be punished with imprisonment of either description for a term which may extend to seven years and must not be less than one year, and shall also be liable to fine.

219. Whoever makes any implement, intending or knowing it to be likely that the same may be used for the purpose of counterfeiting any stamp from which the Government derives a revenue, shall be punished with imprisonment of either description for a term which may extend to seven years and must not be less than one year, and shall also be liable to fine.

220. Whoever sells or offers for sale any stamp which he knows to be a counterfeit of any stamp from which the Government derives a revenue, shall be punished with imprisonment of either description for a term which may extend to seven years and must not be less than one year, and shall also be liable to fine.

221. Whoever has in his possession any stamp which he knows to be a counterfeit of any stamp from which the Government derives a revenue, intending to sell or offer for sale such stamp, shall be punished with imprisonment of either description for a term which may extend to seven years and must not be less than one year, and shall also be liable to fine.

222. Whoever uses as genuine any stamp, knowing it to be a counterfeit of any stamp from which the Government derives a revenue, shall be punished with imprisonment of either description for a term which may extend to six months, or fine, or both.

223. Whoever, intending to cause wrongful loss to the Government, effaces from any substance bearing a stamp any writing for which such stamp has been used, in order that such stamp may be used for a different writing, shall be punished with imprisonment of either description for a term which may extend to three months, or with a fine which may extend to an amount equal to five hundred rupees added to five times the price of such stamp, or with both.

224. Whoever, intending to cause wrongful loss to the Government, uses for any writing, as a stamp which has not been used before, a stamp which he knows to have been before used for a different writing, shall be punished with imprisonment of either description for a term which may extend to three months, or with a fine which may extend to an amount equal to five hundred rupees added to five times the price of such stamp, or with both.

225. Whoever establishes or maintains any illegal post for the purpose of conveying letters or packets from place to place for hire, or receives any letter or packet in order to the conveying of the same by such illegal post, or conveys the same by such illegal post, or delivers the same after the conveyance of the same by such illegal post, shall be punished with imprisonment of either description for a term which may extend to three months, or fine which may extend to one thousand rupees, or both.

226. Whoever, being in charge of any letter or packet which is on board of any vessel, and being legally bound to deliver such letter or packet into the keeping of any officer in charge of a Post Office, intentionally omits so to deliver the same, at the time and in the manner directed by law, shall be punished with fine.

227. Whoever, being in charge of any vessel, refuses to receive on board for the purpose of conveyance any letter or packet which he is required to receive on board by any public servant, or any body of public servants, legally competent as such to require him so to receive the same, shall be punished with fine which may extend to five hundred rupees.

228. Whoever, being legally authorised by license from any public servant, as such, or from any body of public servants, as such, to cultivate, to collect, to manufacture, to import, to export, to convey from place to place, to sell, or to have in his possession any article, disobeys any direction of law, or any condition imposed by the lawful authority of the public servant, or body of public servants from whom such license was obtained, as to the way in which he is to act as such licensed person, shall be punished with fine which may extend to two hundred rupees.

Illustrations.

(a) A, a licensed stamp vender, being bound, as such licensed stamp vender, to have the schedule of stamps affixed in a conspicuous situation in his shop, omits to have that schedule so affixed. A has committed the offence defined in this Clause.

(b) A, a proprietor of salt covered by a rowannah, being legally bound daily to certify on the back of his rowannah the quantity sold by him, omits to do so. A has committed the offence defined in this Clause.

229. The punishments provided by this Chapter are independent of any confiscation to which the property, with respect to which the offences defined in this Chapter have been committed, is liable under any law.

CHAPTER XII.*

OF OFFENCES RELATING TO COIN.

230. Coin is metal used as money, and bearing some mark that it is issued by the authority of some Government in order to be so used.

Illustrations.

(a) Cowries are not coin, as not being metal.

(b) Lumps of unstamped copper, though used as money, are not coin, inasmuch as they bear no mark of the authority which issues them.

(c) An ancient Denarius is not now coin, inasmuch as such pieces are not now used as money.

(d) Medals are not coin, inasmuch as they are not intended to be used as money.

(e) Bank tokens issued by a private Bank are not coin, inasmuch as they are not put forth by the authority of any Government.

231. Coin first issued by the authority of the Government of India, or of the Government of any Presidency, to be used as money within the territories of the East India Company, is designated as Company's coin.

232. Whoever counterfeits coin shall be punished with imprisonment of either description for a term which may extend to three years and must not be less than six months, and shall also be liable to fine.

Explanation. A person may commit this offence by causing a genuine coin to appear like a different coin.

233. Whoever counterfeits the King's or the Company's coin shall be punished with imprisonment of either description for a term which may extend to seven years and must not be less than one year, and shall also be liable to fine.

234. Whoever makes any die for the purpose of counterfeiting coin, or of enabling any other person to counterfeit coin, shall be punished with imprisonment of either description for a term which may extend to three years and must not be less than six months, and shall also be liable to fine.

235. Whoever makes any die for the purpose of counterfeiting the King's or the Company's coin, or of enabling any other person to counterfeit the King's or the Company's coin, shall be punished with imprisonment of either description for a term which may extend to seven years and must not be less than two years, and shall also be liable to fine.

236. Whoever is in possession of any implement or material with the intention of employing the same for the purpose of committing any of the offences defined in any of

* See Note I.

the four Clauses last preceding, shall be punished with imprisonment of either description for a term which may extend to three years and must not be less than six months, and shall also be liable to fine.

237. Whoever previously abets by instigation, conspiracy, or aid, the counterfeiting, without the territories of the East India Company, of the King's or the Company's coin, shall be punished with imprisonment of either description for a term which may extend to seven years and must not be less than two years, and shall also be liable to fine.

238. Whoever imports into the territories of the East India Company, or exports from the said territories any coin which he knows to be counterfeit, intending or knowing it to be likely that such coin may pass as genuine, shall be punished with imprisonment of either description for a term which may extend to three years and must not be less than six months, and shall also be liable to fine.

239. Whoever imports into the territories of the East India Company, or exports from the said territories any coin which he knows to be a counterfeit of the King's or the Company's coin, intending or knowing it to be likely that such coin may pass as genuine, shall be punished with imprisonment of either description for a term which may extend to seven years and must not be less than two years, and shall also be liable to fine.

240. Whoever, having any counterfeit coin which at the time at which he became possessed of it he knew to be counterfeit, delivers the same to any other, or attempts to induce any other to receive it, with the intention that such counterfeit coin shall pass as genuine, shall be punished with imprisonment of either description for a term which may extend to three years and must not be less than six months, and shall also be liable to fine.

241. Whoever, having any counterfeit coin which is a counterfeit of the King's or the Company's coin, and which at the time at which he became possessed of it he knew to be a counterfeit of the King's or the Company's coin, delivers the same to any other, or attempts to induce any other to receive it, with the intention that such counterfeit coin shall pass as genuine, shall be punished with imprisonment of either description for a term which may extend to seven years and must not be less than two years, and shall also be liable to fine.

242. Whoever, knowing any coin to be counterfeit, delivers the same to any other person as genuine, or attempts to induce any other person to receive it as genuine, shall be punished with fine to an amount which may extend to ten times the value of the coin of which such counterfeit coin is a counterfeit.

Illustration.

A, a coiner, delivers counterfeit Company's rupees to his accomplice B, for the purpose of uttering them. B sells the rupees to C, another utterer, who buys them knowing them to be counterfeit. C pays away the rupees for goods to D, who receives them not knowing them to be counterfeit. D, after receiving the rupees, discovers that they are counterfeit, and pays them away as if they were good. Here, A, B, and C, are guilty of the offence defined in the last preceding Clause. D is guilty only of the offence defined in this Clause.

243. Whoever is in possession of counterfeit coin, having known at the time when he became possessed thereof that such coin was counterfeit, and intending or knowing it to be likely that such counterfeit coin may pass as genuine, shall be punished with imprisonment of either description for a term which may extend to three years and must not be less than six months, and shall also be liable to fine.

244. Whoever is in possession of counterfeit coin which is a counterfeit of the King's or the Company's coin, having known at the time when he became possessed of it that it was counterfeit, and intending or knowing it to be likely that such counterfeit coin may pass as genuine, shall be punished with imprisonment of either description for a term which may extend to seven years and must not be less than two years, and shall also be liable to fine.

245. Whoever, being employed in any mint lawfully established within the territories of the East India Company, does any act, or omits what he is legally bound to do, with the intention of causing any coin issued from that mint to be of different weight or composition from the weight or composition fixed by law, shall be punished with imprisonment of either description for a term which may extend to seven years and must not be less than two years, and shall also be liable to fine.

246. Whoever performs on any coin any operation which diminishes the weight or

alters the composition of that coin, with the intention that the said coin shall pass as if its weight had not been so diminished or its composition so altered, shall be punished with imprisonment of either description for a term which may extend to one year and must not be less than three months, and shall also be liable to fine.

Explanation. A person who scoops out part of the coin, and puts any thing else into the cavity, changes the composition of that coin.

247. Whoever performs on any of the King's or the Company's coin any operation which diminishes the weight or alters the composition of that coin, with the intention that the said coin shall pass as if its weight had not been so diminished or its composition so altered, shall be punished with imprisonment of either description for a term which may extend to three years and must not be less than one year, and shall also be liable to fine.

248. Whoever is in possession of any implement or material, intending to employ the same for the purpose of committing any of the offences defined in either of the three last preceding Clauses, shall be punished with imprisonment of either description for a term which may extend to one year and must not be less than three months, and shall also be liable to fine.

249. Whoever, having coin in his possession with respect to which the offence defined in Clause 246 has been committed, and having known at the time when he became possessed of such coin that such offence had been committed with respect to it, delivers such coin to any other or attempts to induce any other to receive the same, with the intention that such coin may pass as if no offence had been committed with respect to it, shall be punished with imprisonment of either description for a term which may extend to one year and must not be less than three months, and shall also be liable to fine.

250. Whoever, having coin in his possession with respect to which the offence defined in Clause 247 has been committed, and having known at the time when he became possessed of such coin that such offence had been committed with respect to it, delivers such coin to any other or attempts to induce any other to receive the same, with the intention that such coin may pass as if no such offence had been committed with respect to it, shall be punished with imprisonment of either description for a term which may extend to three years and must not be less than one year, and shall also be liable to fine.

251. Whoever is in possession of coin with respect to which the offence defined in Clause 246 has been committed, having known at the time of becoming possessed thereof that such offence had been committed with respect to such coin, and intending to cause the same to be in circulation, shall be punished with imprisonment of either description for a term which may extend to one year and must not be less than three months, and shall also be liable to fine.

252. Whoever is in possession of coin with respect to which the offence defined in Clause 247 has been committed, having known at the time of becoming possessed thereof that such offence had been committed with respect to such coin, and intending to cause the same to be in circulation, shall be punished with imprisonment of either description for a term which may extend to three years, and must not be less than one year, and shall also be liable to fine.

CHAPTER XIII.

OF OFFENCES RELATING TO WEIGHTS AND MEASURES.

253. Whoever, in dealing, fraudulently uses any balance which he knows to be false, shall be punished with imprisonment of either description for a term which may extend to one year, or fine, or both.

254. Whoever, in dealing, fraudulently uses any false weight or false measure of length or capacity, or fraudulently uses any weight or any measure of length or

F

capacity as a different weight or measure from what it is, shall be punished with imprisonment of either description for a term which may extend to one year, or fine, or both.

255. Whoever is in possession of any balance, or of any weight, or of any measure of length or capacity, which he knows to be false, and which he intends to use fraudulently in dealing, shall be punished with imprisonment of either description for a term which may extend to one year, or fine, or both.

256. Whoever makes any balance, or weight, or measure of length or capacity, which he knows to be false, intending the same to be fraudulently used in dealing, shall be punished with imprisonment of either description for a term which may extend to one year, or fine, or both.

CHAPTER XIV.

OF OFFENCES AFFECTING THE PUBLIC HEALTH, SAFETY, AND CONVENIENCE.

257. Whoever malignantly or wantonly does any act which he knows to be likely to spread the infection of any disease dangerous to life, shall be punished with imprisonment of either description for a term which may extend to six months, or fine, or both.

258. Whoever knowingly disobeys any rule made and promulgated according to law by the Government of India, or by the Government of any Presidency, for putting any vessel into a state of quarantine, or for regulating the intercourse of vessels in a state of quarantine with the shore, or with other vessels, or for regulating the intercourse between places where an infectious disease prevails and other places, shall be punished with imprisonment of either description for a term which may extend to six months, or fine, or both.

259. Whoever adulterates any article of food or drink, so as to make such article noxious as food or drink, intending or knowing it to be likely that such article may be sold as wholesome food or drink, shall be punished with imprisonment of either description for a term which may extend to six months, or fine which may extend to five hundred rupees, or both.

260. Whoever sells or offers for sale, as wholesome, any food or drink, knowing the same to be noxious, shall be punished with imprisonment of either description for a term which may extend to six months, or fine which may extend to five hundred rupees, or both.

261. Whoever adulterates any drug or medical preparation, in such a manner as to lessen the efficacy or change the operation of such drug or medical preparation, or to make it noxious, intending or knowing it to be likely that such drug or medical preparation may be sold or issued from any dispensary, as if it had not undergone such adulteration, shall be punished with imprisonment of either description for a term which may extend to six months, or fine which may extend to one thousand rupees, or both.

262. Whoever, knowing any drug or medical preparation to have been adulterated in such a manner as to lessen its efficacy, to change its operation, or to render it noxious, sells the same, or offers it for sale, or issues it from any dispensary, as unadulterated, shall be punished with imprisonment of either description for a term which may extend to six months, or fine which may extend to one thousand rupees, or both.

263. Whoever knowingly sells, or offers for sale, or issues from any dispensary, any drug or medical preparation, as a different drug or medical preparation, shall be punished with imprisonment of either description for a term which may extend to six months, or fine which may extend to one thousand rupees, or both.

264. Whoever, by any act, or by omitting to take order with property in his possession, voluntarily causes the atmosphere in any public way to be in a state noxious to health, or offensive to the senses, shall be punished with imprisonment of either description for

a term which may extend to one month, or fine which may extend to five hundred rupees, or both.

265. Whoever drives any vehicle, or rides, on any public way in a manner so rash or negligent as to indicate a want of due regard for human life, shall be punished with imprisonment of either description for a term which may extend to six months, or fine which may extend to two thousand rupees, or both.

266. Whoever navigates any vessel in a manner so rash or negligent as to indicate a want of due regard for human life, shall be punished with imprisonment of either description for a term which may extend to six months, or fine which may extend to two thousand rupees, or both.

267. Whoever, being in charge of any vessel, conveys for hire any person by water in that vessel, when that vessel is in such a state or so loaded as to endanger the life of that person, shall be punished with imprisonment of either description for a term which may extend to six months, or fine which may extend to two thousand rupees, or both.

268. Whoever does with any poisonous substance any act so rash or negligent as to indicate a want of due regard for human life, or omits to take such order with any poisonous substance in his possession as he believes to be sufficient to guard against any probable danger to human life from such poisonous substance, shall be punished with imprisonment of either description for a term which may extend to six months, or fine which may extend to two thousand rupees, or both.

269. Whoever does with fire or any combustible matter any act so rash or negligent as to indicate a want of due regard to human life, or omits to take such order with any fire or any combustible matter in his possession as he believes to be sufficient to guard against any probable danger to human life from such fire or combustible matter, shall be punished with imprisonment of either description for a term which may extend to six months, or fine which may extend to two thousand rupees, or both.

270. Whoever does with any explosive substance any act so rash or negligent as to indicate a want of due regard for human life, or omits to take such order with any explosive substance in his possession as he believes to be sufficient to guard against any probable danger to human life from that substance, shall be punished with imprisonment of either description for a term which may extend to six months, or fine which may extend to two thousand rupees, or both.

271. Whoever does with any machinery any act so rash or negligent as to indicate a want of due regard for human life, or omits to take such order with any machinery in his possession or under his care as he believes to be sufficient to guard against any probable danger to human life from such machinery, shall be punished with imprisonment of either description for a term which may extend to six months, or fine which may extend to two thousand rupees, or both.

272. Whoever, having such a right over any building as entitles him to pull down or repair that building, omits to take such order with that building as he believes to be sufficient to guard against any probable danger to human life from the fall of that building, or of any part thereof, shall be punished with imprisonment of either description for a term which may extend to six months, or fine which may extend to two thousand rupees, or both.

273. Whoever omits to take such order with any animal in his possession as he believes to be sufficient to guard against any probable danger to human life, or any probable danger of grievous hurt, from such animal, shall be punished with imprisonment of either description for a term which may extend to six months, or fine which may extend to two thousand rupees, or both.

274. Whoever by doing any act in any public way or public line of navigation, or by omitting to take order with any property in his possession, which property is in any public way or public line of navigation, voluntarily causes danger, annoyance, or obstruction to those who pass along that way or line of navigation or who reside in the neighbourhood of that way or line of navigation, shall be punished with fine which may extend to two hundred rupees.

CHAPTER XV.*

OF OFFENCES RELATING TO RELIGION AND CASTE.

275. Whoever destroys, damages, or defiles any place of worship, or any object held sacred by any class of persons, with the intention of thereby insulting the religion of any class of persons, or with the knowledge that any class of persons are likely to consider such destruction, damage, or defilement as an insult to their religion, shall be punished with imprisonment of either description for a term which may extend to seven years and must not be less than one year, and shall also be liable to fine.

276. Whoever voluntarily causes disturbance to any assembly lawfully engaged in the performance of religious worship, or religious ceremonies, if in causing such disturbance he assaults any person, or makes shew of assaulting any person, or threatens to assault any person engaged in such worship or ceremonies, shall be punished with imprisonment of either description for a term which may extend to three years and must not be less than six months, and shall also be liable to fine.

277. If any person, by doing any thing whereby he commits an offence under the last preceding Clause, also commits an offence under any Clause contained in any other Chapter of this Code, the punishment shall be cumulative.

278. Whoever, in any place of worship, does any thing whereby he voluntarily causes disturbance to any assembly lawfully met therein for the performance of religious worship or religious ceremonies, shall be punished with imprisonment of either description for a term which may extend to one year, or fine, or both.

279. If any person, by doing any thing whereby he commits an offence under the last preceding Clause, also commits an offence under any Clause contained in any other Chapter of this Code, the punishment shall be cumulative.

280. Whoever, with the intention of wounding the feelings or insulting the religion of any person, commits any trespass on any place of sepulture, offers any indignity to any human corpse, or causes disturbance to any assembly assembled for the performance of funeral ceremonies, shall be punished with imprisonment of either description for a term which may extend to one year, or fine, or both.

281. If any person, by doing any thing whereby he commits an offence under the last preceding Clause, also commits an offence under any Clause contained in any other Chapter of this Code, the punishment shall be cumulative.

282. Whoever, with the deliberate intention of wounding the religious feelings of any person, utters any word or makes any sound in the hearing of that person, or makes any gesture in the sight of that person, or places any object in the sight of that person, shall be punished with imprisonment of either description for a term which may extend to one year, or fine, or both.

283. Whoever does any act with the intention of causing it to be believed in any quarter that, by doing that act, he renders some other person an object of divine displeasure, or of causing it to be believed that by doing that act he obliges some other person, on pain of the divine displeasure, to do any thing which that person is not legally bound to do, or to omit any thing which that person is legally entitled to do, or threatens any person with doing any act which would, in any quarter, be believed to render the person threatened an object of divine displeasure, shall be punished with imprisonment of either description for a term which may extend to one year, or fine which may extend to one thousand rupees, or both.

Illustrations.

(a) A sits Dhurna at Z's door, with the intention of causing it to be believed that by so sitting he renders Z an object of divine displeasure. A has committed the offence defined in this Clause.

(b) A threatens Z that, unless Z performs a certain act, A will kill one of A's own children, under such circumstances that the killing would be believed to render Z an object of divine displeasure. A has committed the offence defined in this Clause.

* See Note J.

284. Whoever, with the intention of causing any person to lose caste, commits any assault which causes that person to lose caste, or induces that person to do ignorantly any thing whereby that person incurs loss of caste, shall be punished with imprisonment of either description for a term which may extend to six months, or fine which may extend to two thousand rupees, or both.

Illustration.

A, with the intention of causing Z, a Brahmin, to lose caste, mixes beef broth with Z's food. Z swallows it in ignorance, and thereby loses caste. A has committed the offence defined in this Clause.

285. Whoever intentionally causes any food belonging to any person to be in a state in which that person, according to the rules of his religion or caste, cannot use it as food, shall be punished with fine which may extend to fifty rupees.

286. Whoever, having been convicted of the offence defined in the Clause last preceding, again commits the offence defined in the Clause last preceding, shall be punished with imprisonment of either description for a term which may extend to one month, or fine which may extend to two hundred rupees, or both.

CHAPTER XVI.*

OF ILLEGAL ENTRANCE INTO AND RESIDENCE IN THE TERRITORIES OF THE EAST INDIA COMPANY.

287. Whoever, being a subject of the King and not a native of the Territories of the East India Company, on his arrival by sea in any place within the said Territories omits to make known in writing his name, place of destination, and object of pursuit in India, to the Chief Officer of Customs, or other Officer authorised for that purpose at the place at which such subject of the King has arrived, shall be punished with fine which may extend to one thousand rupees.

288. Whoever, being a subject of the King and not a native of the Territories of the East India Company, enters the said Territories by land not being legally authorised so to do, shall be punished with simple imprisonment for a term which may extend to three months, or fine which may extend to two thousand rupees, or both.

289. Whoever, being a subject of the King and not a native of the Territories of the East India Company, and not having such a license as is by law necessary to authorise such a subject of the King to reside in a certain part of the said Territories, enters or resides in that part of the said Territories, shall be punished with simple imprisonment for a term which may extend to three months, or fine which may extend to two thousand rupees, or both.

290. Whoever, having been convicted of the offence defined in the Clause last preceding, again commits the offence defined in the Clause last preceding, shall be punished with banishment for life, or for any term, or with simple imprisonment for a term which may extend to one year, to which banishment or imprisonment and fine may be added.

* See Note K.

CHAPTER XVII.*

OF OFFENCES RELATING TO THE PRESS.

291. Whoever keeps in his possession a press for the printing of books or papers, not having made and subscribed the declaration required by law to be made and subscribed by every person keeping such a press in his possession, shall be punished with simple imprisonment for a term which may extend to two years, or fine which may extend to five thousand rupees, or both.

292. Whoever prints or publishes any book or paper which has not printed legibly on it the name of the printer, the name of the publisher, and the place of the printing and publication, shall be punished with simple imprisonment for a term which may extend to two years, or fine which may extend to five thousand rupees, or both.

293. Whoever prints or publishes any periodical work whatever containing public news, or comments on public news, otherwise than in conformity to the rules of law whereby the printing and publishing of such works is regulated, shall be punished with simple imprisonment for a term which may extend to two years, or fine which may extend to five thousand rupees, or both.

CHAPTER XVIII.†

OF OFFENCES AFFECTING THE HUMAN BODY.

OF OFFENCES AFFECTING LIFE.

294. Whoever does any act or omits what he is legally bound to do, with the intention of thereby causing, or with the knowledge that he is likely thereby to cause the death of any person, and does by such act or omission cause the death of any person, is said to commit the offence of " voluntary culpable homicide."

Illustrations.

(*a*) A lays sticks and turf over a pit, with the intention of thereby causing death, or with the knowledge that death is likely to be thereby caused. Z, believing the ground to be firm, treads on it, falls in, and is killed. A has committed the offence of voluntary culpable homicide.

(*b*) A, with the intention or knowledge aforesaid, relates agitating tidings to Z, who is in a critical stage of a dangerous illness. Z dies in consequence. A has committed the offence of voluntary culpable homicide.

(*c*) A, with the intention or knowledge aforesaid, gives Z his choice whether Z will kill himself, or suffer lingering torture. Z kills himself in consequence. A has committed the offence of voluntary culpable homicide.

(*d*) A, with the intention or knowledge aforesaid, falsely deposes before a Court of Justice that he saw Z commit a capital crime. Z is convicted and executed in consequence. A has committed the offence of voluntary culpable homicide.

(*e*) A is hired to guide Z through a jungle. In the midst of the jungle A, no circumstance having occurred to release him from his legal obligation to guide Z through the jungle, with such intention or knowledge as aforesaid, leaves Z. Z dies in consequence. A has committed the offence of voluntary culpable homicide.

(*f*) A, being legally bound to furnish food to Z, who is the mother of a sucking child, omits to furnish her with food, intending or knowing it to be likely that Z's death may be the consequence of the omission. Z survives, but the child is starved to death in consequence of the failure of milk which is caused by A's omission. Here, even if A did not know of the existence of the child, he has committed the offence of voluntary culpable homicide.

(*g*) A keeps Z in wrongful confinement, and is therefore legally bound (see Clause 338) to furnish Z with what he knows to be necessary to prevent Z from being in danger of death. A

* See Note L. † See Note M.

knowing that Z is likely to die if medical advice be not procured, illegally omits to procure such advice. Z dies in consequence. A has committed the offence of voluntary culpable homicide.

(h) A knows Z to be behind a bush. B does not know it. A, intending to cause or knowing himself to be likely to cause Z's death, induces B to fire at the bush. B fires and kills Z. Here, B may be guilty of no offence, or if his firing was, under the circumstances, a rash act, he may be guilty of the offence defined in Clause 304. But A has committed the offence of voluntary culpable homicide.

295. Voluntary culpable homicide is "murder" unless it be of one of the three mitigated descriptions hereinafter enumerated; That is to say,

First, Manslaughter;

Secondly, Voluntary culpable homicide by consent;

Thirdly, Voluntary culpable homicide in defence.

296. If a person, by doing any thing which he intends or knows to be likely to cause death, commits voluntary culpable homicide on a person whose death he neither intends nor knows himself to be likely to cause, the voluntary culpable homicide committed by the offender is of the same description of which it would have been if he had caused the death which he intended or knew himself to be likely to cause.

297. Voluntary culpable homicide is " manslaughter," when it is committed on grave and sudden provocation, by causing the death of the person who gave that provocation.

Explanation. Provocation is designated as "grave," when it is such as would be likely to move a person of ordinary temper to violent passion, and is not given by any thing done in obedience to the law, or by any thing authorised by the law of Civil or Criminal Procedure, or by any thing done by a public servant in the exercise of the lawful powers of such public servant, or by any thing done by any person in the exercise of the right of private defence against the offender.

Illustrations.

(a) A, under the influence of passion excited by a provocation given by Z, intentionally kills Y, Z's child. This is not manslaughter, but murder.

(b) A is lawfully arrested by Z, a bailiff. A is excited to sudden and violent passion by the arrest, and voluntarily kills Z. This is not manslaughter, but murder.

(c) A appears as a witness before Z, a Magistrate. Z says that he does not believe a word of A's deposition, and that A has perjured himself. A is moved to sudden passion by these words, and kills Z. This is not manslaughter but murder.

(d) A attempts to pull Z's nose. Z in the exercise of the right of private defence, strikes A. A is moved to sudden and violent passion by the blow, and kills Z. This is not manslaughter, but murder.

(e) Z strikes B. B is by this provocation excited to violent rage. A, a bystander, intending to take advantage of B's rage in order to cause Z's death, puts a knife into B's hand. B kills Z with the knife. Here, B may have committed only manslaughter, but A has committed murder.

(f) Y gives grave and sudden provocation to A. A, on this provocation, fires a pistol at Y, neither intending nor knowing himself to be likely to kill Z, who is near him, but out of sight. A kills Z. Here, A has committed manslaughter.

298. Voluntary culpable homicide is " voluntary culpable homicide by consent" when the person whose death is caused, being above twelve years of age, suffers death, or takes the risk of death, by his own choice:

Provided,

First, That the offender does not induce the person whose death is caused to make that choice by directly or indirectly putting that person in fear of any injury;

Secondly, That the person whose death has been caused is not, from youth, mental imbecility, derangement, intoxication, or passion, unable to understand the nature and consequences of his choice;

Thirdly, That the offender does not know that the person whose death is caused was induced to make the choice by any deception, or concealment;

Fourthly, That the offender does not conceal from the person whose death is caused any thing which the offender knew to be likely to cause that person to change his mind.

Explanation. Voluntary culpable homicide committed by inducing a person voluntarily to put himself to death is voluntary culpable homicide by consent, except when it is murder.

Illustrations.

(a) Z, a Hindoo Widow, consents to be burned with the corpse of her husband. A kindles the pile. Here A has committed voluntary culpable homicide by consent.

(b) A, by instigation, voluntarily causes Z, a child under twelve years of age, to commit suicide.

Here, on account of Z's youth, the offence cannot be voluntary culpable homicide by consent. A has therefore committed murder.

(c) A, by deceiving Z into a belief that Z's family have perished at sea, voluntarily causes Z to commit suicide. Here, on account of the deception practised by A, the offence cannot be voluntary culpable homicide by consent. A has therefore committed murder.

299. Voluntary culpable homicide is " voluntary culpable homicide in defence" when it is committed by causing death under such circumstances that such causing of death would be no offence if the right of private defence extended to the voluntary causing of death in cases of assault not falling under any of the descriptions enumerated in Clause 76, or in cases of theft, mischief, or criminal trespass not falling under any of the descriptions enumerated in Clause 79.

Illustrations.

(a) Z attempts to horsewhip A, not in such a manner as to cause grievous hurt to A. A draws out a pistol. Z persists in the assault. A believing in good faith that he can by no other means prevent himself from being horsewhipped, shoots Z dead. A has committed voluntary culpable homicide in defence.

(b) Z commits simple theft on A's horse, and rides away with it. Here A has a right of private defence which lasts till either Z can effect his retreat with the property, or till A can recover his horse, but which does not extend to the infliction of death, in as much as A is in no danger of death or hurt. A pursues Z, and, not being able to overtake him, shoots him dead. A has committed voluntary culpable homicide in defence.

(c) Z commits an assault not of a dangerous description on A. A, knowing that he can defend himself from the assault without killing Z, kills Z. Here, as A's act would be an offence even if the right of private defence in cases of assault of the descriptions not enumerated in Clause 76 extended to the voluntary infliction of death, A has committed voluntary culpable homicide which is not voluntary culpable homicide in defence, but which, according to the circumstances, will be manslaughter, or murder.

300. Whoever commits murder shall be punished with death, or transportation for life, or rigorous imprisonment for life, and shall also be liable to fine.

301. Whoever commits manslaughter shall be punished with imprisonment of either description for a term which may extend to fourteen years, or fine, or both.

302. Whoever commits voluntary culpable homicide by consent shall be punished with imprisonment of either description for a term which may extend to fourteen years and must not be less than two years, and shall also be liable to fine.

303. Whoever commits voluntary culpable homicide in defence shall be punished with imprisonment of either description for a term which may extend to fourteen years, or fine, or both.

304. Whoever causes the death of any person by any act or any illegal omission, which act or omission was so rash or negligent as to indicate a want of due regard for human life, shall be punished with imprisonment of either description for a term which may extend to two years, or fine, or both.

305. If the act or illegal omission whereby death is caused in the manner described in the last preceding Clause be, apart from the circumstance of its having caused death, an offence other than the offence defined in Clause 327, or an attempt to commit an offence, the offender shall be liable to the punishment of the offence so committed or attempted in addition to the punishment provided by the last preceding Clause.

Explanation. In cases in which the doing of a certain thing and the attempting to do that thing are distinct offences, if the offence defined in the last preceding Clause be committed in the attempting to do that thing, the additional punishment to which the offender is liable is the punishment not of attempting to do that thing but of doing that thing.

Illustration.

A uses force to Z, a woman, intending to ravish her. He does not ravish her, but commits the offence defined in Clause 304. Here, the term of imprisonment to which A has made himself liable is to be regulated not by the term of imprisonment assigned to the offence of attempting to ravish but by the term of imprisonment assigned to actual rape, that is to say, A is liable to rigorous imprisonment for a term of not more than sixteen nor less than two years.

306. If any child under twelve years of age, any insane person, any delirious person, any idiot, or any person in a state of intoxication, commits suicide, whoever previously abets by aid the commission of such suicide shall be punished with death, or transportation for life, or rigorous imprisonment for life, and shall also be liable to fine.

307. If any person commits suicide, whoever previously abets by aid the commission of such suicide shall be punished with imprisonment of either description for a term which

may extend to fourteen years and must not be less than two years, and shall also be liable to fine.

308. Whoever does any act, or omits what he is legally bound to do, with such intention or knowledge and under such circumstances that if he by that act or omission caused death he would be guilty of murder, and carries that act or omission to such a length as at the time of carrying it to that length he contemplates as sufficient to cause death, shall be punished with transportation for life, or with rigorous imprisonment for a term which may extend to life, and must not be less than seven years, and shall also be liable to fine.

Illustrations.

(a) A, intending to murder Z by means of a spring gun, purchases such a gun. A has not yet committed the offence defined in this Clause. A sets the gun loaded in Z's path, and leaves it there. A has committed the offence defined in this Clause.

(b) A, intending to murder Z by poison, purchases poison, and mixes the same with food which remains in A's keeping. A has not yet committed the offence defined in this Clause. A places the food on Z's table, or delivers it to Z's servants to place it on Z's table. A has committed the offence defined in this Clause.

309. Whoever does any act, or omits what he is legally bound to do, with such intention or knowledge and under such circumstances that if he, by that act or omission, caused death he would be guilty of voluntary culpable homicide, and carries that act or omission to such a length as at the time of carrying it to that length he contemplates as sufficient to cause death, shall be punished with imprisonment of either description for a term which may extend to three years, or fine, or both.

Illustrations.

(a) A, on grave and sudden provocation, fires a pistol at Z, under such circumstances that if he thereby caused death he would be guilty of manslaughter. A has committed the offence defined in this Clause.

(b) A lights a pile prepared for a Suttee, under such circumstances that if he thereby caused death he would be guilty of voluntary culpable homicide by consent. A has committed the offence defined in this Clause.

(c) A pursues a thief, and fires at him, under such circumstances that if he killed the thief he would commit voluntary culpable homicide in defence. A has committed the offence defined in this Clause.

310. Whoever belongs or has at any time belonged to any gang of persons associated for the purpose of gaining a livelihood by inveigling and murdering travellers in order to take the property of such travellers, is designated as a "Thug."

311. Whoever is a Thug shall be punished with transportation for life, or imprisonment of either description for life, and shall also be liable to fine.

Of the Causing of Miscarriage.

312. Every woman who, being with child, voluntarily causes herself to miscarry, and every person who voluntarily causes a woman with child to miscarry, shall, if such miscarriage be not caused in good faith for the purpose of saving the life of the woman, be punished with imprisonment of either description for a term which may extend to three years, or fine, or both.

313. If any person commits the offence defined in the last preceding Clause without the free and intelligent consent of the woman, the punishment of causing the miscarriage shall be in excess of any punishment to which the offender may be liable by reason of any hurt which he may have caused or attempted to cause to the woman.

Of Hurt.

314. All bodily pain, disease, and infirmity, is designated as "hurt."

315. The following kinds of hurt are designated as "grievous:"

First, Emasculation;

Secondly, Permanent privation of the sight of either eye;

Thirdly, Permanent privation of the hearing of either ear;

Fourthly, Privation of any member or joint;

Fifthly, Destruction or permanent impairing of the powers of any member, or joint;

Sixthly, Permanent disfiguration of the head, or face;

Seventhly, Fracture or dislocation of any bone other than a tooth;

Eighthly, Such hurt that the sufferer is, during the space of twenty days, in bodily pain, diseased, or unable to follow his ordinary pursuits.

316. Whoever does any act or omits what he is legally bound to do, with the intention of thereby causing hurt to any person, or with the knowledge that he is likely thereby to cause hurt to any person, and does thereby cause hurt to any person, is said " volun- " tarily to cause hurt."

317. Whoever voluntarily causes hurt, if the hurt which he intends to cause or knows himself to be likely to cause is grievous hurt, and if the hurt which he causes is grievous hurt, is said " voluntarily to cause grievous hurt."

Explanation. A person is not said voluntarily to cause grievous hurt except when he both causes grievous hurt, and intends or knows himself to be likely to cause grievous hurt. But he is said voluntarily to cause grievous hurt, if, intending or knowing himself to be likely to cause grievous hurt of one kind, he actually causes grievous hurt of another kind.

Illustration.

A, intending or knowing himself to be likely permanently to disfigure Z's face, gives Z a blow which does not permanently disfigure Z's face, but which causes Z to be diseased during twenty days. A has voluntarily caused grievous hurt.

318. Whoever, except in the case provided for in Clause 325, voluntarily causes hurt, shall be punished with imprisonment of either description for a term which may extend to one year, or fine which may extend to one thousand rupees, or both.

319. Whoever, except in the case provided for in Clause 326, voluntarily causes grievous hurt, shall be punished with imprisonment of either description for a term which may extend to ten years and must not be les than six months, and shall also be liable to fine.

320. Whoever voluntarily causes hurt in an attempt to commit murder shall be punished with transportation for life, or rigorous imprisonment for a term which may extend to life and must not be less than seven years, and shall also be liable to fine.

321. Whoever voluntarily causes hurt for the purpose of extorting from the sufferer, or from any person interested in the sufferer, any property, or of constraining the sufferer of the hurt, or some person interested in such sufferer to give any information which may lead to a wrongful transfer of any property, or to do any thing illegal or disreputable, shall be punished with rigorous imprisonment for a term which may extend to fourteen years and must not be less than one year, and shall also be liable to fine.

322. Whoever voluntarily causes grievous hurt for the purpose of extorting any property, or of constraining the sufferer of the hurt, or some person interested in such sufferer, to give any information which may lead to a wrongful transfer of any property, or to do any thing illegal or disreputable, shall be punished with transportation for life, or rigorous imprisonment for a term which may extend to life and must not be less than seven years, and shall also be liable to fine.

323. Whoever, except in the case provided for in Clause 325, voluntarily causes hurt by means of the edge or point of any sharp instrument, or by means of fire or any heated substance, or by means of any corrosive substance, or by means of any explosive substance, or by means of any substance which it is deleterious to the human body to inhale, to swallow, or to receive into the blood, or by means of any animal, shall be punished with imprisonment of either description for a term which may extend to three years, or fine, or both.

324. Whoever, except in the case provided for in Clause 326, voluntarily causes grievous hurt by means of the edge or point of any sharp instrument, or by means of fire or any heated substance, or by means of any corrosive substance, or by means of any explosive substance, or by means of any substance which it is deleterious to the human body to inhale, to swallow, or to receive into the blood, or by means of any animal, shall be punished with imprisonment of either description for a term which may extend to fourteen years and must not be less than one year, and shall also be liable to fine.

325. Whoever voluntarily causes hurt, on grave* and sudden provocation, if he neither intends nor knows himself to be likely to cause hurt to any person other than the person who gave the provocation, shall be punished with imprisonment of either

---

* For the definition of grave provocation see Clause 297.

description for a term which may extend to one month, or fine which may extend to five hundred rupees, or both.

326. Whoever voluntarily causes grievous hurt, on grave and sudden provocation, if he neither intends nor knows himself to be likely to cause grievous hurt to any person other than the person who gave the provocation, shall be punished with imprisonment of either description for a term which may extend to one year, or fine which may extend to two thousand rupees, or both.

327. Whoever causes grievous hurt to any person by any act or illegal omission, which act or omission is so rash or negligent as to indicate a want of due regard for the safety of others, shall be punished with imprisonment of either description for a term which may extend to six months, or fine which may extend to one thousand rupees, or both.

328. If the act or illegal omission whereby grievous hurt is caused in the manner described in the last preceding Clause be, apart from the circumstance of its having caused grievous hurt, an offence, the punishment shall be cumulative.

329. Whoever does any act, or omits what he is legally bound to do, intending or knowing it to be likely that by such act or omission he may cause grievous hurt, the voluntary causing of which grievous hurt would be an offence other than the offence defined in Clause 326, and carries that act or omission to such a length as, at the time of carrying it to that length, he contemplates as sufficient to cause grievous hurt, shall be punished with imprisonment of either description for a term which may extend to one half of the term of imprisonment to which he would have been liable if he had actually caused the grievous hurt which he intended to cause, or knew himself to be likely to cause, or fine, or both.

Illustrations.

(a) A ties a rope across a road by night, intending or knowing it to be likely that Z's horse may stumble over it, and that grievous hurt to Z may be the consequence. Grievous hurt is not caused. Here, if grievous hurt had been caused, A would have been liable to imprisonment for a term not exceeding ten years. A, therefore, is liable to imprisonment for a term not exceeding five years.

(b) A lays a steel-trap in Z's path, intending or knowing it to be likely that he may thereby cause grievous hurt to Z. Here, if grievous hurt were actually caused to Z, A, as having caused grievous hurt by means of a sharp instrument, would be liable to imprisonment for a term not exceeding fourteen years. If therefore no grievous hurt is caused, A is liable to imprisonment for a term not exceeding seven years.

(c) A puts an explosive substance under the seal of a letter, intending or knowing it to be likely that he shall thereby cause grievous hurt to some person. While A keeps the letter in his own custody he has not committed the offence defined in this Clause. As soon as he sends it to the post, he has committed the offence defined in this Clause. If he actually causes, by these means, grievous hurt to any person, as the hurt is caused by means of an explosive substance, he is liable to imprisonment for a term not exceeding fourteen years. If he does not actually cause grievous hurt to any person he is liable to imprisonment for a term not exceeding seven years.

Of Wrongful Restraint and Wrongful Confinement.

330. Whoever by any act or by any illegal omission voluntarily obstructs any person so as to prevent that person from proceeding in any direction in which that person has a right to proceed, is said " wrongfully to restrain" that person.

Explanation. A person may obstruct another by causing it to appear to that other impossible, difficult, or dangerous to proceed, as well as by causing it actually to be impossible, difficult, or dangerous for that other to proceed.

Illustrations.

(a) A builds a wall across a path along which Z has a right to pass. Z is thereby prevented from passing. A wrongfully restrains Z

(b) A illegally omits to take proper order with a furious buffalo, which is in his possession, (see Clause 273,) and thus voluntarily deters Z from passing along a road along which Z has a right to pass. A wrongfully restrains Z.

(c) A threatens to set a savage dog at Z, if Z goes along a path along which Z has a right to go. Z is thus prevented from going along that path. A wrongfully restrains Z.

(d) In the last illustration, if the dog is not really savage, but if A voluntarily causes Z to think that it is savage, and thereby prevents Z from going along the path, A wrongfully restrains Z.

331. Whoever wrongfully restrains any person in such a manner as to prevent that

person from proceeding beyond certain circumscribing limits, is said " wrongfully to confine" that person.

Illustrations.

(*a*) A causes Z to go within a walled space, and locks Z in. Z is thus prevented from proceeding in any direction beyond the circumscribing line of wall. A wrongfully confines Z.

(*b*) In the last illustration, if there is in some nook of the walled space a door which is not secured, but which may easily escape observation, as A had voluntarily caused it to appear to Z impossible to proceed beyond the line of wall, A has wrongfully confined Z.

(*c*) A places men with fire arms at the outlets of a building, and tells Z that they will fire at Z, if Z attempts to leave the building. A wrongfully confines Z.

332. Whoever wrongfully restrains any person shall be punished with imprisonment of either description for a term which may extend to one month, or fine which may extend to five hundred rupees, or both.

333. Whoever wrongfully confines any person shall be punished with imprisonment of either description for a term which may extend to one year, or fine which may extend to one thousand rupees, or both.

334. Whoever wrongfully confines any person for three days, or more, shall be punished with imprisonment of either description for a term which may extend to two years, or fine, or both.

335. Whoever wrongfully confines any person for ten days, or more, shall be punished with imprisonment of either description for a term which may extend to three years, in addition to three days for every day of such wrongful confinement, and must not be less than six months, in addition to one day for every day of such wrongful confinement, and shall also be liable to fine.

336. Whoever keeps any person in wrongful confinement, knowing that a writ for the liberation of that person has been issued in the manner described in the Code of Procedure, shall be punished with imprisonment of either description for a term which may extend to three years and must not be less than one year, in addition to any term of imprisonment to which he may be liable under the last preceding Clause, and shall also be liable to fine.

337. Whoever wrongfully confines any person, for the purpose of extorting from the person confined, or from any person interested in the person confined, any property, or of constraining the person confined, or any person interested in the person confined to give any information which may lead to a wrongful transfer of property, or to do any thing illegal or disreputable, shall be punished with imprisonment of either description for a term which may extend to three years and must not be less than one year, in addition to any term of imprisonment to which he may be liable under either of the two last preceding Clauses, and shall also be liable to fine.

338. Whoever, while keeping any person in wrongful confinement, knowing a certain thing to be necessary to prevent the person confined from being in danger of death, or hurt, voluntarily omits to furnish that thing to the person confined, shall be punished with imprisonment of either description for a term which may extend to one year, or fine, or both.

Illustration.

Z's eyes are in such a state as to require constant medical care. A wrongfully confines Z, and knowing that without medical attendance Z is likely to lose his eye-sight, omits to procure such medical attendance. A has committed the offence defined in this Clause. If Z loses his eye-sight, A has by an illegal omission voluntarily caused Z to lose his eye-sight, and has thus become liable to the punishment of having voluntarily caused grievous hurt to Z.

Of Assault.

339. A person is said to use force to another, if he causes motion, or change of motion, or cessation of motion to that other, or if he causes to any substance such motion, or change of motion, or cessation of motion as brings that substance into contact with any part of that other's body, or with any thing which that other is wearing or carrying, or with any thing so situated that such contact affects that other's sense of feeling:

Provided, that the person causing the motion, or change of motion, or cessation of motion, causes that motion, change of motion, or cessation of motion in one of the three ways hereinafter described;

First, By his own bodily power;

Secondly, By disposing any substances in such a manner that the motion, or change or cessation of motion takes place without any further act on his part, or on the part of any other person ;

Thirdly, By inducing any animal to move, to change its motion, or to cease to move.

340. Whoever intentionally uses force, or attempts to use force to any person, without that person's consent, in order to the committing of any offence, or intending or knowing it to be likely that, by such use of force, he may cause to the person to whom the force is used injury, fear, or annoyance, is said to commit an assault.

Illustrations.

(*a*) Z is sitting in a moored boat on a river. A unfastens the moorings, and thus intentionally causes the boat to drift down the stream. Here, A intentionally causes motion to Z, and he does this by disposing substances in such a manner that the motion is produced without any other act on any person's part. A has therefore intentionally used force to Z ; and if he has done so without Z's consent, in order to the committing of any offence, or intending or knowing it to be likely that this use of force may cause injury, fear, or annoyance to Z, A has committed an assault.

(*b*) Z is riding in a chariot. A lashes Z's horses, and thereby attempts to cause them to quicken their pace. Here, A has attempted to cause change of motion to Z by inducing animals to change their motion. A has therefore attempted to use force to Z, and if A has done this, without Z's consent, intending or knowing it to be likely that he may thereby injure, frighten, or annoy Z, A has committed an assault.

(*c*) Z is riding in a palanquin. A, intending to rob Z, seizes the pole, and stops the palanquin. Here, A has caused cessation of motion to Z, and he has done this by his own bodily power. A has therefore used force to Z. And as A has acted thus, intentionally, without Z's consent, in order to the commission of an offence, A has committed an assault.

(*d*) A intentionally pushes against Z in the street. Here, A has by his own bodily power moved his own person so as to bring it into contact with Z. He has therefore intentionally used force to Z ; and if he has done so without Z's consent, intending or knowing it to be likely that he may thereby injure, frighten, or annoy Z, he has committed an assault.

(*e*) A throws a stone, intending or knowing it to be likely that the stone will be thus brought into contact with Z, or with Z's clothes, or with something carried by Z, or that it will strike water, and dash up the water against Z, or Z's clothes, or something carried by Z. Here, A has attempted to use force to Z, and if he has done so without Z's consent, intending thereby to injure, frighten, or annoy Z, he has committed an assault.

(*f*) A intentionally pulls up a woman's veil. Here, A intentionally uses force to her, and if he does so without her consent, intending or knowing it to be likely that he may thereby injure, frighten, or annoy her, he commits an assault.

(*g*) Z is bathing. A pours into the bath water which he knows to be boiling. Here, A intentionally by his own bodily power causes such motion in the boiling water as brings that water into contact with Z, or with other water so situated that such contact must affect Z's sense of feeling. A has therefore intentionally used force to Z, and if he has done this without Z's consent, intending or knowing it to be likely that he may thereby cause injury, fear, or annoyance to Z, A has committed an assault.

(*h*) A attempts to incite a dog to spring upon Z, without Z's consent. Here, if A intends to cause injury, fear, or annoyance to Z, he commits an assault.

341. Whoever makes any gesture, or any preparation, intending or knowing it to be likely that such gesture or preparation will cause any person present to apprehend that he who makes that gesture or preparation is about to assault that person, is said " to make " shew of assault."

Explanation. Mere words do not amount to a shew of assault. But the words which a person uses may give to his gestures or preparations such a meaning as may make those gestures or preparations amount to shew of assault.

Illustrations.

(*a*) A shakes his fist at Z, intending or knowing it to be likely that he may thereby cause Z to believe that A is about to assault Z. A has made shew of assault.

(*b*) A begins to unloose the muzzle of a ferocious dog, intending or knowing it to be likely that he may thereby cause Z to believe that he is about to assault Z. A has made shew of assault.

(*c*) A takes up a stick, saying to Z " I will give you a beating." Here, though the words used by A could in no case amount to shew of assault, and though the mere gesture, unaccompanied by any other circumstances, might not amount to shew of assault, it is nevertheless possible that the gesture explained by the words may be shew of assault.

342. Whoever assaults any person, otherwise than on grave* and sudden provocation given by that person, shall be punished with imprisonment of either description for a

---

* For the explanation of grave provocation see Clause 297.

term which may extend to three months, or fine which may extend to five hundred rupees, or both.

343. Whoever, in attempting to commit murder, assaults any person, shall be punished with transportation for life, or rigorous imprisonment for a term which may extend to life and must not be less than seven years, and shall also be liable to fine.

344. Whoever, in attempting to commit the offence of kidnapping, assaults any person, shall be punished with imprisonment of either description for a term which may extend to half the term for which the offender would have been liable to be imprisoned if he had committed the kidnapping which he has attempted to commit and must not be less than six months, and shall also be liable to fine.

345. Whoever assaults any person in attempting to cause grievous hurt to that person, otherwise than on grave and sudden provocation given by that person, shall be punished with imprisonment of either description for a term which may extend to one third part of the term for which he might have been imprisoned if he had actually caused such hurt as he attempted to cause, or fine, or both.

346. Whoever assaults any woman, in attempting to commit rape on her, shall be punished with imprisonment of either description for a term which may extend to three years and must not be less than six months, and shall also be liable to fine.

347. Whoever assaults any woman, intending thereby to outrage her modesty, shall be punished with imprisonment of either description for a term which may extend to two years, or fine, or both.

348. Whoever assaults any person, intending thereby to dishonor that person, otherwise than on grave and sudden provocation given by that person, shall be punished with imprisonment of either description for a term which may extend to two years, or fine, or both.

349. Whoever assaults any person, in attempting to commit theft on any property which that person is then wearing or carrying, shall be punished with imprisonment of either description for a term which may extend to two years, or fine, or both.

350. Whoever assaults any person, in attempting wrongfully to confine that person, shall be punished with imprisonment of either description for a term which may extend to one year, or fine which may extend to one thousand rupees, or both.

351. Whoever assaults any person, on grave and sudden provocation given by that person, shall be punished with imprisonment of either description for a term which may extend to one month, or fine which may extend to two hundred rupees, or both.

352. Whoever makes shew of assault, except on grave and sudden provocation given by the person whom he makes shew of being about to assault, shall be punished with imprisonment of either description for a term which may extend to one month, or fine which may extend to two hundred rupees, or both.

Of Kidnapping.

353. " Kidnapping" is of two kinds, kidnapping from the territories of the East India Company, and kidnapping from lawful guardianship.

354. Whoever conveys beyond the limits of the territories of the East India Company, or takes on board of any vessel with the intention of conveying beyond the limits of the said territories, any person without the free and intelligent consent of that person, or of some person legally authorized to consent on behalf of that person, or with such consent, but knowing that such consent has been obtained by deception or concealment as to the place of destination, or the future treatment of that person, is said to " kidnap that person from the territories of the East India Company."

Whoever conveys any child under twelve years of age out of the keeping of the lawful guardian or guardians of such child, without the free and intelligent consent of such guardian or guardians, or with such consent but knowing that such consent has been obtained by deception or concealment as to the place of destination, or the future treatment of the child, or that such consent is the effect of collusion between himself and such guardian or guardians, for any purpose of injury to the child, is said to " kidnap that child from lawful guardianship."

355. Whoever kidnaps any person shall be punished with imprisonment of either description for a term which may extend to seven years and must not be less than one year, and shall also be liable to fine.

356. Whoever kidnaps any person, intending or knowing it to be likely that murder may, in consequence of such kidnapping, be committed on that person, shall be punished with transportation for life, or rigorous imprisonment for a term which may extend to life and must not be less than seven years, and shall also be liable to fine.

Illustration.

A kidnaps Z from the territories of the East India Company, intending or knowing it to be likely that Z may be sacrificed to an idol. A has committed the offence defined in this Clause.

357. Whoever kidnaps any person, intending or knowing it to be likely that the consequence of such kidnapping may be grievous hurt to that person, or the rape of that person, or the subjecting of that person to unnatural lust, or the slavery of that person, shall be punished with imprisonment of either description for a term which may extend to fourteen years and must not be less than two years, and shall also be liable to fine.

358. Whoever, being in charge of any vessel, knowingly suffers any person who cannot without a certain order or permit legally embark on board of such vessel for any place which is not within the territories of the East India Company, to embark on board of the said vessel for any such place, shall be punished with simple imprisonment for a term which may extend to one month for every person so suffered to embark, or fine which may extend to two hundred rupees for every person so suffered to embark, or both.

Of Rape.

359. A man is said to commit " rape" who, except in the case hereinafter excepted, has sexual intercourse with a woman under circumstances falling under any of the five following descriptions ;

First, Against her will ;

Secondly, Without her consent, while she is insensible ;

Thirdly, With her consent, when her consent has been obtained by putting her in fear of death, or of hurt ;

Fourthly, With her consent, when the man knows that her consent is given because she believes that he is a different man to whom she is or believes herself to be married ;

Fifthly, With or without her consent, when she is under nine years of age.

Explanation. Penetration is sufficient to constitute the sexual intercourse necessary to the offence of rape.

Exception. Sexual intercourse by a man with his own wife is in no case rape.

360. Whoever commits rape shall be punished with imprisonment of either description for a term which may extend to fourteen years and must not be less than two years, and shall also be liable to fine.

Of Unnatural Offences.

361. Whoever, intending to gratify unnatural lust, touches, for that purpose, any person, or any animal, or is by his own consent touched by any person, for the purpose of gratifying unnatural lust, shall be punished with imprisonment of either description for a term which may extend to fourteen years and must not be less than two years, and shall also be liable to fine.

362. Whoever, intending to gratify unnatural lust, touches for that purpose any person without that person's free and intelligent consent, shall be punished with imprisonment of either description for a term which may extend to life and must not be less than seven years, and shall also be liable to fine.

CHAPTER XIX.

OF OFFENCES AGAINST PROPERTY.*

OF THEFT.

363. Whoever, intending to take fraudulently any thing which is property, and which is not attached to the earth, out of the possession of any person, without that person's consent, moves that thing in order to such taking, is said to commit "theft."

Explanations. All things fastened to any thing attached to the earth are said to be attached to the earth.

A thing which is attached to the earth becomes capable of being the subject of theft as soon as it is severed from the earth.

A moving effected by the same act which effects the severance may be a theft.

The words to "move a thing" include the cases in which a person causes a thing to move by removing an obstacle which prevented it from moving, or by separating it from any other thing.

A person who by any means induces an animal to move in a direction in which he intends to induce that animal to move, is said to move that animal, and to move every thing which in consequence of the motion so caused is moved by that animal.

The consent mentioned in the definition may be express, or implied, and may be given either by the person in possession, or by any person having for that purpose authority, either express or implied, from the person in possession.

A person may commit theft though he intends to restore the property after taking it.

Illustrations.

(a) A cuts down a tree on Z's ground, with the intention of fraudulently taking the tree out of Z's possession, without Z's consent. Here, as soon as A has severed the tree, in order to such taking, he has committed theft.

(b) A pulls a bung out of a hogshead of liquor in Z's possession, with the intention of fraudulently taking some of the liquor without Z's consent. As soon as the liquor begins to flow, A has committed theft.

(c) A puts a bait for dogs in his pocket, and thus induces Z's dog to follow A. Here, if A's intention be fraudulently to take the dog out of Z's possession, without Z's consent, A has committed theft as soon as Z's dog has begun to follow A.

(d) A drives Z's sheep before him, with the intention of fraudulently taking them out of Z's possession, without Z's consent. As soon as any sheep begins to move in the direction in which A intended that it should move, A has committed theft.

(e) A meets a bullock carrying a box of treasure. He drives the bullock in a certain direction, in order that he may fraudulently take the treasure. As soon as the bullock begins to move in the direction in which A intends it to move, A has committed theft on the treasure.

(f) A, being Z's butler, and entrusted by Z with the care of Z's plate, fraudulently runs away with the plate, without Z's consent. Here, the plate, till carried off by A, was still in Z's possession, though it was also in A's possession. A has therefore committed theft.

(g) Z, going on a journey, entrusts his plate to A, the keeper of a warehouse, till Z shall return. A carries the plate to a goldsmith, and sells it. Here the plate was not in Z's possession. It could not therefore be taken out of Z's possession, and A has not committed theft, though he may have committed criminal breach of trust.

(h) A finds a ring belonging to Z on a table in the house which Z occupies. Here, the ring is in Z's possession, and if A fraudulently removes it, A commits theft.

(i) A finds a ring lying on the high road, not in the possession of any person. A by taking it commits no theft, though he may commit criminal misappropriation of property not in possession.

(j) A sees a ring belonging to Z lying on a table in Z's house. Not venturing to misappropriate the ring immediately, for fear of search and detection, A hides the ring in a place where it is highly improbable that it will ever be found by Z, with the intention of taking the ring from the hiding place, and selling it when the loss is forgotten. Here, A at the time of first hiding the ring, commits theft.

(k) A delivers his watch to Z, a jeweller, to be regulated. Z carries it to his shop. A, not owing to the jeweller any debt for which the jeweller might lawfully detain the watch as a security, enters the shop openly, takes his watch by force out of Z's hand, and carries it away. Here A, though he may have committed criminal trespass, and assault, has committed no theft, inasmuch as what he did was not done fraudulently.

* See Note N.

(*l*) But if A carries away the watch out of Z's possession, with the intention of also recovering the value of the watch from Z, A has acted fraudulently, and has therefore committed theft, though the watch is his own property.

(*m*) Again : if A owes money to Z for repairing the watch, and if Z retains the watch lawfully as a security for the debt, and A takes the watch out of Z's possession with the intention of keeping Z out of the money due to him, he commits theft, inasmuch as he takes it fraudulently.

(*n*) Again : if A, having pawned his watch to Z, takes it out of Z's possession without Z's consent, not having paid what he had borrowed on the watch, he commits theft though the watch is his own property, inasmuch as he takes it fraudulently.

(*o*) A takes an article belonging to Z out of Z's possession, without Z's consent, with the intention of carrying it back to Z and of pretending to have found it, in the hope of thus obtaining a reward from Z. Here A takes fraudulently ; A has therefore committed theft.

(*p*) A, being exasperated at a passage in a book which is lying on the counter of Z, a bookseller, snatches it up, and tears it to pieces. A has not committed theft, as he has not acted fraudulently, though he may have committed criminal trespass, and mischief.

(*q*) A and Z are gardeners. Z has reared a pine-apple of extraordinary size, in hope of obtaining a prize. A takes the pine-apple without Z's consent, produces it before the judges as his own, and obtains the prize. He then sends back the pine-apple to Z. Here, as A took the pine-apple fraudulently, A has committed theft, though he has restored the pine-apple.

(*r*) A takes a gold chain from a child of five years old, with that child's consent, but without the consent of the child's guardians. Here, the chain was in the possession of the child's guardians. A has therefore taken the chain out of the possession of the guardians, without their consent, and if he has done this fraudulently, A has committed theft.

(*s*) A takes a rupee from a gentleman's child of twelve years of age, with the child's consent. Here, it is probable that A conceived the rupee to have been placed entirely at the child's disposal. If this was A's impression, A has not committed theft.

(*t*) A, being on friendly terms with Z, goes into Z's library, in Z's absence, and takes away a book without Z's express consent. Here, it is probable that A may have conceived that he had Z's implied consent to use Z's books. If this was A's impression, A has not committed theft.

(*u*) A asks charity from Z's wife. She gives A money, food, and clothes, which A knows to belong to Z, her husband. Here, it is probable that A may conceive that Z's wife is authorised to give away alms. If this was A's impression, A has not committed theft.

(*v*) A is the paramour of Z's wife. She gives A valuable property which A knows to belong to her husband Z, and to be such property as she has not authority from Z to give. If A takes the property he commits theft.

(*w*) A and Z are joint proprietors of a horse. A takes the horse out of Z's possession, intending to use it for a time. A has not committed theft. But if A takes the horse fraudulently out of Z's possession, intending to carry it away altogether, or to sell it and appropriate the whole price, A commits theft.

(*x*) A, having charge, in trust for the Government, of a public treasury, fraudulently appropriates some of the money to himself. Here, as A has not taken the money out of the possession of any person (see Clause 19), he is not guilty of theft, but he has committed criminal breach of trust.

(*y*) A, believing in good faith that Z owes him a thousand rupees, and only intending to repay himself what is due to him, without injury to any party, takes property out of Z's possession, without Z's consent. A, not acting fraudulently, is not guilty of theft. But he may have committed an offence under the provisions contained in the Chapter entitled " of the illegal pursuit of legal rights."

(*z*) But if A, in the last illustration, intended to take and appropriate more than sufficient to repay himself, or intended, after repaying himself, to prosecute Z for the debt, here, as such intention was fraudulent, A commits theft.

364. Whoever commits theft shall be punished with rigorous imprisonment for a term which may extend to three years, or fine, or both.

365. Whoever commits theft within any building, tent, or vessel, which building, tent, or vessel is used as a human dwelling, or within any building used for the custody of property, in pursuance of a conspiracy, in which conspiracy any person residing or employed within that building, tent, or vessel, and also any person not residing nor employed within that building, tent, or vessel, are engaged, shall be punished with rigorous imprisonment for a term which may extend to three years and must not be less than six months, and shall also be liable to fine.

366. Whoever commits theft on any letter or packet, which, at the time of the committing of the theft, is in the possession of any officer of the Post Office, or on any thing contained in any such letter or packet, shall be punished with rigorous imprisonment for a term which may extend to three years and must not be less than six months, and shall also be liable to fine.

367. Whoever commits theft, having made preparation for causing death, or hurt, or restraint, or fear of death, or of hurt, or of restraint to any person, in order to the committing of such theft, or in order to retiring after the committing of such theft, or in order to the retaining of property taken by such theft, shall be punished with rigorous im-

prisonment for a term which may extend to seven years and must not be less than one year, and shall also be liable to fine.

Illustrations.

(*a*) A commits theft on property in Z's possession, and while committing this theft he has a loaded pistol under his garment, having provided this pistol for the purpose of hurting or terrifying Z in case Z should resist. A has committed the offence defined in this Clause.

(*b*) A picks Z's pocket, having posted several of his companions near him, in order that they may hustle Z, if Z should perceive what is passing, and should resist, or should attempt to detain A. A has committed the offence defined in this Clause.

Of Extortion.

368. Whoever intentionally puts any person in fear of any injury to that person, or to any other, and thereby fraudulently induces the person so put in fear to deliver any property to any person, or to consent that any person shall retain any property, or to affix a seal to any substance, or to make, alter, or destroy the whole or any part of any document which is or purports to be a valuable security, is said to commit " extortion."

Illustrations.

(*a*) A threatens to publish a defamatory life of Z, unless Z gives him money. He thus induces Z to give him money. A has committed extortion.

(*b*) A threatens Z that he will keep Z's child in wrongful confinement, unless Z will sign a promissory note binding Z to pay certain monies to A. Z signs the note. A has committed extortion.

(*c*) A threatens to send bludgeon-men to plough up Z's field, unless Z will sign a bond binding himself under a penalty to deliver certain produce to B. Z signs the bond. A has committed extortion.

(*d*) A has lent Z money. Z has repaid the money. A has given Z a receipt. A afterwards threatens Z with bearing false evidence against him on a trial, unless Z will burn the receipt. Z burns the receipt. A has committed extortion.

(*e*) A, by putting Z in fear of injury, fraudulently induces Z to affix his seal to a blank paper. A has committed extortion.

369. Whoever commits extortion shall be punished with imprisonment of either description for a term which may extend to three years, or fine or both.

370. Whoever, in order to the committing of extortion, puts any person in fear, or attempts to put any person in fear, shall be punished with imprisonment of either description for a term which may extend to one year, or fine, or both.

371. Whoever commits extortion by putting any person in fear, for that person or for any other, of death or of grievous hurt, shall be punished with imprisonment of either description for a term which may extend to fourteen years and must not be less than two years, and shall also be liable to fine.

372. Whoever, in order to the committing of extortion, puts any person in fear, or attempts to put any person in fear, for that person or for any other, of death or of grievous hurt, shall be punished with imprisonment of either description for a term which may extend to seven years and must not be less than one year, and shall also be liable to fine.

373. Whoever commits extortion by putting any person in fear of being falsely accused or defamed as a person under the influence of unnatural lust, shall be punished with imprisonment of either description for a term which may extend to fourteen years and must not be less than two years, and shall also be liable to fine.

374. Whoever, in order to the committing of extortion, puts any person in fear, or attempts to put any person in fear, of being falsely accused or defamed as a person under the influence of unnatural lust, shall be punished with imprisonment of either description for a term which may extend to seven years and must not be less than one year, and shall also be liable to fine.

Of Robbery and Dacoity.

375. In all robbery there is either theft, or extortion.

Theft is " robbery" if, in order to the committing of the theft, or in committing the theft, or ih carrying away or attempting to carry away property obtained by the theft, the offender, for that end, voluntarily causes or attempts to cause to any person death, hurt, or wrongful restraint, or fear of instant death, of instant hurt, or of instant wrongful restraint.

Extortion is " robbery" if the offender, at the time of committing the extortion, is in the presence of the person put in fear, and commits the extortion by putting that person in fear of instant death, of instant hurt, or of instant wrongful restraint, to that person, or to some other person present at the time of committing the extortion, and, by so putting in fear, induces the person so put in fear then and there to deliver up any property.

Illustrations.

(*a*) A holds Z down, and fraudulently takes Z's money and jewels from Z's clothes, without Z's consent. Here, A has committed theft, and, in order to the committing of that theft, has voluntarily caused wrongful restraint to Z. A has therefore committed robbery.

(*b*) A meets Z on the high road, shews a pistol, and demands Z's purse. Z surrenders his purse. Here, A has extorted the purse from Z by putting the person on whom the extortion has been committed in fear of instant hurt. A has therefore committed robbery.

(*c*) A meets Z, and Z's child, on the high road. A takes the child, and threatens to fling it down a precipice, unless Z delivers his purse. Z delivers his purse. Here A has extorted the purse from Z, by causing Z to be in fear of instant hurt to the child who is there present. A has therefore committed robbery on Z.

(*d*) But if A obtains property from Z by saying, " your child is in the hands of my gang, and " will be put to death unless within a month you send us ten thousand rupees,"—this is extortion, punishable under Clause 371, but it is not robbery.

376. Where six or more persons, conjointly, commit or attempt to commit a robbery, or where the whole number of persons conjointly committing or attempting to commit a robbery, and persons present and aiding such commission or attempt, amounts to six or more, every person so committing, attempting, or aiding, is said to commit " Dacoity."

377. Whoever commits robbery shall be punished with rigorous imprisonment for a term which may extend to fourteen years and must not be less than two years, and shall also be liable to fine.

378. Whoever attempts to commit robbery shall be punished with rigorous imprisonment for a term which may extend to seven years, and must not be less than one year, and shall also be liable to fine.

379. Whoever commits dacoity shall be punished with transportation for life, or with rigorous imprisonment for a term which may extend to life and must not be less than three years, and shall also be liable to fine.

380. If any one of six or more persons who are conjointly committing dacoity, commits murder in so committing dacoity, every one of those persons shall be punished with death, or transportation for life, or rigorous imprisonment for a term which may extend to life and must not be less than seven years, and shall also be liable to fine.

381. Whoever is one of six or more persons assembled for the purpose of committing dacoity, shall be punished with rigorous imprisonment for a term which may extend to seven years and must not be less than one year, and shall also be liable to fine.

382. If any person voluntarily causes hurt in committing or attempting to commit robbery, or in committing dacoity, the punishment shall be cumulative.

Illustration.

A in robbing Z of his ear-rings, tears them from his ears, and in so doing causes grievous hurt to Z. A is liable both to the punishment of voluntarily causing grievous hurt, and to the punishment of robbery.

Of Criminal Misappropriation of Property not in possession.

383. Whoever fraudulently takes into his possession any property which is in no person's possession, is said, except in the case hereinafter excepted, " criminally to misap- " propriate property not in possession."

Exception. If the person taking the property into his possession neither knows, nor has reason to believe, that any particular party has a better right than himself to the property, or that any particular person can direct him to any such party, he is not guilty of the offence above defined.

Illustrations.

(*a*) A finds a rupee on the high road, not knowing, nor having reason to believe, that the rupee belongs to any particular party, or that any particular person can direct him to the party to whom the rupee belongs. A takes the rupee. Here, A has not committed the offence defined in this Clause.

(*b*) A finds a letter on the road containing a bank note. From the direction and the contents of the letter he learns to whom the note belongs. He appropriates the note. Here, he criminally misappropriates property not in possession.

(*c*) A finds a cheque payable to bearer. He can form no conjecture as to the person who has lost the cheque. But the name of the person who has drawn the cheque appears. A knows that this person can direct him to the party in whose favor the cheque was drawn. A appropriates the cheque. Here, he criminally misappropriates property not in possession.

384. Whoever criminally misappropriates property not in possession shall be punished with imprisonment of either description for a term which may extend to two years, or fine, or both.

385. Whoever criminally misappropriates property not in possession, knowing that such property was in the possession of a deceased person at the time of that person's decease, and has not since been in the possession of any person legally entitled to such possession, shall be punished with imprisonment of either description for a term which may extend to three years and must not be less than six months, and shall also be liable to fine.

Illustration.

Z dies in possession of furniture and money. His servant, A, before the money comes into the possession of any person entitled to such possession, fraudulently takes possession of it. A has committed the offence defined in this Clause.

Of Criminal Breach of Trust.

386. Whoever, being entrusted with the keeping of any property, or with any dominion over any property, and intending fraudulently to cause wrongful loss or risk of wrongful loss to any party for whom he is in trust, disobeys any direction of law prescribing the mode in which such trust is to be discharged, or violates any legal contract express or implied which he has made touching the discharge of such trust with any party from whom such trust was derived, is said to commit " criminal breach of trust."

Illustrations.

(a) A, being executor to the will of a deceased person, fraudulently disobeys the law which directs him to divide the effects according to the will, and absconds with them. A has committed criminal breach of trust.

(b) A is a warehouse-keeper. Z, going on a journey, entrusts his furniture to A, under a contract that it shall be returned on payment of a stipulated sum for warehouse room. Z on his return tenders the sum. A fraudulently retains the goods. A has committed criminal breach of trust.

(c) A, residing at Calcutta, is agent for Z, residing at Delhi. There is an express or implied contract between A and Z that all sums remitted by Z to A shall be invested by A according to Z's direction. Z remits a lac of rupees to A, with directions to A to invest the same in Company's paper. A fraudulently disobeys the directions, and employs the money in his own business. A has committed criminal breach of trust.

(d) But if A, in the last illustration, not fraudulently, but believing that it will be more for Z's advantage to hold shares in the Bank of Bengal, disobeys Z's directions, and buys shares in the Bank of Bengal for Z, instead of buying Company's paper, here, though Z should suffer loss, and should be entitled to bring a civil action against A on account of that loss, yet A, not having acted fraudulently, has not committed criminal breach of trust.

(e) A, a revenue Officer, is entrusted with public money, and is either directed by law, or bound by a contract express or implied with the Government, to pay into a certain treasury all the public money which he holds. A fraudulently appropriates the money. A has committed criminal breach of trust.

387. Whoever commits criminal breach of trust shall be punished with imprisonment of either description for a term which may extend to three years, or fine, or both.

388. Whoever, being a public servant in the Post Office Department, and being, as such, entrusted with the keeping of any letter or packet, commits criminal breach of trust by misappropriating such letter or packet, or any thing contained therein, shall be punished with imprisonment of either description for a term which may extend to three years and must not be less than six months, and shall also be liable to fine.

Of the receiving of Stolen Property.

389. Property the possession whereof has been transferred by theft, or by robbery, or by criminal misappropriation of property not in possession, or which, being specific property, and having been entrusted to the keeping of a public servant, as such public servant, has been so misappropriated by that public servant that he has thereby committed a criminal breach of trust, is designated as " stolen property." But if such property subsequently comes into the possession of a person legally entitled to the possession thereof, it then ceases to be stolen property.

390. Whoever fraudulently receives any stolen property, knowing the same to be stolen property, shall be punished with imprisonment of either description for a term which may extend to three years, or fine, or both.

391. Whoever fraudulently receives any stolen property the possession whereof he knows to have been transferred in the commission of dacoity, shall be punished with transportation for life, or with rigorous imprisonment for a term which may extend to life and must not be less than three years, and shall also be liable to fine.

Of Cheating.

392. Whoever, by intentionally deceiving any person, fraudulently induces the person so deceived to deliver any property to any person, or to consent that any person shall retain any property, or to affix a seal to any substance, or to make, alter, or destroy the whole or any part of any document which is or purports to be a valuable security, is said to " cheat."

Illustrations.

(a) A, by presenting to Z a bill of exchange which A knows to be forged, intentionally deceives Z, and thereby fraudulently induces Z to discount the bill. A cheats.

(b) A, by falsely pretending to be a Civil Servant of the East India Company, intentionally deceives Z, and thus fraudulently induces Z to let him have on credit goods for which he does not mean to pay. A cheats.

(c) A, by putting a counterfeit mark on an article, intentionally deceives Z into a belief that this article was made by a certain celebrated manufacturer, and thus fraudulently induces Z to buy and pay for the article. A cheats.

(d) A, by exhibiting to Z a false sample of an article, intentionally deceives Z into believing that the article corresponds with the sample, and thereby fraudulently induces Z to buy and pay for the article. A cheats.

(e) A, by tendering in payment for an article a bill on a house with which A keeps no money, and by which A expects that the bill will be dishonoured, intentionally deceives Z, and thereby fraudulently induces Z to deliver the article, intending not to pay for it. A cheats.

(f) A, by pledging ornaments of paste to Z, as diamonds, intentionally deceives Z, and thereby fraudulently induces Z to lend money. A cheats.

(g) A intentionally deceives Z into a belief that A means to repay any money that Z may lend to him, and thereby fraudulently induces Z to lend him money. A cheats.

(h) A intentionally deceives Z into a belief that A means to deliver to Z a certain quantity of indigo plant, and thereby fraudulently induces Z to advance money. A cheats.

(i) A intentionally deceives Z into a belief that A has performed A's part of a contract made with Z, and thereby fraudulently induces Z to pay money. A cheats.

(j) A intentionally deceives Z into a belief that A is attached to Z, and thereby induces Z to give him pecuniary assistance. Here, A has, by intentionally deceiving Z, induced Z to deliver up property, but he has not fraudulently induced Z to deliver up property, inasmuch as the property delivered by Z to A becomes, by the delivery, A's property, notwithstanding the deception by which it had been obtained. Therefore A does not cheat.

(k) A, by exaggerating the excellence of an article on sale, intentionally deceives Z, and induces Z to buy and pay for that article. Here, A has, by intentionally deceiving Z, induced Z to deliver up property. The question whether A has cheated will depend on the question whether he acted fraudulently, that is to say, whether he intended to cause wrongful gain to himself by means of wrongful loss to Z. If the deception practised by A were such that A has, notwithstanding the deception, a legal right to the price as soon as it has been delivered to him by Z, no gain which the law pronounces to be wrongful has been intended. A, therefore, has not acted fraudulently, and has not cheated. But if the deception practised by A were such that Z has a legal right to have back the price which he has paid, there is wrongful loss and wrongful gain; and if A intended to cause such wrongful loss and wrongful gain he has acted fraudulently, and has cheated.

393. A person is said to " cheat by personation" if he cheats in any of the ways hereinafter enumerated, namely;

First, By pretending to be some other person;

Second, By taking a name not his own;

Third, By taking any title or addition to which he has not a right;

Fourth, By dropping any title or addition to which he has a right, and which is ordinarily annexed to the names of those who have a right to it;

Fifth, By pretending to be of a country of which he is not;

Sixth, By pretending to be of a calling of which he is not;

Seventh, By pretending to be of a family of which he is not;

Eighth, By falsely pretending to hold or to have held any office, real or imaginary;

Ninth, By falsely pretending to be related by blood or marriage to any person, real or imaginary;

Tenth, By falsely pretending to be in the employ of any party, real or imaginary.

Illustrations.

(a) A cheats by pretending to be a certain rich banker of the same name. A cheats by personation.

(b) A cheats by pretending to be B, a person who is deceased. A cheats by personation.

(c) John Smith cheats by calling himself Thomas Brown. John Smith cheats by personation.

(d) A cheats by taking the title of Rajah, having no right to that title. He cheats by personation.

(e) John Smith cheats by falsely calling himself Lieutenant Colonel John Smith. He cheats by personation.

(f) Doctor Smith cheats by dropping the addition of Doctor. He cheats by personation.

(g) A, an East Indian, cheats by pretending to be an Afghan. He cheats by personation.

(h) A cheats by falsely pretending to be a Clergyman. He cheats by personation.

(i) A cheats by falsely pretending to be a member of one of the sovereign Houses of India. He cheats by personation.

(j) A cheats by falsely pretending to be or to have been Governor of Macao, which is a real office, or French Consul at Singapore, which is an imaginary office. A cheats by personation.

(k) A cheats by falsely pretending to be married to B, an heiress. A cheats by personation.

(l) A cheats by falsely pretending to be the agent of a great commercial house in Europe. He cheats by personation.

(m) A cheats by falsely pretending to be the Vakeel of a Native Prince. A cheats by personation.

394. Whoever cheats shall be punished with imprisonment of either description for a term which may extend to one year, or fine, or both.

395. Whoever cheats with the knowledge that he is likely thereby to cause wrongful loss to a party whose interest in the transaction to which the cheating relates he was bound, either by law, or by legal contract, to protect, shall be punished with imprisonment of either description for a term which may extend to two years, or fine, or both.

396. Whoever cheats by personation shall be punished with imprisonment of either description for a term which may extend to two years, or fine, or both.

397. Whoever attempts to cheat by personation shall be punished with imprisonment of either description for a term which may extend to one year, or fine, or both.*

Of Fraudulent Insolvency.

398. Whoever, being an insolvent trader, or being a trader who contemplates it as likely that he may become insolvent, fraudulently removes, conceals, delivers to any party, or causes to be transferred to any party any property, intending thereby to prevent, or knowing it to be likely that he may thereby prevent the distribution of that property according to law among his creditors, shall be punished with imprisonment of either description for a term which may extend to seven years and must not be less than one year, and shall also be liable to fine.

Of Mischief.

399. Whoever causes the destruction of any property, or any such change in any property, or in the situation of any property, as destroys or diminishes the value of such property, intending thereby to cause wrongful loss to any party, is said, except in the case hereinafter excepted, to commit " mischief."

Explanation. A person may commit mischief on his own property.

Exception. Nothing is mischief which a person does openly, and with the intention in good faith of thereby saving any person from death or hurt, or of thereby preventing a greater loss of property than that which he occasions.

Illustrations.

(a) A voluntarily burns a valuable security belonging to Z, intending to cause wrongful loss to Z. A has committed mischief.

(b) A introduces water into an ice house belonging to Z, and thus causes the ice to melt, intending wrongful loss to Z. A has committed mischief.

(c) A voluntarily throws into a river a ring belonging to Z, with the intention of thereby causing wrongful loss to Z. A has committed mischief.

(d) A, knowing that his effects are about to be taken in execution in order to satisfy a debt due from him to Z, destroys those effects, with the intention of thereby preventing Z from obtaining satisfaction of the debt, and of thus causing wrongful loss to Z. A has committed mischief.

(e) A, having insured a ship, voluntarily causes the same to be cast away, with the intention of causing wrongful loss to the underwriters. A has committed mischief.

(f) A causes a ship to be cast away, intending thereby to cause wrongful loss to Z, who has lent money on bottomry on the ship. A has committed mischief.

---

* For some of the aggravated forms of cheating, see the Chapters of Offences relating to the Coin, to Weights and Measures, to Documents, and to Property-marks.

(g) A, having joint property with Z in a horse, shoots the horse, intending thereby to cause wrongful loss to Z. A has committed mischief.

(h) A, in a storm, throws overboard property of Z, in spite of Z's prohibition, but intending in good faith to save the lives of the crew, or to save property of greater value than that which is thrown overboard. Here, A has not committed mischief.

(i) A, in a great fire, pulls down houses in order to prevent the conflagration from spreading. He does this openly, and with the intention in good faith of saving human life, or of saving property of more value than the value of the property sacrificed. A has not committed mischief.

400. Whoever commits mischief shall be punished with fine which may extend to ten times the amount of the wrongful loss which he has caused by such mischief.

401. Whoever commits mischief, having taken precautions not to be detected, shall be punished with imprisonment of either description for a term which may extend to six months, or fine, or both.

402. Whoever commits mischief, and thereby voluntarily causes wrongful loss to the amount of five rupees, or upwards, shall be punished with imprisonment of either description for a term which may extend to six months, or fine, or both.

403. Whoever commits mischief, and thereby voluntarily causes wrongful loss to the amount of one hundred rupees, or upwards, shall be punished with imprisonment of either description for a term which may extend to two years, or fine, or both.

404. Whoever commits mischief, intending thereby to enhance the value of any article, or directly or indirectly to affect the event of any competition so as to cause gain to any person, shall be punished with imprisonment of either description for a term which may extend to two years, or fine, or both.

Illustrations.

(a) A and Z are competitors for an agricultural prize. A, knowing that a cow belonging to Z is the finest that is likely to be exhibited, poisons it, in order to secure the prize to himself. A has committed the offence defined in this Clause.

(b) A, having an article to sell, intending to raise the price of that article, destroys a quantity of that article which belongs to Z. A has committed the offence defined in this Clause.

405. Whoever commits mischief with the deliberate intention of thereby insulting or annoying the person to whom he intends to cause wrongful loss, shall be punished with imprisonment of either description for a term which may extend to two years, or fine, or both.

Illustration.

A, with the deliberate intention of insulting or annoying Z, destroys a book which Z values as a rarity, a picture which Z values on account of its resemblance to a friend, a keepsake, a family relic, an animal to which Z is attached. A has in each of these cases committed the offence defined in this Clause.

406. Whoever commits or attempts to commit mischief by killing, wounding, or poisoning any animal or animals to the value of ten rupees or upwards, shall be punished with imprisonment of either description for a term which may extend to three years, or fine, or both.

407. Whoever commits or attempts to commit mischief on any natural or artificial channel or reservoir of water, intending or knowing it to be likely that he may thereby cause a diminution of cultivation, or of agricultural produce, or a failing of the supply of water required for purposes of food or drink by human beings, or by animals which are property, or for purposes of cleanliness, or for the carrying on of any manufacture, shall be punished with imprisonment of either description for a term which may extend to three years, or fine, or both.

408. Whoever commits or attempts to commit mischief on any road, bridge, or navigable channel natural or artificial, intending or knowing it to be likely that he may thereby render it less safe or easy to travel or to convey property by such road, bridge, or navigable channel, shall be punished with imprisonment of either description for a term which may extend to three years, or fine, or both.

409. Whoever commits or attempts to commit mischief, intending or knowing it to be likely that such mischief may cause an inundation attended with loss to the amount of one hundred rupees or upwards, shall be punished with imprisonment of either description for a term which may extend to three years, or fine, or both.

410. Whoever commits or attempts to commit mischief on any light-house, sea-mark, or buoy, intending or knowing it to be likely that such mischief may render such light-house, sea-mark, or buoy, less useful, as such light-house, sea-mark, or buoy, shall be

punished with imprisonment of either description for a term which may extend to three years, or fine, or both.

411. Whoever commits or attempts to commit mischief on any land-mark, intending or knowing it to be likely that he may thereby render such land-mark less useful, as such, shall be punished with imprisonment of either description for a term which may extend to one year, or fine, or both.

412. Whoever commits or attempts to commit mischief by fire, intending or knowing it to be likely that he may thereby cause the destruction of any property which is not kept within any building, the value of which property amounts to one hundred rupees or upwards, shall be punished with imprisonment of either description for a term which may extend to seven years and must not be less than six months, and shall also be liable to fine.

413. Whoever commits or attempts to commit mischief by fire, intending or knowing it to be likely that he may thereby cause the destruction of any building which is ordinarily used as a human dwelling or as a place for the custody of property, shall be punished with imprisonment of either description for a term which may extend to fourteen years and must not be less than one year, and shall also be liable to fine.

414. Whoever commits or attempts to commit mischief by fire, intending or knowing it to be likely that buildings ordinarily used as human dwellings, to the number of not less than five, may be consumed, shall be punished with transportation for life, or rigorous imprisonment which may extend to life and must not be less than seven years, and shall also be liable to fine.

415. Whoever commits or attempts to commit mischief on any decked vessel, intending or knowing it to be likely that he may thereby destroy that decked vessel, or render that decked vessel unsafe, shall be punished with imprisonment of either description for a term which may extend to fourteen years and must not be less than two years, and shall also be liable to fine.

416. Whoever commits or attempts to commit mischief, having made preparation for causing to any person death, or hurt, or wrongful restraint, or fear of death, or of hurt, or of wrongful restraint, while committing or attempting to commit such mischief, or while retiring after committing it, shall be punished with imprisonment of either description for a term which may extend to three years and must not be less than six months, and shall also be liable to fine.

417. If any person, by doing any thing which is an offence under the last preceding Clause, also commits an offence under any other Clause of this Code, the punishment shall be cumulative.*

OF CRIMINAL TRESPASS.

418. Whoever exercises any dominion over any property, not having a legal right independent of the consent of any other party to exercise such dominion, and not having the consent, express or implied, of any party legally entitled to give a consent which would authorize the exercise of such dominion, is said to " trespass."

Illustrations.

(a) A walks into a building, not having a right of entry there, and not having the consent of any person entitled to authorize such entry. A trespasses.

(b) A goes across Z's field, not having a right of way there, and not having the consent of any person entitled to authorise A so to do. A trespasses.

(c) A takes up a book belonging to Z, and reads it, not having any right over the book, and not having the consent of any person entitled to authorize A so to do. A trespasses.

(d) A throws rubbish into Z's garden, not having any right over the garden, and not having the consent of any person entitled to authorize A so to do. A trespasses.

(e) A climbs up behind Z's carriage, not having a right so to do, and not having the consent of any person entitled to authorize him so to do. A trespasses.

(f) A goes into Z's field with Z's consent, but remains in the field after he has been directed by Z to withdraw. A trespasses.

419. Whoever knowingly trespasses in order to the injuring by any offence, to the intimidating, to the insulting, or to the annoying of any possessor of the property which is the subject of the trespass, or of any person who, by the permission express or implied of such possessor, is exercising any dominion over such property, is said to commit " criminal trespass."

* For mischief to certain Documents, see the Chapter of Offences relating to Documents.

420. Whoever commits criminal trespass by entering or remaining in any building, tent, or vessel, used as a human dwelling, or any building used as a place for worship, or as a place for the custody of property, is said to commit " house-trespass."

Explanations. The introduction of any part of the criminal trespasser's body is entering sufficient to constitute house-trespass.

A person who enters, not as a house-trespasser, may remain as a house-trespasser.

421. Whoever commits house-trespass, taking precautions to conceal such house-trespass from some person who has a right to exclude or eject the trespasser from the building, tent, or vessel which is the subject of the trespass, is said to commit " lurking house-" trespass."

Explanation. A person who enters, not as a lurking house-trespasser, may remain as a lurking house-trespasser.

422. Whoever commits lurking house-trespass after sunset and before sunrise, is said to commit " lurking house-trespass by night."

Explanation. A person who enters, not by night, may remain as a lurking house-trespasser by night.

423. A person is said to commit " housebreaking" who commits house-trespass in any of the six ways hereinafter described; namely,

First, If he enters through a passage made by himself, or by any previous abettor of the house-trespass, in order to the committing of the house-trespass;

Second, If he enters through any passage not intended for human entrance;

Third, If he enters through any passage which he or any previous abettor of the house-trespass has opened in order to the committing of the house-trespass by any means by which that passage was not intended to be opened;

Fourth, If he enters by opening any lock with a key which he did not find in the lock, or with a key which was left in the lock in order to the committing of the house-trespass;

Fifth, If he effects his entrance by committing an assault, or by making shew of assault, or by threatening any person with assault;

Sixth, If he enters by any passage which he knows to have been fastened against such entrance, and to have been unfastened from within by a previous abettor of the house-trespass.

Illustrations.

(*a*) A commits house-trespass by digging through the wall of Z's house, and putting his hand through the aperture. This is housebreaking.

(*b*) A commits house-trespass by creeping into a ship at a port hole between decks. This is housebreaking.

(*c*) A commits house-trespass by entering Z's house through a window. This is housebreaking.

(*d*) A commits house-trespass by entering Z's house through the door, having opened the door with a false key. This is housebreaking.

(*e*) A commits house-trespass by entering Z's house through the door, having lifted the latch by putting a wire through a hole in the door. This is housebreaking.

(*f*) A finds the key of Z's house door, which Z had lost, and commits house-trespass by entering Z's house having opened the door with that key. This is housebreaking.

(*g*) Z is standing in his door way. A forces a passage by knocking Z down, and commits house-trespass by entering the house. This is housebreaking.

(*h*) Z, the porter of Y, is standing in Y's doorway. A commits house-trespass by entering the house, having deterred Z from opposing him by shaking a stick at Z. This is housebreaking.

424. Whoever commits house-breaking after sunset and before sunrise, is said to commit " house-breaking by night."

425. Whoever commits criminal trespass shall be punished with imprisonment of either description for a term which may extend to one month, or fine which may extend to five hundred rupees, or both.

426. Whoever commits house-trespass shall be punished with imprisonment of either description for a term which may extend to one year, or fine which may extend to one thousand rupees, or both.

427. If any person commits house-trespass in order to the committing of any other offence, and actually commits that other offence, the punishment shall be cumulative.

428. Whoever commits house-trespass in order to the committing of any offence punishable with death, or of an offence punishable with transportation for life, shall be punished with transportation for life, or with rigorous imprisonment for a term which may extend to life and must not be less than three years, and shall also be liable to fine.

I

429. Whoever commits house-trespass in order to the committing of any offence punishable with imprisonment, shall be punished with imprisonment of either description for a term which may extend to one year added to a term which may extend to one third of the longest time for which he would have been liable to be imprisoned if he had committed the offence in order to the committing of which he committed the house-trespass, or fine, or both.

430. Whoever commits house-trespass having made preparation for causing hurt to any person, or for assaulting any person, or for wrongfully restraining any person, or for putting any person in fear of hurt, or of assault, in order to the committing of such house-trespass, or during the continuance of such house-trespass, shall be punished with imprisonment of either description for a term which may extend to two years, or fine, or both.

431. Whoever commits lurking house-trespass, or house-breaking, shall be punished with imprisonment of either description for a term which may extend to two years, or fine, or both.

432. If any person commits lurking house-trespass, or house-breaking, in order to the committing of any other offence, and actually commits that other offence, the punishment shall be cumulative.

433. Whoever commits lurking house-trespass, or house-breaking, in order to the committing of any offence punishable with imprisonment, shall be punished with imprisonment of either description for a term which may extend to two years added to a term which may extend to one half of the longest time for which he would have been liable to be imprisoned if he had committed the offence in order to the committing of which he committed such lurking house-trespass or house-breaking, and must not be less than one half of the shortest time for which he would have been liable to be imprisoned if he had committed that offence, and shall also be liable to fine.

434. Whoever commits lurking house-trespass, or house-breaking, having made preparation for causing hurt to any person, or for assaulting any person, or for wrongfully restraining any person, or for putting any person in fear of hurt, or of assault, in order to the committing of such lurking house-trespass, or house-breaking, or during the continuance of the house-trespass which has been begun by such lurking house-trespass, or house-breaking, shall be punished with imprisonment of either description for a term which may extend to three years and must not be less than three months, and shall also be liable to fine.

435. Whoever commits lurking house-trespass by night, or house-breaking by night, in order to the committing of any other offence, and actually commits that other offence, shall be punished with imprisonment of either description for a term which may extend to three years, or fine, or both.

436. If any person commits lurking house-trespass by night, or house-breaking by night, the punishment shall be cumulative.

437. Whoever commits lurking house-trespass by night, or house-breaking by night, in order to the committing of any offence punishable with imprisonment, shall be punished with imprisonment of either description for a term which may extend to three years, added to a term which may extend to two thirds of the longest time for which he would have been liable to be imprisoned if he had committed the offence in order to the committing of which he committed such lurking house-trespass by night, or house-breaking by night, and must not be less than the shortest time for which he would have been liable to be imprisoned if he had committed that offence, and shall also be liable to fine.

438. Whoever commits lurking house-trespass by night, or housebreaking by night, having made preparation for causing hurt to any person, or for assaulting any person, or for wrongfully restraining any person, or for putting any person in fear of hurt or of assault, in order to the committing of such house-trespass, or during the continuance of the house-trespass which has been begun by such lurking house-trespass by night, or house-breaking by night, shall be punished with imprisonment of either description for a term which may extend to seven years and must not be less than six months, and shall also be liable to fine.

439. Whoever commits criminal trespass by opening any closed receptacle which contains or which he believes to contain property, by any means by which that receptacle or any fastening of that receptacle is damaged, or by opening any lock, shall be punished

with imprisonment of either description for a term which may extend to two years, or fine, or both.

440. Whoever, being entrusted either by law, or in pursuance of a contract made by him, with the keeping of any closed receptacle which contains or which he believes to contain property, commits criminal trespass by opening with a fraudulent intention that receptacle by any means by which that receptacle or any fastening of that receptacle is damaged, or by opening any lock, shall be punished with imprisonment of either description for a term which may extend to three years, or fine, or both.

CHAPTER XX.

OF OFFENCES RELATING TO DOCUMENTS.

441. A person is said to commit forgery who,

First, Makes any document, or any part of any document, or any mark which may appear to identify or authenticate any document, intending that it may be believed, in any quarter, that such document, part, or mark was made by some other person, or at some other time, or by some authority by which it was not made ;

Or, *Secondly*, Having engaged to make any document by the authority and according to the direction of another, voluntarily omits to insert therein any thing which he is directed by that other to insert, intending that it may be believed in any quarter that the document is made according to that other's direction ;

Or, *Thirdly*, Cancels any document, or any part of any document, intending that it may be believed in any quarter that such cancellation was made by some other person, or at some other time, or by some authority by which it was not made ;

Or, *Fourthly*, Causes any part of any document or any mark which may appear to identify or authenticate any document to disappear, intending that it may be believed in any quarter that such part or mark never existed, or was caused to disappear by some other person, or at some other time, or by some authority by which it was not caused to disappear ;

Or, *Fifthly*, Makes any mark, not in handwriting, nor meant to be taken for handwriting, which mark at the time when it is made is not part of a document, intending that such mark may become part of a document, or may appear to identify or authenticate a document, and may be believed in any quarter to have been made by some other person, or at some other time, or by some authority by which it was not made.

Illustrations.

(*a*) A writes a letter, and signs it with Z's name, intending that it may be believed that Z wrote the same. A has committed forgery under the first head of the definition.

(*b*) A has a letter of credit for 10000 Rupees written by Z. A adds a cypher to the 10000 and makes the sum 100000, intending that it may be believed that Z so wrote the letter. A has committed forgery under the first head of the definition.

(*c*) A affixes Z's seal to a document, intending that it may be believed that Z affixed the same. A has committed forgery under the first head of the definition.

(*d*) A signs his own name to a bill of exchange, intending that it may be believed that the bill was drawn by another person of the same name. A has committed forgery under the first head of the definition.

(*e*) A, a trader, in anticipation of insolvency, lodges effects with B, and, in order to give a color to the transaction, writes a promissory note binding himself to pay to B a sum for value received, and antedates the note, intending that it may be believed to have been made before A was on the point of insolvency. A has committed forgery under the first head of the definition.

(*f*) Z dictates his will to A. A writes down a different legatee from the legatee named by Z, intending that it may be believed that what he writes was written by Z's authority. A has committed forgery under the first head of the definition, inasmuch as he makes a part of a document, intending that it may be believed that such part was made by an authority by which it was not made.

(*g*) A, having engaged to write Z's will according to Z's direction, and being directed by Z to write that Z leaves the residuum of his property equally between J, K, and L, omits the name of K, intending that it may be believed that the document is made according to Z's direction. A has committed forgery under the second head of the definition.

(*h*) Z's will contains these words—" I direct that all my remaining property be equally divided " between A, B, and C." A scratches out B's name, intending that it may be believed that the whole was left to himself and C. A has committed forgery under the fourth head of the definition.

(*i*) A makes an engraved border in imitation of the border of a Government promissory note, intending that the paper on which the border is engraved may afterwards, by the addition of handwriting, or of an imitation of handwriting, become a document, and that this document may be believed to be a Government promissory note. A has committed forgery under the fifth head of the definition.

442. A document made in whole or in part by forgery is designated as a " forged document."

A document altered by forgery, marked by forgery, or cancelled in whole or in part by forgery, is designated as a " document falsified by forgery."

443. Whoever, with the intention of causing any injury to any party, or of rendering any illegal act or omission easier or safer than it would otherwise be, or of obtaining for any person any employment either in the service of the public or of an individual, commits forgery, or uses as genuine any document which he knows to be forged or falsified by forgery, shall be punished with imprisonment of either description for a term which may extend to two years, or fine, or both.

Illustrations.

(*a*) A, a British-born subject of the King, forges a license to reside at Delhi, intending thereby to render it easier for him to violate the law which forbids him to reside there without a license. A has committed the offence defined in this Clause.

(*b*) A presents to Z a certificate of character which A knows to be forged, intending thereby to obtain employment under Z. A has committed the offence defined in this Clause.

444. Whoever, with the intention of causing any injury to any party, forges or falsifies by forgery any document which is or purports to be a valuable security, or uses as genuine any document which he knows to be forged or falsified by forgery, and which is or purports to be a valuable security, shall be punished with imprisonment of either description for a term which may extend to fourteen years and must not be less than two years and shall also be liable to fine.

445. Whoever commits forgery, intending or knowing it to be likely that the document forged or falsified by such forgery may be used as genuine for the purpose of cheating, or uses as genuine for the purpose of cheating any document which he knows to have been forged or falsified by forgery, shall be punished with imprisonment of either description for a term which may extend to seven years and must not be less than one year, and shall also be liable to fine.

446. Whoever commits forgery, intending or knowing it to be likely that the document forged or falsified by such forgery may harm the reputation of any party, or uses as genuine, for the purpose of harming the reputation of any party, any document which he knows to have been forged or falsified by forgery, shall be punished with imprisonment of either description for a term which may extend to three years and must not be less than six months, and shall also be liable to fine.

447. Whoever makes any apparatus or material for engraving, or any seal, intending or knowing it to be likely that the same may be used for the purpose of committing any forgery which it would be an offence under any Clause of this Chapter to commit, shall be punished with imprisonment of either description for a term which may extend to fourteen years and must not be less than two years, and shall also be liable to fine.

448. Whoever has in his possession any plate, or material, or implement for engraving, or any seal, intending or knowing it to be likely that the same may be used for the purpose of committing any forgery which it would be an offence under any Clause of this Chapter to commit, shall be punished with imprisonment of either description for a term which may extend to fourteen years and must not be less than two years, and shall also be liable to fine.

449. Whoever has in his possession any document which he knows to be forged, or falsified by forgery, and which is or purports to be a valuable security, intending or knowing it to be likely that the same may be used as genuine to the injury of any party, shall be punished with imprisonment of either description for a term which may extend to fourteen years and must not be less than two years, and shall also be liable to fine.

450. Whoever has in his possession any thing which is not a document, but which has been marked by forgery, intending that the same may be made a document purporting to be a valuable security, and intending or knowing it to be likely that such document

mãy be used as genuine to the injury of any party, shall be punished with imprisonment of either description for a term which may extend to fourteen years and must not be less than two years, and shall also be liable to fine.

451. Whoever fraudulently destroys or. defaces, or fraudulently attempts to destroy or deface, or fraudulently secretes any document which is or purports to be a will, shall be punished with imprisonment of either description for a term which may extend to fourteen years and must not be less than two years, and shall also be liable to fine.

452. Whoever fraudulently destroys or defaces, or fraudulently attempts to destroy or deface, or fraudulently secretes any document which purports to be a valuable security, shall be punished with imprisonment of either description for a term which may extend to three years and must not be less than six months, and shall also be liable to fine.

453. Whoever, being a public servant in the Post Office Department, and being, as such, entrusted with the keeping of any fastened letter or any fastened packet containing any document, intentionally opens the same, knowing that he has not legal authority so to do, shall be punished with imprisonment of either description for a term which may extend to two years, or fine, or both.

454. Whoever opens any fastened letter or any fastened packet containing any document, knowing that it does not belong to him, and that he has not the consent, express or implied, of any party legally entitled to give a consent which would authorize such opening of such letter or packet, shall be punished with imprisonment of either description for a term which may extend to six months, or fine which may extend to five hundred rupees, or both.

CHAPTER XXI.

OF OFFENCES RELATING TO PROPERTY-MARKS.

455. Every mark put on any property for the purpose of distinguishing the property marked from other property, or for the purpose of indicating to what party the property marked, or any dominion over the property marked belongs, or for the purpose of indicating that any payment is due or has been made in respect of the property marked, or that the property marked is entitled to any exemption, is designated as a " property- " mark."

456. Whoever makes any counterfeit property-mark, intending or knowing it to be likely that such counterfeit property-mark may be used as genuine to the injury of any party, or uses as genuine any counterfeit property-mark knowing the same to be counterfeit, and intending or knowing it to be likely that, by so using that property-mark, he may cause injury to some party, shall be punished with imprisonment of either description for a term which may extend to one year, or fine, or both.

Illustration.

A marks Z's sheep with a mark which Y is in the habit of affixing to Y's sheep, intending or knowing it to be likely that Z's sheep may be confounded with Y's, and that injury may thus be caused to Z. A has committed the offence defined in this Clause.

457. Whoever makes any counterfeit property-mark, which is a counterfeit of any property-mark affixed by the lawful authority of some public servant, as such, or some body of public servants, as such, intending or knowing it to be likely that such counterfeit property-mark may be used as genuine to the injury of any party, or uses as genuine any such counterfeit property-mark, knowing the same to be counterfeit, and intending or knowing it to be likely that, by so using that counterfeit property-mark, he may cause injury to some party, shall be punished with imprisonment of. either description for a term which may extend to three years and must not be less than six months, and shall also be liable to fine.

Illustration.

A, intending to cause Z to believe that a threatening letter comes from a place from which it does not come, and thus to injure Z, by annoying and terrifying him, counterfeits the post-mark of the Post Office of that place. A has committed the offence defined in this Clause.

458. Whoever makes any counterfeit property-mark, intending or knowing it to be likely that such counterfeit property-mark may be used as genuine for the purpose of cheating, or uses as genuine for the purpose of cheating any property-mark which he knows to be counterfeit, shall be punished with imprisonment of either description for a term which may extend to two years, or fine, or both.

Illustration.

A counterfeits the mark of a cutler at Sheffield on cutlery made by himself in India, intending thereby to cheat. A has committed the offence defined in this Clause.

459. Whoever puts any property-mark on any property, intending or knowing it to be likely that such property-mark may be used for the purpose of cheating, or uses any property-mark for the purpose of cheating, shall be punished with imprisonment of either description for a term which may extend to one year, or fine, or both.

CHAPTER XXII.*

OF THE ILLEGAL PURSUIT OF LEGAL RIGHTS.

460. Whoever, in good faith, believing a debt to be legally due, takes or attempts to take any property from the person whom he believes to owe that debt, not fraudulently, but in order to satisfy that debt, under such circumstances that if his intention were fraudulent he would be guilty of theft, or robbery, shall be punished with imprisonment of either description for a term which may extend to one year, or fine, or both.

Illustrations.

(a) A, believing in good faith that Z owes him one hundred rupees, in order to satisfy the debt takes property belonging to Z, not fraudulently, but under such circumstances that if he took it fraudulently he would be guilty of theft. A sells that property for one hundred and fifty rupees, and sends back fifty rupees to Z. A has committed the offence defined in this Clause.

(b) But if A, at the time of taking, intended to keep the whole sum of one hundred and fifty rupees, he acted fraudulently, and has committed theft.

(c) If A meant, after repaying himself, to sue Z for the debt, A acted fraudulently, and has committed theft.

461. Whoever takes property in the manner described in the last preceding Clause, and keeps that property or any part thereof fraudulently, shall be punished with the punishment to which he would have been liable if the taking had been fraudulent.

Illustration.

A takes property in the manner described in Clause 460, intending to repay himself a debt due to him by Z, and to refund the surplus. A subsequently changes his mind, and fraudulently keeps the whole. A is liable to be punished as if he had taken the property fraudulently.

462. If any person voluntarily causes hurt in doing any thing which is an offence under any Clause of this Chapter, the punishment shall be cumulative.

CHAPTER XXIII.†

OF THE CRIMINAL BREACH OF CONTRACTS OF SERVICE.

463. Whoever, being bound by a lawful contract to convey or conduct any person, or any property, from one place to another place, illegally omits so to do, intending or knowing it to be likely that such illegal omission will cause injury to some party, shall

be punished with imprisonment of either description for a term which may extend to one month, or fine which may extend to one hundred rupees, or both.

Illustrations.

(*a*) A, a palanquin bearer, being bound by legal contract to carry Z from one place to another, runs away in the middle of the stage. A has committed the offence defined in this Clause.

(*b*) A, a cooly, being bound by lawful contract to carry Z's baggage from one place to another, throws the baggage away. A has committed the offence defined in this Clause.

(*c*) A, a proprietor of bullocks, being bound by legal contract to convey goods on his bullocks from one place to another, illegally omits to do so. A has committed the offence defined in this Clause.

464. Whoever, being a seaman, bound by a lawful contract to serve on board of a merchant vessel, illegally leaves that vessel, or illegally remains absent from that vessel, or illegally disobeys any order of any officer of that vessel, shall be punished with imprisonment of either description for a term which may extend to three months, or fine which may extend to one hundred rupees, or both.

465. Whoever, being bound by a lawful contract to attend on any person who by reason of youth, or of unsoundness of mind, or of disease, is helpless or incapable of providing for his own safety, or to supply the wants of any such person, illegally omits so to do, shall be punished with imprisonment of either description for a term which may extend to six months, or fine which may extend to five hundred rupees, or both.

CHAPTER XXIV.*

OF OFFENCES RELATING TO MARRIAGE.

466. Every man who by deceit causes any woman, who is not lawfully married to him according to the law of marriage under which she lives, to believe that she is lawfully married to him according to that law, and to cohabit with him in that belief, shall be punished with imprisonment of either description for a term which may extend to fourteen years and must not be less than two years, and shall also be liable to fine.

467. Every woman who by deceit causes any man to believe that he is lawfully married to her according to the law of marriage under which he lives, and to cohabit with her in consequence of that belief, shall be punished with simple imprisonment for a term which may extend to one year, or fine, or both.

468. Whoever, with any fraudulent intention, goes through the ceremony of being married according to any law in force in the Territories of the East India Company, knowing that he is not thereby lawfully married, shall be punished with imprisonment of either description for a term which may extend to three years and must not be less than six months, and shall also be liable to fine.

CHAPTER XXV.†

OF DEFAMATION.

469. Whoever, by words either spoken or intended to be read, or by signs, or by visible representations, attempts to cause any imputation concerning any person to be believed in any quarter, knowing that the belief thereof would harm the reputation of that person in that quarter, is said, except in the cases excepted in the nine Clauses next following, to defame that person.

* See Note Q.   † See Note R.

Explanations. An imputation is not defamatory unless it be such as, if believed in that quarter in which it is intended to be believed, would harm the reputation of the person concerning whom it is intended to be believed.

Hence an imputation which is defamatory when directed against one person, is not necessarily defamatory when directed against another person ; and an imputation which is defamatory when intended to be believed in one quarter is not necessarily defamatory when intended to be believed in another quarter.

Also, it may be defamation to repeat or circulate an imputation which it was not defamation originally to make ; and it is not necessarily defamation to repeat or circulate an imputation which it was defamation originally to make.

A deceased person may be defamed.*

A collection of persons cannot, as such, be defamed. But an individual may be defamed by means of an imputation thrown on a collection of persons of whom he is one, or by means of an imputation made in the form of an alternative.

If the imputation be such that, if it were believed in the quarter in which it was intended to be believed, the reputation of the person concerning whom it is intended to be believed would not be harmed, then, though that person may suffer in his interest, he has not been defamed.

" Harm the reputation." No imputation is said to harm a person's reputation unless that imputation directly or indirectly lowers the moral or intellectual character of that person, or lowers the character of that person in respect of his caste or of his calling, or lowers the commercial credit of that person if he is engaged in trade, or causes it to be believed that the body of that person is in a loathsome state, or in a state generally considered as disgraceful.

Illustrations.

(*a*) A says—" Z is an honest man ; he never stole B's watch ;" intending to cause it to be believed that Z did steal B's watch. This is defamation, unless it fall within one of the exceptions.

(*b*) A is asked who stole B's watch. A points to Z, intending to cause it to be believed that Z stole B's watch. This is defamation, unless it fall within one of the exceptions.

(*c*) A draws a picture of Z running away with B's watch, intending it to be believed that Z stole B's watch. This is defamation, unless it fall within one of the exceptions.

(*d*) A says of Z that Z drinks wine. Here, the question whether A has defamed Z may turn on the question whether Z is a Musulman, or a Christian.

(*e*) It may be defamation to say of a Sheeah that he has turned a Soonee. It may also be defamation to say of a Soonee that he has turned a Sheeah.

(*f*) A says of Z that Z is a coward. The question whether this is defamation, or not, may depend on the question whether Z be a soldier or a woman.

(*g*) A says of Z, a Hindoo, that it is highly probable that he will be converted to Mahomedanism. The question whether this is defamation, or not, may depend on the question whether the communication was made to the Hindoo relatives of Z, or to a Musulman.

(*h*) A journeyman printer who sets the types for printing defamatory matter, a bookseller who sells books containing defamatory matter, a person who lends a defamatory newspaper or repeats defamatory verses, does not commit defamation unless he has the intention described in the definition of defamation.

(*i*) The Bank of Bengal, the Civil Service, the Army, cannot be defamed, as such. But it may be defamation of every Judge of the Sudder to say—" The whole Sudder Court is corrupt."

(*j*) A says—" X, Y, or Z must be a thief. I do not know which committed the theft. But it " was one of the three." This may be defamation of every one of the three persons named.

(*k*) A falsely tells B, who is a public servant having an office at his disposal, that Z, to whom B intends to offer that office, will not accept it. B, in consequence, gives that office to another. Here Z, though he suffers in his interests, is not harmed in his reputation, and therefore is not defamed.

470. *First Exception.* It is not defamation to attempt to cause any thing which is true to be believed in any quarter, concerning any person.

471. *Second Exception.* It is not defamation to express in good faith any opinion whatever respecting the conduct of a public servant in the discharge of his public functions, or respecting his character so far as his character appears in that conduct, and no further.

472. *Third Exception.* It is not defamation to express in good faith any opinion whatever respecting the conduct of any person touching any public question, and respecting his character so far as his character appears in that conduct, and no further.

---

* The course of proceeding in such a case belongs to the Law of Criminal Procedure.

Illustrations.

It is not defamation in A to express in good faith any opinion whatever respecting Z's conduct in petitioning Government on a public question, in signing a requisition for a meeting on a public question, in presiding or attending at such a meeting, in forming or joining any society which invites the public support, in voting or canvassing for a particular candidate for any situation in the efficient discharge of the duties of which the public is interested.

473. *Fourth Exception.* It is not defamation to express in good faith any opinion whatever respecting the merits of any case, civil or criminal, which has been brought before any Court of Justice, or respecting the conduct of any person as a party, witness, or agent, in any such case, or respecting the character of such person, as far as his character appears in that conduct, and no further.

Illustrations.

(*a*) A says—" I think Z's evidence on that trial is so contradictory that he must be stupid or " dishonest." A is within this exception if he says this in good faith ; inasmuch as the opinion which he expresses respects Z's character as it appears in Z's conduct as a witness, and no further.

(*b*) But if A says—" I do not believe what Z asserted at that trial, because I know him to be " a man without veracity ;"—A is not within this exception, inasmuch as the opinion which he expresses of Z's character is an opinion not founded on Z's conduct as a witness.

474. *Fifth Exception.* It is not defamation to express in good faith any opinion respecting the merit of any performance which its author has submitted to the judgment of the public, or respecting the character of the author so far as his character appears in such performance, and no further.

Explanation. A performance may be submitted to the judgment of the public expressly, or by acts on the part of the author which imply such submission to the judgment of the public.

Illustrations.

(*a*) A person who publishes a book submits that book to the judgment of the public.

(*b*) A person who makes a speech in public submits that speech to the judgment of the public.

(*c*) An actor or singer who appears on a public stage submits his acting or singing to the judgment of the public.

(*d*) A says of a book published by Z, " Z's book is foolish, Z must be a weak man. Z's book " is indecent, Z must be a man of impure mind." A is within this exception, if he says this in good faith, in as much as the opinion which he expresses of Z respects Z's character only so far as it appears in Z's book, and no further.

(*e*) But if A says—" I am not surprised that Z's book is foolish, and indecent, for he is a weak " man, and a libertine ;"—A is not within this exception in as much as the opinion which he expresses of Z's character is an opinion not founded on Z's book.

475. *Sixth Exception.* It is not defamation in a person having over another any authority, either conferred by law, or arising out of a lawful contract made with that other, to pass in good faith any censure on the conduct of that other in matters to which such lawful authority relates.

Illustrations.

A judge censuring in good faith the conduct of a witness, or an officer of the Court; a head of a department censuring in good faith those who are under his orders ; a parent censuring in good faith a child in the presence of other children ; a schoolmaster, whose authority is derived from a parent, censuring in good faith a pupil in the presence of other pupils ; a master censuring a servant in good faith for remissness in service ; a banker censuring in good faith the cashier of his Bank for the conduct of such cashier, as such cashier ; are within this exception.

476. *Seventh Exception.* It is not defamation to prefer, in good faith, an accusation against any person to any of those who have lawful authority over that person with respect to the subject matter of accusation.

Illustrations.

If A in good faith accuses Z before a Magistrate ; if A in good faith complains of the conduct of Z, a servant, to Z's master ; if A in good faith complains of the conduct of Z, a child, to Z's father ; A is within this exception..

477. *Eighth Exception.* It is not defamation in a person giving directions for the management of his concerns to make an imputation on the character of another, provided that the imputation be made in good faith for the protection of the interests of the person making it.

Illustration.

A, a shopkeeper, says to B his foreman—" sell nothing to Z unless he pays you ready money, for I have no opinion of his honesty." A is within the exception, if he has made this imputation on Z in good faith, for the protection of his own interests.

478. *Ninth Exception.* It is not defamation to convey a caution, in good faith, to one person against another, provided that such caution be intended for the good of the person to whom it is conveyed, or of some party in whom that person is interested.

479. Whoever defames another shall be punished with simple imprisonment for a term which may extend to two years, or fine, or both.

480. Wherever defamation is committed by means of any printed or engraved substance, whoever at the time of printing or engraving the defamatory matter was a possessor of the machinery whereby such defamatory matter was printed or engraved, shall, except in the case hereinafter excepted, be punished with simple imprisonment for a term which may extend to two years, or fine, or both.

Exception. No person shall be liable to punishment as a possessor of the machinery by which defamatory matter was printed or engraved, if such defamatory matter were printed or engraved contrary to his directions, or if the printing or engraving were purposely concealed from him.

481. Wherever defamation is committed by means of any printed or engraved substance, whoever first sells or offers for sale that printed or engraved substance, shall be punished with simple imprisonment for a term which may extend to two years, or fine, or both.

CHAPTER XXVI.

OF CRIMINAL INTIMIDATION, INSULT, AND ANNOYANCE.

482. Whoever deliberately threatens any person to murder that person or any other in whom that person is interested, or to commit the offence of voluntarily causing hurt to that person or to any other person in whom that person is interested, or to commit mischief by fire on that person's property, or to kill or wound any animal which is that person's property, or to commit the offence of housebreaking on any building, tent, or vessel which is that person's property, or wherein that person resides, or to commit any mischief or trespass injurious to that person by means of a riotous assembly, or falsely to impute unnatural lust to that person, or falsely to impute unchastity to that person if that person be a woman, with the intention of causing, by such threat, distress or terror to the person to whom such threat is conveyed, or of inducing that person to do any act which that person is not legally bound to do, or to omit the doing of any act which that person has a legal right to do, is said to commit the offence of " criminal intimidation."

483. Whoever commits the offence of criminal intimidation shall be punished with imprisonment of either description for a term which may extend to two years, or fine, or both.

484. Whoever commits the offence of criminal intimidation, having taken precaution to conceal the quarter from whence the threat comes, shall be punished with imprisonment of either description for a term which may extend to three years and must not be less than six months, and shall also be liable to fine.

485. Whoever utters any word, makes any sound, makes any gesture, or exhibits any object, intending that such word or sound shall be heard, or that such gesture or object shall be seen by any person, and intending thereby to insult that person, shall be punished with imprisonment of either description for a term which may extend to three months, or fine which may extend to one thousand rupees or both.

Explanations. A person may exhibit an object by sending it to another as well as by placing it before the eyes of another.

The making of an imputation which is not defamatory because it falls under one of the exceptions appended to the definition of defamation, may be an offence under this Clause.

Illustrations.

(*a*) Z has been guilty of an offence, and has been punished for it, A follows him reproaching him with that offence. Here, A is not guilty of defamation, inasmuch as he has imputed to Z only what was true. But if A has used words, intending them to be heard by Z, and intending thereby to insult Z, he has committed the offence defined in this Clause.

(b) A forces himself into the presence of a Magistrate, crying out that the Magistrate is a tyrant. Here, though A is not guilty of defamation if in good faith he accuses a public servant of tyranny, yet if he uses those words intending that the Magistrate may hear them, and intending thereby to insult the Magistrate, A commits the offence defined in this Clause.

486. Whoever utters any word, makes any sound, makes any gesture, or exhibits any object, intending that such word or sound shall be heard, or that such gesture or object shall be seen by any woman, and intending thereby to insult the modesty of that woman, shall be punished with imprisonment of either description for a term which may extend to two years, or fine, or both.

Illustration.

A, intending to outrage the modesty of a woman, exposes his person indecently to her, or uses obscene words intending that she should hear them, or sends to her obscene drawings by post. A has committed the offence defined in this Clause.

487. Whoever utters any word, makes any sound, makes any gesture, or exhibits any object, intending that such word or sound shall be heard, or that such gesture or object shall be seen by any person, and malignantly and wantonly intending thereby to annoy that person, shall be punished with imprisonment of either description which may extend to one month, or fine which may extend to one hundred rupees, or both.

Illustrations.

(a) A follows Z in the street, hooting him, malignantly and wantonly intending thereby to annoy Z. A has committed the offence defined in this Clause.

(b) A beats a gong under Z's window by night, malignantly and wantonly intending to annoy Z. A has committed the offence defined in this Clause.

488. Whoever, in a state of intoxication, appears in any public place, or in any place which it is a trespass in him to enter, and there conducts himself in such a manner as to cause annoyance to any person, shall be punished with simple imprisonment for a term which may extend to twenty-four hours, or fine which may extend to ten rupees, or both.

NOTES.

NOTE A.

ON THE CHAPTER OF PUNISHMENTS.

First among the punishments provided for offences by this Code stands death. No argument that has been brought to our notice has satisfied us that it would be desirable wholly to dispense with this punishment. But we are convinced that it ought to be very sparingly inflicted, and we propose to employ it only in cases where either murder, or the highest offence against the State has been committed.

We are not apprehensive that we shall be thought by many persons to have resorted too frequently to capital punishment. But we think it probable that many even of those who condemn the English statute book as sanguinary may think that our Code errs on the other side. They may be of opinion that gang-robbery, the cruel mutilation of the person, and possibly rape, ought to be punished with death. These are doubtless offences which, if we looked only at their enormity, at the evil which they produce, at the terror which they spread through society, at the depravity which they indicate, we might be inclined to punish capitally. But atrocious as they are, they cannot, as it appears to us, be placed in the same class with murder. To the great majority of mankind nothing is so dear as life. And we are of opinion that to put robbers, ravishers, and mutilators on the same footing with murderers is an arrangement which diminishes the security of life.

There is in practice a close connection between murder and most of those offences which come nearest to murder in enormity. Those offences are almost always committed under such circumstances that the offender has it in his power to add murder to his guilt. They are often committed under such circumstances that the offender has a temptation to add murder to his guilt. The same opportunities, the same superiority of force, which enabled a man to rob, to mangle, or to ravish, will enable him to go farther and to dispatch his victim. As he has almost always the power to murder, he will often have a strong motive to murder, inasmuch as by murder he may often hope to remove the only witness of the crime which he has already committed. If the punishment of the crime which he has already committed be exactly the same with the punishment of murder, he will have no restraining motive. A law which imprisons for rape and robbery, and hangs for murder, holds out to ravishers and robbers a strong inducement to spare the lives of those whom they have injured. A law which hangs for rape and robbery, and which only hangs for murder, holds out, indeed, if it be rigorously carried into effect, a strong motive to deter men from rape and robbery, but as soon as a man has ravished or robbed, it holds out to him a strong motive to follow up his crime with a murder.

If murder were punished with something more than simple death, if the murderer were broken on the wheel, or burned alive, there would not be the same objection to punishing with death those crimes which in atrocity approach nearest to murder. But such a system would be open to other objections so obvious that it is unnecessary to point them out. The highest punishment which we propose is the simple privation of life; and the highest punishment, be it what it may, ought not, for the reason which we have given, to be assigned to any crime against the person who stops short of murder. And it is hardly necessary to point out to his Lordship in Council how great a shock would be given to public feeling if, while we propose to exempt from the punishment of death the most atrocious personal outrages which stopt short of murder, we were to inflict that punishment even in the worst cases of theft, cheating, or mischief.

It will be seen that, throughout the Code, wherever we have made any offence punishable by transportation, we have provided that the transportation shall be for life. The consideration which has chiefly determined us to retain that mode of punishment is our persuasion that it is regarded by the natives of India, particularly by those who live at a distance from the sea, with peculiar fear. The pain which is caused by punishment is unmixed evil. It is by the terror which it inspires that it produces good: and perhaps no punishment inspires so much terror in proportion to the actual pain which it causes as the punishment of transportation in this country. Prolonged imprisonment may be more painful in the actual indurance: but it is not so much dreaded before hand; nor does a sentence of imprisonment strike either the offender or the by-standers with so much horror as a sentence of exile beyond what they call the Black Water. This feeling, we believe, arises chiefly from the mystery which overhangs the fate of the transported convict. The separation resembles that which takes place at the moment of death. The criminal is taken for ever from the society of all who are acquainted with him, and conveyed by means of which the natives have but an indistinct notion over an element which they regard with extreme awe, to a distant country of which they know nothing, and from which he is never to return. It is natural that his fate should impress them with a deep feeling of terror. It is on this feeling that the efficacy of the punishment depends, and this feeling would be greatly weakened if transported convicts should frequently return, after an exile of seven or fourteen years, to the scene of their offences, and to the society of their former friends.

We may observe that the rule which we propose to lay down is already in force in almost every part of British India. The Courts established by the Royal Charters, and Courts Martial, are at present the only Courts which sentence offenders to transportation for any term short of life. In the case of European offenders who are condemned to long terms of imprisonment, we allow the Government to commute imprisonment for transportation not perpetual. But in that case we are of opinion that in general the transported criminal ought not, after the expiration of the term for which he is transported, to be allowed to return to India. This rule and the reasons for it will be considered hereafter.

Of imprisonment we propose to institute two grades; rigorous imprisonment and simple imprisonment. But we do not think the Penal Code the proper place for describing with minuteness the nature of either kind of punishment.

We entertain a confident hope that it will shortly be found practicable greatly to reduce the terms of imprisonment which we propose. Where a good system of prison-discipline exists, where the criminal, without being subject to any cruel severities, is strictly restrained, regularly employed in labor not of an attractive kind, and deprived of every indulgence not necessary to his health, a year's confinement will generally prove as efficacious as confinement for two years in a gaol where the superintendence is lax, where the work exacted is light, and where the convicts find means of enjoying as many luxuries as if they were at liberty. As the intensity of the punishment is increased its length may safely be diminished. As members of the committee which is now employed in investigating the system followed in the gaols of this country, we have had access to information which enables us to say with confidence that in this department of the administration extensive reforms are greatly needed, and may easily be made. The researches of that committee will, we hope, enable the Law Commission hereafter to prepare such a Code of Prison-Discipline, as, without shocking the humane feelings of the community, may yet be a terror to the most hardened wrong doers. Whenever such a Code shall come into operation, we conceive that it will be advisable greatly to shorten many of the terms of imprisonment which we have proposed.

It will be seen that we have given to the Government a power of commuting sentences in certain cases without the consent of the offender. Some of the rules which we have laid down on this subject will be universally allowed to be proper. It is evidently fit that the Government should be empowered to commute the sentence of death for any other punishment provided by the Code. It seems to us also very desirable that the Government should have the power of commuting perpetual transportation for perpetual imprisonment. Many circumstances of which the executive authorities ought to be accurately informed, but which must often be unknown to the ablest judge, may, at particular times, render it highly inconvenient to carry a sentence of transportation into effect. The state of those remote Provinces of the Empire in which convict settlements are established, and the way in which the interest of those Provinces may be affected by any addition to the convict population, are matters which lie altogether out of the cognizance of the tribunals by which those sentences are passed, and which the Government only is competent to decide.

The provisions contained in Clauses 43 and 44 are more likely to cause difference of opinion. We are satisfied that both humanity and policy require that those provisions, or provisions very similar to them, should be adopted.

The physical difference which exists between the European and the native of India renders it impossible to subject them to the same system of prison-discipline. It is most desirable, indeed, that in the treatment of offenders convicted of the same crime and sentenced to the same punishment there should be no apparent inequality. But it is still more desirable that there should be no real inequality, and there must be real inequality unless there be apparent inequality. It would be cruel to subject an European for a long period to a severe prison-discipline, in a country in which existence is almost constant misery to an European who has not many indulgences at his command. If not cruel it would be impolitic. It is unnecessary to point out to his Lordship in Council how desirable it is that our national character should stand high in the estimation of the inhabitants of India, and how much that character would be lowered by the frequent exhibition of Englishmen of the worst description, placed in the most degrading situations, stigmatized by the Courts of Justice, and engaged in the ignominious labour of a gaol.

As there are strong reasons for not punishing Europeans with imprisonment of the same description with which we propose to punish natives, so there are reasons equally strong for not suffering Europeans who have been convicted of serious crimes to remain in this country. As we are satisfied that nothing can add more strength to the Government, or can be more beneficial to the people, than the free admission of honest, industrious, and intelligent Englishmen, so we are satisfied that no greater calamity could befall either the Government or the people, than the influx of Englishmen of lawless habits and blasted character. Such men are of the same race and color with the rulers of the country, they speak the same language, they wear the same garb. In all these things they differ from the great body of the population. It is natural and inevitable that in the minds of a people accustomed to be governed by Englishmen, the idea of an Englishman should be associated with the idea of government. Every Englishman participates in the power of Government though he holds no office. His vices reflect disgrace on the Government though the Government gives him no countenance.

It was probably on these grounds that Parliament, at the same time at which it threw open a large part of India to British-born subjects of the King, directed the local legislature to provide against those dangers which might be expected from an influx of such settlers. No regulation can, in our opinion, promote more effectually, or in a more unexceptionable manner, the end which Parliament had in view, than that which we now propose.

We recommend that whenever a person not both of Asiatic birth and of Asiatic blood commits an offence so serious that he is sentenced to two years of simple imprisonment, or to one year of rigorous imprisonment, it shall be competent to the Government to commute that punishment for banishment from the Territories of the East India Company.

If a person of unmixed European blood should commit an offence so heinous as to be visited with a sentence of imprisonment for seven years, or more, we would give to the Government the power of substituting an equal term of transportation for that term of imprisonment, and of excluding the offender, after the expiration of the term of transportation, from the Territories of the East India Company. The Government would doubtless make arrangements for transporting such offenders to some British colony situated in a temperate climate.

In the great majority of cases we believe that this commutation of punishment would be most welcome to an European offender. But, however this may be, we are satisfied that it is for the interest both of the British Government, and of the Indian people, that the executive authorities should possess the power which we propose to confide to them.

The forfeiture of property is a punishment which we propose to inflict only on persons guilty of high political offences. The territorial possessions of such persons often enable them to disturb the public peace, and to make head against the Government; and it seems reasonable that they should be deprived of so dangerous a power.

Fine is one of the most common punishments in every part of the world, and it is a punishment the advantages of which are so great and obvious that we propose to authorise the Courts to inflict it in every case, except where forfeiture of all property is necessarily part of the punishment. Yet the punishment of fine is open to some objections. Death, imprisonment, transportation, banishment, solitude, compelled labour, are not, indeed, equally disagreeable to all men. But they are so disagreeable to all men that the legislature, in assigning these punishments to offences, may safely neglect the differences produced by temper and situation. With fine the case is different. In imposing a fine it is always necessary to have as much regard to the pecuniary circumstances of the offender, as to the character and magnitude of the offence. The mulct which is ruinous to a labourer is easily borne by a tradesman, and is absolutely unfelt by a rich zemindar.

It is impossible to fix any limit to the amount of a fine which will not either be so high as to be ruinous to the poor, or so low as to be no object of terror to the rich. There are many millions in India who would be utterly unable to pay a fine of fifty rupees; there are hundreds of thousands from whom such a fine might be levied, but whom it would reduce to extreme distress; there are thousands to whom it would give very little uneasiness; there are hundreds to whom it would be a matter of perfect indifference, and who would not cross a room to avoid it. The number of the poor in every country exceeds in a very great ratio the number of the rich. The number of poor criminals exceeds the number of rich criminals in a still greater ratio. And to the poor criminal it is a matter of absolute indifference whether the fine to which he is liable be limited or not, unless it be so limited as to render it quite inefficient as a mode of punishing the rich. To a man who has no capital, who has laid by nothing, whose monthly wages are just sufficient to provide himself and his family with their monthly rice, it matters not whether the fine for assault be left to be settled by the discretion of the Courts, or whether a hundred rupees be fixed as the maximum. There are no degrees in impossibility. He is no more able to pay a hundred rupees than to pay a lac. A just and wise judge, even if entrusted with a boundless discretion, will not, under ordinary circumstances, sentence such an offender to a fine of a hundred rupees. And the limit of a hundred rupees would leave it quite in the power of an unjust or inconsiderate judge to inflict on such an offender all the evil which can be inflicted on him by means of fine.

If, in imitation of Mr. Livingston, we provide that no fine shall exceed one fourth of the amount of the offender's property, no serious fine will ever be imposed in this country without a long and often a most unsatisfactory investigation, in which it would be necessary to decide many obscure questions of right purposely darkened by every artifice of chicanery. And even if this great practical difficulty did not exist, we should see strong objections to such a provision in a very large class of cases. Take the case of a corrupt judge who has accumulated a lac of rupees by his illicit practices. A fine which should deprive such a man of the whole of his fortune would not appear to us excessive. And certainly we should think it most undesirable that he should be allowed to retain 75,000 rupees of his ill-gotten gains. Again: take the case of a man who has been suborned to commit perjury, and has received a great bribe for doing so. Such a man may have little, or no property, except what he has received as a bribe. Yet it is evidently desirable that he should be compelled to disgorge the whole. No man ought ever to gain by breaking the law; and if Mr. Livingston's rule were adopted in this country, many would gain by breaking the law. To punish a man for a crime, and yet to leave in his possession three fourths of the consideration which tempted him to commit the crime, is to hold out at once punishments for crime, and inducements to crime. It appears to us that the punishment of fine is a peculiarly appropriate punishment for all offences to which men are prompted by cupidity. For it is a punishment which operates directly on the very feeling which impels men to such offences. A man who has been guilty of great offences arising from cupidity, of forging a bill of exchange for example, of keeping a receptacle for stolen goods, or of extensive embezzlement, ought, we conceive, to be so fined as to reduce him to poverty. That such a man should, when his imprisonment is over, return to the enjoyment of three fourths of his property, a property which may be very large, and which may have been accumulated by his offences, appears to us highly objectionable Those persons who are most likely to commit such offences would often be less deterred by knowing that the offender had passed several years in imprisonment, than encouraged by seeing him, after his liberation, enjoying the far larger part of his wealth.

We have never seen any general rule for the limiting of fine, which we are disposed to adopt. The difficulty of framing a rule has evidently been felt by many eminent men. The authors of the Bill of Rights, with many instances of gross abuse fresh in their re collection, could devise no other rule than that excessive fines should not be imposed. And the authors of the Constitution of the United States, after the experience of another century, contented themselves with repeating the words of the Bill of Rights.

It will be seen that in cases which are not very heinous we propose to limit the amount of fine which the Courts may impose. But in serious cases we have left the amount of fine absolutely to their discretion; and we feel, as we have said, that, even in the cases where we have proposed a limit, such a limit will be no protection to the poor, who in every community are also the many. We feel that the extent of the discretion which we have thus left to the Courts is an evil, and that no sagacity and no rectitude of inten- tion can secure a judge from occasional error. We conceive, however, that if fine is to be employed as a punishment,—and no judicious person, we are persuaded, would pro- pose to dispense with it,—this evil must be endured. We shall attempt in the Code of Procedure to establish such a system of appeal as may prevent gross or frequent injustice from taking place.

The next question which it became our duty to consider was this;—when a fine has been imposed, what measures shall be adopted in default of payment? And here two modes of proceeding, with both of which we were familiar, naturally occurred to us. The offender may be imprisoned, till the fine is paid ; or he may be imprisoned for a cer- tain term, such imprisonment being considered as standing in place of the fine. In the former case the imprisonment is used in order to compel him to part with his money. In the latter case the imprisonment is a punishment substituted for another punishment. Both modes of proceeding appear to us to be open to strong objections. To keep an of- fender in imprisonment till his fine is paid is, if the fine be beyond his means, to keep him in imprisonment all his life. And it is impossible for the best judge to be certain that he may not sometimes impose a fine which shall be beyond the means of an offender. Nohting could make such a system tolerable, except the constant interference of some authority empowered to remit sentences : and such constant interference we should con- sider as in itself an evil. On the other hand to sentence an offender to fine, and to a certain fixed term of imprisonment in default of payment, and then to leave it to himself to determine whether he will part with his money, or lie in gaol, appears to us to be a very objectionable course. The high authority of Mr. Livingston is here against us. He allows the criminal, if sentenced to a fine exceeding one fourth of his property, to com- pel the judge to commute the excess for imprisonment at the rate of one day of imprison- ment for every two dollars of fine, and he adds that such imprisonment must in no case exceed ninety days. We regret that we cannot agree with him. The object of the penal law is to deter from offences, and this can only be done by means of inflictions disagree- able to offenders. The law ought not to inflict punishments unnecessarily severe. But it ought not, on the other hand, to call the offender into council with his judges, and to allow him an option between two punishments. In general the circumstance that he pre- fers one punishment raises a strong presumption that he ought to suffer the other. The circumstance that the love of money is a stronger passion in his mind than the love of personal liberty is, as far as it goes, a reason for our availing ourselves rather of his love of money than of his love of personal liberty for the purpose of restraining him from crime. To look out systematically for the most sensitive part of a man's mind, in order that we may not direct our penal sanctions towards that part of his mind, seems an inju- dicious policy.

We are far from thinking that the course which we propose is unexceptionable. But it appears to us to be less open to exception that any other which has occurred to us. We propose that, at the time of imposing a fine, the Court shall also fix a certain term of imprisonment which the offender shall undergo in default of payment. In fixing this term the Court will in no case be suffered to exceed a certain maximum, which will vary according to the nature of the offence. If the offence be one which is punishable with

L

imprisonment as well as fine, the term of imprisonment in default of payment will not exceed one fourth of the longest term of imprisonment fixed by the Code for the offence. If the offence be one which, by the Code, is punishable only with fine, the term of imprisonment for default of payment will in no case exceed seven days.

But we do not mean that this imprisonment shall be taken in full satisfaction of the fine. We cannot consent to permit the offender to choose whether he will suffer in his person or in his property. To adopt such a course would be to grant exemption from the punishment of fine to those very persons on whom it is peculiarly desirable that the punishment of fine should be inflicted, to those very persons who dislike that punishment most, and whom the apprehension of that punishment would be most likely to restrain. We therefore propose that the imprisonment which an offender has undergone shall not release him from the pecuniary obligation under which he lies. His person will, indeed, cease to be answerable for the fine. But his property will for a time continue to be so. What we recommend is that, at any time during a certain limited period, the fine may be levied on his effects by distress. If the fine is paid or levied while he is imprisoned for default of payment, his imprisonment will immediately terminate, and if a portion of the fine be paid during the imprisonment, a proportional abatement of the imprisonment will take place.

It may perhaps appear to some persons harsh to imprison a man for non-payment of a fine, and after he has endured his imprisonment to take his property by distress in order to realize the fine. But this harshness is rather apparent than real. If the offender, having the means of paying the fine, chooses rather to lie in prison than to part with his money, his case is the very case in which it is most desirable that the fine should be levied, and he is the very convict who has least claim to indulgence. The confinement which he has undergone may be regarded as no more than a reasonable punishment for his obstinate resistance to the due execution of his sentence. If the offender has not the means of paying the fine while he continues liable to it, he will be quit for his imprisonment. There remains another case, that of an offender who, being really unable to pay his fine, lies in prison for a term, and within six years after his sentence acquires property. This case is the only case in which it can with any plausibility be maintained that the law, as we have framed it, would operate harshly. Even in this case, it is evident that our law will operate far less harshly than a law which should provide that an offender sentenced to a fine should be imprisoned till the fine should be paid. Under both laws imprisonment is inflicted, under both a fine is exacted. But the one law liberates the offender on payment of the fine, and also fixes a limit beyond which he cannot be detained in gaol whether the fine be paid or no. The other law keeps him in confinement till the money is actually paid. It is therefore at least as severe as ours on his property, and is immeasurably more severe on his person.

In fact we treat an offender who has been sentenced to fine more leniently than the law now treats a debtor either in England or in this country. By the English law an insolvent not in trade is kept in confinement till he has surrendered all his property; till he has answered interrogatories respecting it, till the Court is satisfied that he has paid all that he can pay. Even when his person is liberated his future acquisitions still continue to be liable to the claims of his creditors. The law throughout British India is in principle the same with the law of England. The offender who has been sentenced to fine must be considered as a debtor, and as a debtor not entitled to any peculiar lenity. It will be difficult to shew on what principles a creditor ought to be allowed to employ, for the purpose of recovering a debt from a person who is perhaps only unfortunate, a more stringent mode of procedure than that which the State employs for the purpose of realizing a fine from the property of a criminal. If a temporary imprisonment for debt ought not to cancel the claim of the private creditor, neither ought a temporary imprisonment in default of payment of a fine to cancel the claims of public justice.

It is undoubtedly easy to put cases in which this part of the law will operate more severely than we could wish; and so it is easy to put cases in which every penal Clause in the Code would operate more severely than we could wish. This is an evil inseparable from all legislation. General rules must be framed; and it is absolutely impossible to frame general rules which shall suit all particular cases. It is sufficient if the rule be, on the whole, more beneficial than any other general rule which can be suggested. Those particular cases in which a rule generally beneficial may operate too harshly must be left to the merciful consideration of the Executive Government. We are satisfied that the punishment of fine would, under the arrangement which we propose, be found to be a most efficacious punishment in a large class of cases. We are satisfied that if offenders are allowed to choose between imprisonment and fine, fine will lose almost its whole efficacy, and will never be inflicted on those who dread it most.

Closely connected with these questions respecting the punishment of fine is another question of the highest importance, which indeed belongs rather to the law of civil rights and to the law of procedure than to the penal law, but respecting which we are desirous to place on record the opinion which we have formed after much reflection and discussion.

In a very large proportion of criminal cases there is good ground for a civil as well as for a penal proceeding. The English law, most erroneously in our opinion, allows no civil claim for reparation in cases where injury has been caused by an offence amounting to felony. Thus a person is entitled to reparation for what he has lost by petty fraud, but to none if he has been cheated by means of a forged bill of exchange. He is entitled to reparation if his coat has been torn; but to none if his house has been maliciously burned down. He is entitled to reparation for a slap on the face, but to none for having his nose maliciously slit, or his ears cut off. A woman is entitled to reparation for a breach of promise of marriage; but to none for a rape. To us it appears that of two sufferers he who has suffered the greater harm has, *cæteris paribus*, the stronger claim to compensation; and that of two offences that which produces the greater harm ought, *cæteris paribus*, to be visited with the heavier punishment. Hence it follows that in general the strongest claims to compensations will be the claims of persons who have been injured by highly penal acts; and that to refuse reparation to all sufferers who have been injured by highly penal acts is to refuse reparation to that very class of sufferers who have the strongest claims to it.

We are decidedly of opinion that every person who is injured by an offence ought to be legally entitled to a compensation for the injury. That the offence is a very serious one, far from being a reason for thinking that he ought to have no compensation, is *prima facie* a reason for thinking that the compensation ought to be very large.

Entertaining this opinion, we are desirous that the law of criminal procedure should be framed in such a manner as to facilitate the obtaining of reparation by the sufferer. We are inclined to think that an arrangement might be adopted under which one trial would do the work of two. We conceive that, in every case in which fine is part of the punishment of an offence, it ought to be competent to the tribunal which has tried the offender, acting under proper checks, to award the whole or part of the fine to the sufferer, provided that the sufferer signifies his willingness to receive what is so awarded in full satisfaction of his civil claim for reparation. If the Criminal Court shall not make such an award, or if the sufferer shall not be satisfied with such an award, he must be left to his civil action. But if, in such an action, he recovers damages, the fine ought, in our opinion, to be employed, as far as the fine will go, in satisfying those damages.

The plan we propose would not be open to the strong and indeed unanswerable objections which Mr. Livingston has urged against the plan of blending a civil and criminal trial together. Yet we think it likely that our plan would in a great majority of cases render a civil proceeding unnecessary. We are happy to be able to quote the high authority of Mr. Livingston in favour of the doctrine that every fine imposed for an offence ought to be expended, as far as it will go, in paying any damages which may be due in consequence of injury caused by that offence.

This course seems to be the only course consistent with justice to either party. It is most unjust to the man who has been disabled by a wound, or ruined by a forgery, that the Government should take, under the name of fine, so large a portion of the offender's property as to leave nothing to the sufferer. In general, the greater the injury the greater ought to be the fine. On the other hand, the greater the injury the greater ought to be the compensation. If, therefore, the Government keeps whatever it can raise in the way of fine, it follows that the sufferer who has the greatest claim to compensation will be least likely to obtain it. By empowering the Courts to grant damages out of the fine, and by making the fine after it has reached the treasury of the Government answerable for the damages which the sufferer may recover in a Civil Court, we avoid this injustice.

Nor is this arrangement required only by justice to the sufferer. It is also required by justice to the offender. However atrocious his crime may have been, he ought not to be subjected to any punishment beyond what the public interest demands. And we depart from this principle if, when a single payment would effect all that is required both in the way of punishment and in the way of reparation, we impose two distinct payments, the one by pay of punishment and the other by way of reparation.

The principles on which a Court proceeds in imposing a fine are quite different from those on which it proceeds in assessing damages. A fine is meant to be painful to the person paying it. But civil damages are not meant to cause pain to the person who pays them. They are meant solely to compensate the plaintiff for evil suffered. They cause pain undoubtedly to the person who has to pay them. But this pain is merely incidental; nor ought the amount of damages at all to depend on the degree of depravity which the wrongdoer has shewn, except in so far as that depravity may have increased the evil endured by the sufferer. If A, by mere inadvertence, drives the pole of his carriage against Z's valuable horse, and thus kills the horse, A has committed an action infinitely less reprehensible than if he kills the horse by laying poison secretly in its food. The former act would probably not fall at all under the cognizance of the Criminal Courts. The latter act would be severely punished. But the payment to which Z has a civil claim is in both cases exactly the same, the value of the horse, and a compensation for any expence and inconvenience which the loss of the horse may have occasioned. That A has committed no offence is no reason for giving Z less than his full damages; that A has committed a most wicked and malignant offence is no reason for giving Z more than his full damages. If a mere inadvertence cause a great loss, the damages ought to be high. If the most atrocious crime cause a small loss, the damages ought to be low. They are fixed on a principle quite different from that according to which penal laws are framed and administered.

Here then are two payments required from one person on account of one transaction. The object of the one payment is to give him pain, and the amount of that payment must be supposed to be sufficient to give him as much pain as it is desirable to inflict on him in that form. The object of the other payment is not at all to give pain to the payer, but solely to save another person from loss. It does, indeed, incidentally give pain to the payer; but it is not imposed for that end, nor is it proportioned to the degree in which it may be fit that the payer should suffer pain. Surely under such circumstances justice to the payer requires that the former payment should, as far as it will go, serve both purposes, and that if, in the very act of enduring punishment he can make reparation, he should be permitted to do so.

We have now said all that we at present think it necessary to say respecting the punishments provided in the Code. It may be fit that we should explain why some others are omitted.

We have thought it unnecessary to place incapacitation for office, or dismissal from office, in the list of punishments. It will always be in the power of the Government to dismiss from office and to exclude from office even persons againt whom there is no legal evidence of guilt. It will always be in the power of the Government, by an act of grace, to admit to office even those who may have been dismissed. We therefore propose that the power of inflicting this penalty shall be left in form, as it must be left in reality, to the Government.

We also considered whether it would be advisable to place in the list of punishments the degrading public exhibition of an offender on a pillory after the English fashion, or on an ass in the manner usual in this country. We are decidedly of opinion that it is not advisable to inflict that species of punishment.

Of all punishments this is evidently the most unequal. It may be more severe than any punishment in the Code. It may be no punishment at all. If inflicted on a man who has quick sensibility it is generally more terrible than death itself. If inflicted on a hardened and impudent delinquent, who has often stood at the bar, and who has no character to lose, it is a punishment less serious than an hour of the treadmill. It derives all its terrors from the higher and better parts of the character of the sufferer: its severity is therefore in inverse proportion to the necessity for severity. An offender who, though he has been drawn into crime by temptation, has not yet wholly given himself up to wickedness and discarded all regard for reputation, is an offender with whom it is generally desirable to deal gently. He may still be reclaimed. He may still become a valuable member of society. On the other hand the criminal for whom disgrace has no terrors, who dreads nothing but physical suffering, restraint, and privation, and who laughs at infamy, is the very criminal against whom the whole rigour of the law ought to be put forth. To employ a punishment which is more bitter than the bitterness of death to the man who has still some remains of virtuous and honorable feeling, and which is mere matter of jest to the utterly abandoned villain, appears to us most unreasonable.

If it were possible to devise a punishment which should give pain proportioned to the degree in which the offender was shameless, hard-hearted, and abandoned to vice, such a punishment would be the most effectual means of protecting society. On the other hand of all punishments the most absurd is that which produces pain proportioned to the degree in which the offender retains the sentiments of an honest man.

This argument proceeds on the supposition that the public exposure of the criminal has no other terrors than those which it derives from his sensibility to shame. The English pillory, indeed, had terrors of a very different kind. The offender was, even in our own time, given up with scarcely any protection to the utmost ferocity of the mob. Such a mode of punishment is, indeed, free from one objection which we have urged against simple exposure ; for it is an object of terror to the most hardened criminal. But it is open to other objections so obvious that it is unnecessary to bring them to the notice of his Lordship in Council. That the amount of punishment should be determined, not by the law or by the tribunals, but by a throng of people accidentally congregated, among whom the most ignorant and brutal would always on such an occasion be the most forward, would be a disgrace to an age and country pretending to civilization. We take it for granted that the punishment which we are considering, if inflicted in any part of India subject to the British Government, would consist in degrading exposure and nothing more. That punishment, we repeat, while it would be a mere subject of mockery to shameless and abandoned delinquents, would, when inflicted on men who have filled respectable stations and borne respectable characters, be so cruel that it would become justly more odious to the public than the very offences which it was intended to repress.

We have not thought it desirable to place flogging in the list of punishments. If inflicted for atrocious crimes with a severity proportioned to the magnitude of those crimes, that punishment is open to the very serious objections which may be urged against all cruel punishments, and which are so well known that it is unnecessary for us to recapitulate them. When inflicted on men of mature age, particularly if they be of decent stations in life, it is a punishment of which the severity consists, to a great extent, in the disgrace which it causes ; and, to that extent, the arguments which we have used against public exposure apply to flogging.

It has been represented to us by some functionaries in Bengal that the best mode of stimulating the lower officers of Police to the active discharge of their duties is by flogging, and that since the abolition of that punishment in this Presidency, the Magistrates of the lower provinces have found great difficulty in managing that class of persons.

This difficulty has not been experienced in any other part of India. We, therefore, cannot, without much stronger evidence than is now before us, believe that it is impracticable to make the Police Officers of the lower provinces efficient without resorting to corporal punishment. The objections to the old system are obvious. To inflict on a public servant who ought to respect himself and to be respected by others, an ignominious punishment which leaves an indelible mark, and to suffer him still to remain a public servant, to place a stigma on him which renders him an object of contempt to the mass of the population, and to continue to intrust him with any portion, however small, of the powers of Government, appears to us to be a course which nothing but the strongest necessity can justify.

The moderate flogging of young offenders for some petty offences is not open, at least in any serious degree, to the objections which we have stated. Flogging does not inflict on a boy that sort of ignominy which it causes to a grown man. Up to a certain age boys, even of the higher classes, are often corrected with stripes by their parents and guardians ; and this circumstance takes away a considerable part of the disgrace of stripes inflicted on a boy by order of a Magistrate. In countries where a bad system of prison discipline exists, the punishment of flogging has in such cases one great advantage over that of imprisonment. The young offender is not exposed even for a day to the contaminating influence of an ill regulated gaol. It is our hope and belief, however, that the reforms which are now under consideration will prevent the gaols of India from exercising any such contaminating influence; and, if that should be the case, we are inclined to think that the effect of a few days passed in solitude or in hard and monotonous labour would be more salutary than that of stripes.

Being satisfied, therefore, that the punishment of flogging can be proper only in a few cases, and not being satisfied that it is necessary in any, we are unwilling to advise the Government to retrace its steps, and to re-establish throughout the British territories a parctice which, by a policy unquestionably humane and by no means proved to have been injudicious, has recently been abolished through a large part of those territories.

The only remaining point connected with this Chapter to which we wish to call the attention of his Lordship in Council is the provision contained in Clause 61. This provision is intended to prevent an offender whose guilt is fully established from eluding punishment on the ground that the evidence does not enable the tribunals to pronounce with certainty under what penal provision his case falls.

Where the doubt is merely between an aggravated and mitigated form of the same offence, the difficulty will not be great. In such cases the offender ought always to be convicted of the minor offence. But the doubt may be between two offences neither of which is a mitigated form of the other. The doubt, for example, may lie between murder and the aiding of murder. It may be certain, for example, that either A or B murdered Z, and that whichever was the murderer was aided by the other in the commission of the murder. But which committed the murder, and which aided the commission, it may be impossible to ascertain. To suffer both to go unpunished, though it is certain that both are guilty of capital crimes, merely because it is doubtful under what Clause each of them is punishable, would be most unreasonable. It appears to us that a conviction in the alternative has this recommendation, that it is altogether free from fiction, that it is exactly consonant to the truth of the facts. If the Court find both A and B guilty of murder, or of aiding murder, the Court affirms that which is not literally true: and in all occasions, but especially in judicial proceedings, there is a strong presumption in favor of literal truth. If the Court finds that A has either murdered Z or aided B to murder Z, and that B has either murdered Z or aided A to murder Z, the Court finds that which is the literal truth; nor will there, under the rule which we have laid down, be the smallest difficulty in prescribing the punishment.

It is chiefly in cases where property has been fraudulently appropriated that the necessity for such a provision as that which we are considering will be felt. It will often be certain that there has been a fraudulent appropriation of property; and the only doubt will be whether this fraudulent appropriation was a theft or a criminal breach of trust. To allow the offender to escape unpunished on account of such a doubt would be absurd. To subject him to the punishment of theft, which is the higher of the two crimes between which the doubt lies, would be grossly unjust. The punishment to which he ought to be liable is evidently that of criminal breach of trust. But that a Court should convict an offender of a criminal breach of trust, when the opinion of the Court perhaps is that it is an even chance or more than an even chance that no trust was ever reposed in him, seems to us an objectionable mode of proceeding. We will not, in this stage of our labors, venture to lay it down as an unbending rule that the tribunals ought never to employ phrases which, though literally false, are conventionally true. Yet we are fully satisfied that the presumption is always strongly in favor of that form of expression which accurately sets forth the real state of the facts. In the case which we have supposed the real state of the facts is that the offender has certainly committed either theft or criminal breach of trust, and that the Court does not know which. This ought, therefore, in our opinion, to be the form of the judgment.

The details of the law on this subject must, of course, be reserved for the Code of Procedure. But the provision which directs the manner in which the punishment is to be calculated appears properly to belong to the Penal Code.

NOTE B.

ON THE CHAPTER OF GENERAL EXCEPTIONS.

This Chapter has been framed in order to obviate the necessity of repeating in every penal clause a considerable number of limitations.

Some limitations relate only to a single provision, or to a very small class of provisions. Thus the exception in favour of true imputations on character (Clause 470) is an exception which belongs wholly to the law of defamation, and does not affect any other part of the Code. The exception in favour of the conjugal rights of the husband (Clause 359) is an exception which belongs wholly to the law of rape, and does not affect any other part of the Code. Every such exception evidently ought to be appended to the rule which it is intended to modify.

But there are other exceptions which are common to all the penal Clauses of the Code or to a great variety of Clauses dispersed over many Chapters. Such are the exceptions in favor of infants, lunatics, idiots, persons under the influence of delirium; the exceptions in favour of acts done by the direction of the law, of acts done in the exercise of the right of self-defence, of acts done by the consent of the party harmed by them. It would obviously be inconvenient to repeat these exceptions several times in every page. We have, therefore, placed them in a separate Chapter, and we have provided that every definition of an offence, every penal provision, and every illustration of a definition or penal provision, shall be construed subject to the provisions contained in that Chapter. Most of those explanations appear to us to require no explanation or defence. But the meaning and the ground of the rules laid down in Clause 69 and in the three following Clauses may not be obvious at first sight. On these therefore we wish to make a few observations.

We conceive the general rule to be that nothing ought to be an offence by reason of any harm which it may cause to a person of ripe age who, undeceived, has given a free and intelligent consent to suffer that harm or to take the risk of that harm. The restrictions by which the rule is limited affect only cases where human life is concerned. Both the general rule and the restrictions may, we think, be easily vindicated.

If Z, a grown man, in possession of all his faculties, directs that his valuable furniture shall be burned, that his pictures shall be cut to rags, that his fine house shall be pulled down, that the best horses in his stable shall be shot, that his plate shall be thrown into the sea, those who obey his orders, however capricious those orders may be, however deeply Z may afterwards regret that he gave them, ought not, as it seems to us, to be punished for injuring his property. Again, if Z chooses to sell his teeth to a dentist, and permits the dentist to pull them out, the dentist ought not to be punished for injuring Z's person. So if Z embraces the Mahomedan religion, and consents to undergo the painful rite which is the initiation into that religion, those who perform the rite ought not to be punished for injuring Z's person.

The reason on which the general rule which we have mentioned rests is this, that it is impossible to restrain men of mature age and sound understanding from destroying their own property, their own health, their own comfort, without restraining them from an infinite number of salutary or innocent actions. It is by no means true that men always judge rightly of their own interest. But it is true that, in the vast majority of cases, they judge better of their own interest than any lawgiver, or any tribunal, which must necessarily proceed on general principles, and which cannot have within its contemplation the circumstances of particular cases and the tempers of particular individuals, can judge for them. It is difficult to conceive any law which should be effectual to prevent men from wasting their substance on the most chimerical speculations, and yet which should not prevent the construction of such works as the Duke of Bridgwater's Canals. It is difficult to conceive any law which should prevent a man from capriciously destroying his property, and yet which should not prevent a philosopher, in a course of chemical experiments, from dissolving a diamond, or an artist from taking ancient pictures to pieces, as Sir Joshua Reynolds did, in order to learn the secret of the coloring. It is difficult to conceive any law which should prevent a man from capriciously injuring his own health, and yet which should not prevent an artisan from employing himself in callings which are useful and indeed necessary to society, but which tend to impair the constitutions of those who follow them, or a public-spirited physician from inoculating himself with the virus of a dangerous disease. It is chiefly, we conceive, for this reason that almost all Governments have thought it sufficient to restrain men from harming others, and have left them at liberty to harm themselves.

But though in general we would not punish an act on account of any harm which it might cause to a person who had consented to suffer that harm, we think that there are exceptions to this rule, and that the case in which death is intentionally inflicted is an exception.

It appears to us that the reasons which render it highly inexpedient to inflict punishment in ordinary cases of harm done by consent of the person harmed do not exist here. The thing prohibited is not, like the destruction of property, or like the mutilation of the person, a thing which is sometimes pernicious, sometimes innocent, sometimes highly useful. It is always, and under all circumstances, a thing which a wise lawgiver would desire to prevent, if it were only for the purpose of making human life more sacred to the multitude. We cannot prohibit men from destroying the most valuable effects, or from disfiguring the person of one who has given his unextorted and intelligent consent to such destruction or such disfiguration, without prohibiting at the same time gainful speculations, innocent luxuries, manly exercises, healing operations. But by prohibiting a man from intentionally causing the death of another, we prohibit nothing which we think it desirable to tolerate.

It seems to us clear, therefore, that no consent ought to be a justification of the intentional causing of death. Whether such intentional causing of death ought or ought not to be punished as murder is a distinct question; and will be considered elsewhere.

The next point which we have here to consider is how far consent ought to be a justification of the causing of death, when that causing of death is, in our nomenclature, voluntary, yet not intentional, that is to say when the person who caused the death did not mean to cause it but knew that he was likely to cause it.

In general we have made no distinction between cases in which a man causes an effect designedly, and cases in which he causes it with a knowledge that he is likely to cause it. If, for example, he sets fire to a house in a town at night, with no other object than that of facilitating a theft, but being perfectly aware that he is likely to cause people to be burned in their beds, and thus causes the loss of life, we punish him as a murderer. But there is, as it appears to us, a class of cases in which it is absolutely necessary to make a distinction. It is often the wisest thing that a man can do to expose his life to great hazard. It is often the greatest service that can be rendered to him to do what may very probably cause his death. He may labor under a cruel and wasting malady which is certain to shorten his life, and which renders his life, while it lasts, useless to others and a torment to himself. Suppose that under these circumstances he, undeceived, gives his free and intelligent consent to take the risk of an operation which in a large proportion of cases has proved fatal, but which is the only method by which his disease can possibly be cured, and which, if it succeeds, will restore him to health and vigor. We do not conceive that it would be expedient to punish the surgeon who should perform the operation, though by performing it he might cause death, not intending to cause death, but knowing himself to be likely to cause it. Again; if a person attacked by a wild beast should call out to his friends to fire, though with imminent hazard to himself, and they were to obey the call, we do not conceive that it would be expedient to punish them, though they might by firing cause his death, and though when they fired they knew themselves to be likely to cause his death.

We propose therefore that it shall be no offence to do even what the doer knows to be likely to cause death if the sufferer being of ripe age has, undeceived, given a free and intelligent consent to stand the risk, and if the doer did not intend to cause death, but on the contrary intended in good faith the benefit of the sufferer.

We have now explained the provisions contained in Clauses 69 and 70. The cases to which the two next Clauses relate bear a close affinity to those which we have just considered.

A lunatic may be in a state which makes it proper that he should be put into a strait waistcoat. A child may meet with an accident which may render the amputation of a limb necessary. But to put a strait waistcoat on a man without his consent is, under our definition, to commit an assault. To amputate a limb is by our definition voluntarily to cause grievous hurt, and, as sharp instruments are used, is a very highly penal offence. We have therefore provided by Clause 71, that the consent of the guardian of a sufferer who is an infant or who is of unsound mind shall, to a great extent, have the effect which the consent of the sufferer himself would have, if the sufferer were of ripe age and sound mind.

That there should be some provision of this sort is evidently necessary. On the other hand we feel that there is a considerable danger in allowing people to assume the office of judging for others in such cases. Every man always intends in good faith his own benefit, and has a deeper interest in knowing what is for his own benefit than any body else can have. That he gives a free and intelligent consent to suffer pain or loss, creates a strong presumption that it is good for him on the whole to suffer that pain or loss. But we cannot safely confide to him the interest of his neighbours, in the same unreserved manner in which we confide to him his own, even when he sincerely intends to benefit his neighbours. Even parents have been known to deliver their children up to slavery in a foreign country, to inflict the most cruel mutilations on their male children, to sacrifice the chastity of their female children, and to do all this declaring, and perhaps with truth, that their object was something which they considered as advantageous to the children. We have therefore not thought it sufficient to require that on such occasions the guardian should act in good faith for the benefit of the ward. We have imposed several additional restrictions which, we conceive, carry their defence with them.

There yet remains a kindred class of cases which are by no means of rare occurrence. For example, a person falls down in an apoplectic fit. Bleeding alone can save him, and he is unable to signify his consent to be bled. The Surgeon who bleeds him commits an act falling under the definition of an offence. The Surgeon is not the patient's guardian; and has no authority from any such guardian. Yet it is evident that the Surgeon ought not to be punished. Again, a house is on fire. A person snatches up a child too young to understand the danger, and flings it from the house top, with a faint hope that it may be caught in a blanket below, but with the knowledge that it is highly probable that it will be dashed to pieces. Here, though the child may be killed by the fall, though the person who threw it down knew that it would very probably be killed, and though he was not the child's parent or guardian, he ought not to be punished.

In these examples there is what may be called a temporary guardianship justified by the exigency of the case and by the humanity of the motive. This temporary guardianship bears a considerable analogy to that temporary magistracy with which the law invests every person who is present when a great crime is committed, or when the public peace is concerned. To acts done in the exercise of this temporary guardianship, we extend by Clause 72 a protection very similar to that which we have given to the acts of regular guardians.

Clause 73 is intended to provide for those cases which, though, from the imperfections of language, they fall within the letter of the penal law, are yet not within its spirit, and are all over the world considered by the public, and for the most part dealt with by the tribunals, as innocent. As our definitions are framed, it is theft to dip a pen in another man's ink, mischief to crumble one of his wafers, an assault to cover him with a cloud of dust by riding past him, hurt to incommode him by pressing against him in getting into a carriage. There are innumerable acts without performing which men cannot live together in society, acts which all men constantly do and suffer in turn, and which it is desirable that they should do and suffer in turn, yet which differ only in degree from crimes. That these acts ought not to be treated as crimes is evident, and we think it far better expressly to except them from the penal clauses of the Code than to leave it to the Judges to except them in practice. For if the Code is silent on the subject, the Judges can except these cases only by resorting to one of two practices which we consider as most pernicious, by making law, or by wresting the language of the law from its plain meaning.

We propose (Clauses 74 to 84) to except from the operation of the penal clauses of the Code large classes of acts done in good faith for the purpose of repelling unlawful aggressions. In this part of the Chapter we have attempted to define, with as much exactness as the subject appears to us to admit, the limits of the right of private defence. It may be thought that we have allowed too great a latitude to the exercise of this right; and we are ourselves of opinion that if we had been framing laws for a bold and high-spirited people, accustomed to take the law into their own hand, and to go beyond the line of moderation in repelling injury, it would have been fit to provide additional restrictions. In this country the danger is on the other side. The people are too little disposed to help themselves. The patience with which they submit to the cruel depreda-tions of gang-robbers, and to trespass and mischief committed in the most outrageous manner by bands of ruffians, is one of the most remarkable, and at the same time one of the most discouraging symptoms which the state of society in India presents to us. Under these circumstances we are desirous rather to rouse and encourage a manly spirit among the people than to multiply restrictions on the exercise of the right of self-defence. We are of opinion that all the evil which is likely to arise from the abuse of that right is far less serious than the evil which would arise from the execution of one person for overstepping what might appear to the Courts to be the exact line of modera-tion in resisting a body of dacoits.

We think it right however to say that there is no part of the Code with which we feel less satisfied than this. We cannot accuse ourselves of any want of diligence or care, No portion of our work has cost us more anxious thought or has been more frequently re-written. Yet we are compelled to own that we leave it still in a very imperfect state, and though we do not doubt that it may be far better executed than it has been by us, we are inclined to think that it must always be one of the least exact parts of every system of criminal law.

We have now made such observations as appear to us to be required on the general exceptions which we propose. It is proper that we should next explain why we have not proposed any exception in favor of some classes of acts which, as some persons may think, are entitled to indulgence

We long considered whether it would be advisable to except from the operation of the Penal Clauses of the Code acts committed in good faith from the desire of self-preser-vation : and we have determined not to except them.

We admit indeed that many acts falling under the definition of offences ought not to be punished when committed from the desire of self-preservation : and for this reason, that, as the Penal Code itself appeals solely to the fears of men, it never can furnish them with motives for braving dangers greater than the dangers with which it threatens them. Its utmost severity will be inefficacious for the purpose of preventing the mass of mankind from yielding to a certain amount of temptation. It can, indeed, make those who have yielded to the temptation miserable afterwards. But misery which has no tendency to prevent crime is so much clear evil. It is vain to rely on the dread of a remote and contingent evil as sufficient to overcome the dread of instant death, or the sense of actual torture. An eminently virtuous man indeed will prefer death to crime. But it is not to our virtue that the penal law addresses itself: nor would the world stand in need of penal laws, if men were virtuous. A man who refuses to commit a bad action, when he sees preparations made for killing or torturing him unless he complies, is a man who does not require the fear of punishment to restrain him. A man on the other hand who is withheld from committing crimes solely or chiefly by the fear of punishment, will never be withheld by that fear when a pistol is held to his forehead or a lighted torch applied to his fingers for the purpose of forcing him to commit a crime.

It would, we think, be mere useless cruelty to hang a man for voluntarily causing the death of others by jumping from a sinking ship into an overloaded boat. The suffering caused by the punishment is, considered by itself, an evil, and ought to be inflicted only for the sake of some preponderating good. But no preponderating good, indeed no good whatever, would be obtained by hanging a man for such an act. We cannot expect that the next man who feels the ship in which he is left descending into the waves, and sees a crowded boat putting off from it, will submit to instant and certain death from fear of a remote and contingent death. There are men, indeed, who in such circumstances would sacrifice their own lives rather than risk the lives of others. But such men act from the influence of principles and feelings which no penal laws can produce, and which, if they were general, would render penal laws unnecessary. Again, a gang of dacoits, finding a house strongly secured, seize a smith, and by torture and threats of death induce him to take his tools and to force the door for them. Here, it appears to us that to punish the smith as a housebreaker would be to inflict gratuitous pain. We cannot trust to the deterring effect of such punishment. The next smith who may find himself in the same situation will rather take his chance of being, at a distant time, arrested, convicted, and sentenced to imprisonment, than incur certain and immediate death.

In the cases which we have put some persons may perhaps doubt whether there ought to be impunity. But those very persons would generally admit that the extreme danger was a mitigating circumstance to be considered in apportioning the punishment. It might however with no small plausibility be contended that if any punishment at all is inflicted in such cases, that punishment ought to be not merely death, but death with torture. For the dread of being put to death by torture might possibly be sufficient to prevent a man from saving his own life by a crime, but it is quite certain, as we have said, that the mere fear of capital punishment which is remote, and which may never be inflicted at all, will never prevent him from saving his life. And a fortiori the dread of a milder punishment will not prevent him from saving his life. Laws directed against offences to which men are prompted by cupidity ought always to take from offenders more than those offenders expect to gain by crime. It would obviously be absurd to provide that a thief or a swindler should be punished with a fine not exceeding half the sum which he had acquired by theft or swindling. In the same manner laws directed against offences to which men are prompted by fear ought always to be framed in such a way as to be more terrible than the dangers which they require men to brave. It is on this ground, we apprehend, that a Soldier who runs away in action is punished with a rigor altogether unproportioned to the moral depravity which his offence indicates. Such a Soldier may be an honest and benevolent man, and irreproachable in all the relations of civil life. Yet he is punished as severely as a deliberate assassin, and more severely than a robber or a kidnapper. Why is this? Evidently because, as his offence arises from fear, it must be punished in such a manner that timid men may dread the punishment more than they dread the fire of the enemy.

If all cases in which acts falling under the definition of offences are done from the desire of self-preservation were as clear as the cases which we have put of the man who jumps from a sinking ship into a boat, and of the smith who is compelled by dacoits to force a door for them, we should, without hesitation, propose to exempt this class of acts from punishment. But it is to be observed that in both these cases the person in danger is supposed to have been brought into danger, without the smallest fault on his own part, by mere accident, or by the depravity of others. If a Captain of a Merchantman were to run his ship on shore in order to cheat the insurers, and then to sacrifice the lives of others in order to save himself from a danger created by his own villainy,—if a person who had joined himself to a gang of dacoits with no other intention than that of robbing, were at the command of his leader, accompanied with threats of instant death in case of disobedience, to commit murder, though unwillingly,—the case would be widely different, and our former reasoning would cease to apply. For it is evident that punishment which is inefficacious to prevent a man from yielding to a certain temptation may often be efficacious to prevent him from exposing himself to that temptation. We cannot count on the fear which a man may entertain of being brought to the gallows at some distant time as sufficient to overcome the fear of instant death. But the fear of remote punishment may often overcome the motives which induce a man to league himself with lawless companions in whose society no person who shrinks from any atrocity that they may command can be certain of his life. Nothing is more usual than for pirates, gang-robbers, and rioters to excuse their crimes by declaring that they were in dread of their associates, and durst not act otherwise. Nor is it by any means improbable that this may often be true. Nay, it is not improbable that crews of pirates and gangs of robbers may have committed crimes which every one among them was unwilling to commit, under the influence of mutual fear. But we think it clear that this circumstance ought not to exempt them from the full severity of the law.

Again, nothing is more usual than for thieves to urge distress and hunger as excuses for their thefts. It is certain, indeed, that many thefts are committed from the pressure of distress so severe as to be more terrible than the punishment of theft, and than the disgrace which that punishment brings with it to the mass of mankind. It is equally certain that when the distress from which a man can relieve himself by theft is more terrible than the evil consequences of theft, those consequences will not keep him from committing theft. Yet it by no means follows that it is irrational to punish him for theft. For though the fear of punishment is not likely to keep any man from theft when he is actually starving, it is very likely to keep him from being in a starving state. It is of no effect to counteract the irresistible motive which immediately prompts to theft. But it is of great effect to counteract the motives to that idleness and that profusion which end in bringing a man into a condition in which no law will keep him from committing theft. We can hardly conceive a law more injurious to society than one which should provide that as soon as a man who had neglected his work, or who had squandered his wages in stimulating drugs, or gambled them away, had been thirty-six hours without food, and felt the sharp impulse of hunger, he might, with impunity, steal food from his neighbours.

We should therefore think it in the highest degree pernicious to enact that no act done under the fear even of instant death should be an offence. It would a fortiori be absurd to enact that no act under the fear of any other evil should be an offence.

There are, as we have said, cases in which it would be useless cruelty to punish acts done under the fear of death, or even of evils less than death. But it appears to us impossible precisely to define these cases. We have, therefore, left them to the Government which, in the exercise of its clemency, will doubtless be guided in a great measure by the advice of the Courts.

We considered whether it would be desirable to make any distinction between offences committed against freemen and offences committed against slaves. We certainly entered on the consideration of this important question with a strong leaning to the opinion that no such distinction ought to be made. We thought it our duty however not to come to a decision without obtaining information and advice from those who were best qualified to give it. We have collected information on the subject from every part of India, and we have now in our office a large collection of documents containing much that is curious, and that in future stages of the work in which we are engaged will be useful. At present we have only to consider the subject with reference to the Penal Code.

These documents have satisfied us that there is at present no law whatever defining the extent of the power of a master over his slaves, that every thing depends on the disposition of the particular functionary who happens to be in charge of a district, and that functionaries who are in charge of contiguous districts or who have at different times been in charge of the same district hold diametrically opposite opinions as to what their official duty requires. Nor is this discrepancy found only in the proceedings of subordinate Courts. The Court of Nizamut Adawlut at Fort William lay down the law thus— " A master would not be punished, the Court opine, for inflicting a slight correction on " his legal slave such as a tutor would be justified in inflicting on a scholar, or a father " on a child." The Court of Nizamut Adawlut at Allahabad take a quite different view of the law. " Although," they say, " the Mahomedan Law permits the master to correct " his slave with moderation, the Code by which the Magistrates and other criminal " authorities are bound to regulate their proceedings does not recognize any such power, " and as the Regulations of the Government draw no distinction between the slave and " the freeman in criminal matters, but place them both on a level, it is the practice of " the Courts, following the principles of equal justice, to treat them both alike." The Court of Foujdarry Adawlut at Madras state that it is not the practice of the Courts to make any distinction whatever in cases which come before them, that a Circular Order of the Foujdarry Adawlut recognizes the right of a master to inflict corrections in certain cases, but that in practice no such distinction is made. We own that we entertain some doubts whether the practice be universally such as is supposed by the Foujdarry Adawlut. We perceive that two Magistrates in the Western Division of the Madras Presidency differ from each other in opinion on this subject. The Magistrate of Canara says that " the right of the master to inflict punishment has been allowed, but only to a very small " extent." The Magistrate of Malabar states that " the relation of a master and slave " has never been recognized as justifying acts which would otherwise be punishable, or " as constituting a ground for mitigation of punishment." The Court of Foujdarry

Adawlut at Bombay has given no opinion on the point, and there is a great difference of opinion among the subordinate authorities in the Bombay Presidency. One gentleman conceives that the imposing of personal restraint is the only act otherwise punishable which the Courts would allow a master to commit when a slave might be concerned. Another conceives that a master has a power of correction similar to that of a father. A third goes farther and is of opinion that " all but cases of very aggravated nature would " be considered as entitled to exemption from or mitigation of punishment on this account." On the other hand several gentlemen are of opinion that the relation of master and slave would not be considered by the Courts as a plea for any act which would be an offence if committed against a freeman.

It is clear therefore that we find the law in a state of utter uncertainty. It is equally clear that we cannot leave it in that state. We must either withdraw from a large class of slaves a protection to which the Courts under the jurisdiction of which they live now think them entitled, or we must extend to a large class a protection greater than what they actually enjoy.

We have not the smallest hesitation in recommending to his Lordship in Council that the law throughout all British India should be conformable to what in the opinion of the Court of Nizamut Adawlut at Allahabad is now actually the law in the Presidency of Fort William, and to what in the opinion of the Court of Foujdarry Adawlut at Fort St. George is now actually the practice in the Madras Presidency. That is to say, we recommend that no act falling under the definition of an offence should be exempted from punishment because it is committed by a master against a slave.

The distinction which in the opinion of many respectable functionaries the law now makes between acts committed against a freeman and acts committed against a slave is in itself an evil, and an evil so great that nothing but the strongest necessity, proved by the strongest evidence, could justify any Government in maintaining it. We conceive that the circumstances which we have already stated are sufficient to shew that no such necessity exists. By removing all doubt on the subject, we shall not deprive the master of a power the right to which has never been questioned, but of a power which is and has for some time been, to say the least, of disputable legality, and which has been held by a very precarious tenure.

To leave the question undecided is impossible. To decide the question by putting any class of slaves in a worse situation than that in which they now are is a course which we cannot think of recommending, and which we are certain that the Government will not adopt. The inference seems to be that the question ought to be decided by declaring that whatever is an offence when committed against a freeman shall be also an offence when committed against a slave.

It may perhaps be thought that by framing the law in this manner we do in fact virtually abolish slavery in British India; and undoubtdely, if the law as we have framed it should be really carried into full effect, it will at once deprive slavery of those evils which are its essence, and will insure the speedy and natural extinction of the whole system. The essence of slavery, the circumstance which makes slavery the worst of all social evils, is not in our opinion this, that the master has a legal right to certain services from the slave, but this, that the master has a legal right to enforce the performance of those services without having recourse to the tribunals. He is a judge in his own cause. He is armed with the powers of a Magistrate for the protection of his own private interest against the person who owes him service. Every other Judge quits the bench as soon as his own cause is called on. The judicial authority of the master begins and ends with cases in which he has a direct stake. The moment that a master is really deprived of this authority, the moment that his right to service really becomes, like his right to money which he has lent, a mere civil right which he can enforce only by a civil action, the peculiarly odious and malignant evils of slavery disappear at once. The name of slavery may be retained: but the thing is no longer the same. It is evidently impossible that any master can really obtain efficient service from unwilling labourers by means of prosecution before the Civil tribunals. Nor is there any instance of any country in which the relation of master and servant is maintained by means of such actions. In some states of society the labourer works because the master inflicts instant correction whenever there is any disobedience or slackness. In a different state of society the people labour for a master because the master makes it worth their while. Practically we believe it will be found that there is no third way. A labourer who has neither the motive of the freeman nor that of the slave, who is actuated neither by the hope of wages nor by the dread of stripes, will not work at all. The master may indeed, if he chooses, go before the tribunals, and obtain a decree. But scarcely any master would think it worth while to do so, and scarcely any labourer would be spurred to constant and vigorous exertion by the dread of such a legal proceeding. In fact we are not even able to form to ourselves the idea of a society in which the working classes should have no other motives to industry than the dread of prosecution. We understand how the planter of Mauritius formerly induced his negroes to work. He applied the lash if they loitered. We understand how our grooms and bearers are induced to work at Calcutta. They are gainers by working, and by obtaining a good character: they are losers by being turned away. But in what other way servants can be induced to work, we do not understand.

It appears to us therefore that if we can really prevent the master from exacting service by the use of any violence, or restraint, or by the infliction of any bodily hurt, one of two effects will inevitably follow. Either the master will obtain no service at all, or he will find himself under the necessity of obtaining it by making it a source of advantage to the labourer as well as to himself. A labourer who knows that if he idles his master will not dare to strike him, that if he absconds his master will not dare to confine him, that his master can enforce a claim to service only by taking more trouble, losing more time, and spending more money than the service is worth, will not work for fear. It follows that if the master wishes the labourer to work at all, the master must have recourse to different motives, to the motives of a freeman, to the hope of reward, to the sense of reciprocal benefit. Names are of no consequence. It matters nothing whether the labourer be or be not called a slave. All that is of real moment is that he should work from the motives and feelings of the freeman.

This effect, we are satisfied, would follow if outrages offered to slaves were really punished exactly as outrages offered to freemen are punished. But we are far indeed from thinking that by merely framing the law as we have framed it, we shall produce this effect. It is quite certain that slaves are at present often oppressed by their masters in districts where the Magistrates and Judges conceive that the law now is what we propose that it shall henceforth be. It is therefore evident that they may continue to be oppressed by their masters when the law has been made perfectly clear. To an ignorant labourer, accustomed from his birth to obey a superior for daily food, to submit without resistance to the cruelty and tyranny of that superior, perhaps to be transferred, like a horse or a sheep, from one superior to another, neither the law which we now propose, nor any other law will of itself give freedom. It is of little use to direct the Judge to punish, unless we can teach the sufferer to complain.

We have thought it right to state this, lest we should mislead his Lordship in Council into an opinion that the law, framed as we propose to frame it, will really remove all the evils of slavery, and that nothing more will remain to be done. So far are we from thinking that the law as we propose to frame it will of itself effect a great practical change, that we greatly doubt whether even a law abolishing slavery would of itself effect any great practical change. Our belief is that even if slavery were expressly abolished, it might and would in some parts of India still continue to exist in practice. We trust, therefore, that his Lordship in Council will not consider the measure which we now recommend as of itself sufficient to accomplish the benevolent ends of the British Legislature, and to relieve the Indian Government from its obligation to watch over the interests of the slave population.

NOTE C.

ON THE CHAPTER OF OFFENCES AGAINST THE STATE.

His Lordship in Council will perceive that in this Chapter we have provided only for offences against the Government of India, and that we have made no mention of offences against the General Government of the British Empire. We have done so because it appears to us doubtful to what extent his Lordship in Council is competent to legislate respecting such offences. The Act of Parliament which defines the legislative power of the Council of India especially prohibits that body from making any law " which shall in " any way affect any prerogative of the Crown, or the authority of Parliament, or any " part of the unwritten laws, or constitution of the United Kingdom of Great Britain " and Ireland, whereon may depend, in any degree, the allegiance of any person to the " Crown of the United Kingdom, or the Sovereignty, or Dominion of the said Crown over " any part of the said territories."

It might be argued that these words relate only to laws affecting the rights of the Crown and of Parliament, and not to laws affecting the penal sanctions of those rights, and that, therefore, though the Governor General in Council has no power to absolve the King's subjects from their allegiance, he has power to fix the punishment to which they shall be liable for violating their allegiance. It seems to us, however, that there is the closest connexion in this case between the right, and the penal sanction, that a power to alter the sanction amounts to a power to abolish the right, and that Parliament, which withheld from the Indian Legislature one of those powers, cannot be supposed to have intended to grant the other.

If the Governor General in Council has the legal power to fix the punishment of a subject who should, in the territories of the East India Company, conspire the death of the King, or levy war against the King, then the Governor General in Council has the legal power to fix that punishment at a fine of one anna; and it is plain that a law which should fix such a fine as the only punishment of regicide and rebellion would be a law virtually absolving all subjects within the territories of the East India Company from their allegiance.

This part of the penal law, therefore, we have not ventured to touch. We leave it to the Imperial Legislature. But we trust that we may be permitted to suggest to his Lordship in Council that the early attention of the Home Authorities should be called to this subject.

There is no doubt that the Criminal Statute Law of England is not binding generally on a native of India in the mofussil. Whether the Statute Law relating to treason be binding on such a native is a question with respect to which we do not venture to give a decided opinion. It seems to us exceedingly doubtful whether that part of the Statute Law be binding on such a native. It is quite certain that no Court has ever enforced it against such a native, and that, in the opinion of many respectable and intelligent Judicial Officers in the service of the Company, it could not legally be enforced against such a native. Nor are the Company's Judicial Officers, by whom alone such a native can legally be tried, likely to be accurately acquainted with the Statute Law of England on the subject of treason, or with the mass of constructions and precedents by which that law has been overlaid. If such a native be not punishable under the English Statute Law of treason, it is difficult to say under what law he could be punished for that crime. The Regulations contain nothing on the subject. The Council of India we conceive is not competent to legislate respecting it. The Mahomedan law might possibly be so violently strained as to reach it in Bengal and in the Madras Presidency; and in the Bombay Presidency it might possibly be brought within that Clause, which arms the Courts with an enormous discretion in cases in which they conceive that morality and social order require protection. But there are in our opinion strong reasons against retaining either the Mahomedan penal law, or the sweeping Clause of the Bombay Regulations to which we have referred.

It may be added that the provision of the Bombay Regulations to which we have referred applies only to persons who profess a religion with which a system of penal law is inseparably connected. Unless therefore the English Statute Law on the subject of treason applies to natives in the mofussil, a point respecting which we entertain great doubt, a native christian who should, at Surat, assist the levying of war, not against the Company's Government, but against the British Crown, would be liable to no punishment whatever.

This anomalous state of things may be, in some degree, explained by the singular manner in which the British Empire grew up in India. The East India Company was, during a long course of years, in theory at least, under two masters. It was subject to the King of England. It was subject also to the Great Mogul. It derived its corporate existence from the British Parliament. It held its territorial possessions by a grant from the Durbar of Delhi. The situation of the native subjects of the Company bore some analogy to that of the inhabitants of Mindelheim, while that fief of the Empire was held by the Duke of Marlborough. The inhabitants of Mindelheim were subjects of the Duke of Marlborough, but they owed no allegiance to the English Crown, though their Sovereign was subject to that Crown. It was in this way that the British Empire in India originated. It was long considered as a wise policy to disguise the real power of the English under the forms of vassalage, and to leave to the Mogul and his Viceroys the empty honors of a Sovereignty which was really held by the Company. This policy was abandoned slowly and by imperceptible degrees. The recognition of the supremacy of the King of Delhi appeared on the seal of the British Government down to a late period, and on its coin down to a still later period. A great change has indeed taken place since the grant of the Dewannee of the lower provinces to the Company, but it has taken place so gradually that, though it would be absurd to deny that the natives of British India are now subjects of his Majesty, it would be impossible to point out the particular time when they became so.

To these circumstances we attribute most of the anomalies which are to be found in the legal relation subsisting between the natives of British India and the General Government of the Empire. It seems highly desirable that the Imperial Legislature should do what cannot be done by the Local Legislature, and should pass a Law of high treason for the territories of the East India Company. As far, indeed, as respects the Royal person, the present state of the Law, though in theory unseemly, is not likely to cause any practical evil. It is highly improbable that any English King will visit his Indian dominions, or that any plot having for its object the death of an English King will ever extend its ramifications to India. But it is by no means improbable that persons residing in the territories of the East India Company may be parties to the levying of war against the British Crown, without violating any local regulation. If any insurrection were to take place in any of the British dominions in the Eastern Seas, in Ceylon, for example, or in Mauritius, it is by no means improbable that persons residing within the Company's territories might furnish information and stores to the rebels. And if this were done by a person not subject to the jurisdiction of the Courts established by Royal Charter we are satisfied that there would be the most serious difficulty in bringing the criminal to legal punishment.

We have, his Lordship in Council will perceive, made the abetting of hostilities against the Government in certain cases a separate offence, instead of leaving it to the operation of the general Law laid down in the Chapter on abetment. We have done so for two reasons. In the first place war may be waged against the Government by persons in whom it is no offence to wage such war, by foreign princes and their subjects. Our general rules on the subject of abetment would apply to the case of a person residing in the British territories who should abet a subject of the British Government in waging war against that Government; but they would not reach the case of a person who, while residing in the British territories, should abet the waging of war by any foreign prince against the British Government. In the second place we agree with the great body of legislators in thinking that, though in general a person who has been a party to a criminal design which has not been carried into effect ought not to be punished so severely as if that design had been carried into effect, yet an exception to this rule must be made with respect to high offences against the State. For State-crimes, and especially the most heinous and formidable State-crimes, have this peculiarity, that if they are successfully committed the criminal is almost always secure from punishment. The murderer is in greater danger after his victim is dispatched than before. The thief is in greater danger after the purse is taken than before. But the rebel is out of danger as soon as he has subverted the Government. As the Penal Law is impotent against a successful rebel, it is consequently necessary that it should be made strong and sharp against the first beginnings of rebellion, against treasonable designs which have been carried no further than plots and preparations. We have therefore not thought it expedient to leave such plots and preparations to the ordinary Law of abetment. That Law is framed on principles which, though they appear to us to be quite sound, as respects the great majority of offences, would be inapplicable here. Under that general Law a conspiracy for the subversion of the Government would not be punished at all, if the conspirators were detected before they had done more than discuss plans, adopt resolutions, and interchange promises of fidelity. A conspiracy for the subversion of the Government which should be carried as far as the gunpowder treason, or the assassination plot against William the Third, would be punished very much less severely than the counterfeiting of a rupee, or the presenting of a forged check. We have, therefore, thought it absolutely necessary to make separate provision for the previous abetting of great State offences. The subsequent abetting of such offences may, we think, without inconvenience be left to be dealt with according to the general law.

NOTE D.

ON THE CHAPTER OF OFFENCES RELATING TO THE ARMY AND NAVY.

A few words will explain the necessity of having some provisions of the nature of those which are contained in this Chapter.

It is obvious that a person who, not being himself subject to Military law, exhorts or assists those who are subject to Military law to commit gross breaches of discipline, is a proper subject of punishment. But the general law respecting the abetting of offences will not reach such a person; nor, framed as it is, would it be desirable that it should reach him. It would not reach him, because the Military delinquency which he has abetted is not punishable by this Code, and therefore is not, in our legal nomenclature, an offence. Nor is it desirable that the punishment of a person not Military who has abetted a breach of Military discipline should be fixed according to the principles on which we have proceeded in framing the law of abetment. We have provided that the punishment of the abettor of an offence shall be equal or proportional to the punishment of the person who commits that offence: and this seems to us a sound principle when applied only to the punishments provided by this Code. But the Military penal law is, and must necessarily be, far more severe than that under which the body of the people live. The severity of the Military penal law can be justified only by reasons drawn from the peculiar habits and duties of soldiers, and from the peculiar relation in which they stand to the Government. The extension of such severity to persons not members of the Military profession appears to us altogether unwarrantable. If a person not Military who abets a breach of Military discipline should be made liable to a punishment regulated, according to our general rules, by the punishment to which such a breach of discipline renders a soldier liable, the whole symmetry of the penal law would be destroyed. He who should induce a soldier to disobey any order of a commanding officer would be liable to be punished more severely than a dacoit, a professional thug, an incendiary, a ravisher, or a kidnapper. We have attempted in this Chapter to provide, in a manner more consistent with the general character of the Code, for the punishment of persons who, not being Military, abet Military crimes.

N

NOTE E.

ON THE CHAPTER OF THE ABUSE OF THE POWERS OF PUBLIC SERVANTS.

This Chapter is intended to reach offences which are committed by public servants, and which are of such a description that they can be committed by public servants alone.

We have found considerable difficulty in drawing the line between public servants and the great mass of the community. We hope that the description which we have given in Clause 14 will be found to comprehend all those whom it is desirable to bring under this part of the law, and we trust that, when the Code of procedure is completed, this description may be made both more accurate and more concise.

Those offences which are common between public servants and other members of the community, we leave to the general provisions of the Code. If a public servant embezzles public money, we leave him to the ordinary law of criminal breach of trust. If he falsely pretends to have disbursed money for the public, and by this deception induces the Government to allow it in his accounts, we leave him to the ordinary law of cheating. If he produces forged vouchers to back his statement, we leave him to the ordinary law of forgery. We see no reason for punishing these offences more severely when the Government suffers by them than when private people suffer. A Government, indeed, which does not consider the sufferings of private individuals as its own, is not only selfish, but short-sighted in its selfishness. The revenue is drawn from the wealth of individuals, and every act of dishonest spoliation which tends to render individuals insecure in the enjoyment of their wealth, is really an injury to the revenue. On every account, therefore, we think it desirable that the property of the State should, in general, be protected by exactly the same laws which are considered as sufficient for the protection of the property of the subject.

We are not without apprehension that we may be thought to have treated the transgressions of public servants too favourably, to have passed by without notice some malpractices which deserve punishment, and, where we have provided punishments, to have seldom made those punishments sufficiently severe.

It is true that we have altogether omitted to provide any punishment for some kinds of misconduct on the part of public servants. It is true also that the punishments which we propose in this Chapter are not generally proportioned either to the evil which the abuse of power produces, or to the depravity of a man who, having been entrusted with power for the public benefit, employs that power to gratify his own cupidity, or revenge.

But it is to be remembered that there is a marked distinction between the Penal Clauses contained in this Chapter and the other Penal Clauses of the Code. In general a Penal Clause sets forth the whole punishment which can be inflicted on an offender by any public authority. The penalty of theft, of breach of trust, of cheating, of extortion, of assault, of defamation, has been fixed on the supposition that it is the whole penalty which the criminal is to suffer, and that no power in the State can make any addition to it. But the penalty of an offence committed by a public functionary in the exercise of his public functions has been fixed on the supposition that it will often be only a part, and a small part, of the penalty which he will suffer. It is in the power of the Government to punish him for many acts which the law has not made punishable. It is in the power of the Government to add to any sentence pronounced by the Courts another sentence which will often be even more terrible. To a man whose subsistence is derived from official emoluments, whose habits are formed to official business, and whose whole ambition is fixed on official promotion, degradation to a lower post is a punishment; dismissal from the public service is a punishment sufficient even for a serious offence. The mere knowledge that his character has suffered in the opinion of those superiors on whom his advancement depends probably gives him as much pain as a heavy fine.

This is to a great degree the case in every country, and assuredly not less in India than in any other country. Indeed those servants of the Company by whom all the higher offices in the Indian Government are filled entertain a feeling about their situations very different from that which is found among political men in England. It is natural that they should entertain such a feeling. They are set apart at an early age as persons destined to hold offices in India. Their education is conducted at home with that view. They are transferred when just entering on manhood to the country which they are to govern. They pass the best years of their lives in acquiring knowledge which is most important to men who are to fill high situations in India, but which in any other walk of life would bring little profit and little distinction, in mastering languages which, when they quit this country, are useless to them, in studying a vast and complicated system of revenue which is altogether peculiar to the East, in becoming intimately acquainted with the interests, the resources, and the projects of potentates whose very existence is unknown even to educated men in Europe. To such a man, dismissal from the service of the Indian Government is generally a very great calamity. His life has been thrown away. It has been passed in acquiring information and experience which, in any pursuit to which he may now betake himself, will be of little or no service to him. There are therefore few covenanted servants of the Company who, even if they were men destitute of all honourable feeling, would not look on dismissal from the service as a most severe punishment. But the covenanted servants of the Company are English gentlemen, that is to say they are persons to whom the ruin of their fortunes is less terrible than the ruin of their characters. There are few of them, we believe, to whom an intimation that their integrity was suspected by the Government would not give more pain than a sentence of six months imprisonment for an offence not of a disgraceful kind, and to many of them death itself would appear less dreadful than ignominious expulsion from the body of which they are members.

Thus dismissal from the public service is a punishment exceedingly dreaded by public functionaries, and most dreaded in this country by the highest class of public functionaries. Nor is this all. It is not merely a severe punishment, but it is also a punishment which is far more likely to be inflicted than many punishments which are less severe. Those who are legally competent to inflict it are bound by no rules, except those which their own discretion may impose on them. For what kind and degree of delinquency they shall inflict it, by what evidence that delinquency shall be established, by what tribunals the enquiry shall be conducted, nay whether there shall be any delinquency, any evidence, any tribunal, is absolutely in their breasts. They may inflict this punishment, and may be justified in inflicting it for transgressions which are not susceptible of precise definition, and which have not been substantiated by decisive proof. They may be justified in inflicting it because many petty circumstances, each of which separately would be too trivial for notice, have, when taken together, satisfied them that a functionary is unfit for any public employment. They may be justified in inflicting it because they strongly suspect him of guilt which they cannot bring home to him by evidence to which a Zillah Judge would pay any attention. Most of what we have said of the punishment of dismissal from office applies, though not in the same degree, to the slighter punishments of censure, suspension, and removal from a higher to a lower post.

We have shewn that public funtionaries are liable not only to the punishments provided by this Code, but also to other peculiar punishments of great severity. It seems therefore to follow that, if those who possess the power of inflicting these peculiar punishments can be trusted, some mal-practices of public functionaries may be safely left unnoticed in this Code, and that other mal-practices need not be visited with legal punishment so rigorous as their enormity might seem to merit. The Executive Government, in our opinion, deserves to be trusted. At all events it must be trusted. For it is quite certain that no laws will prevent corruption and oppression on the part of the servants of the Indian Government, if that Government is inclined to screen the offenders. The Government, to say nothing of the vast influence which it can indirectly exert, appoints, promotes, and removes Judges at its discretion. It can remit any sentence pronounced by the Courts. It can, therefore, if it be not honestly disposed to correct official abuses, render any penal clauses directed against such abuses almost wholly inoperative. And if it be honestly disposed, as we firmly believe that it is, to correct official abuses, it will use for that purpose its power of rewarding and punishing its servants.

It will be seen that we propose, under Clause 138, to punish with imprisonment for a term not exceeding three years, or with fine, or both, the corruption of public functionaries. The punishment of fine will, we think, be found very efficacious in cases of this description, if the Judges exercise the power given them as they ought to do, and compel the delinquent to deliver up the whole of his ill-gotten wealth.

The mere taking of presents by a public functionary, when it cannot be proved that such presents were corruptly taken, we have made penal only in one particular case to which we shall hereafter call the attention of His Lordship in Council. We have not made the taking of presents by public functionaries generally penal; because, though we think that it is a practice which ought to be carefully watched and often severely punished, we are not satisfied that it is possible to frame any law on the subject which would not be rendered inoperative either by its extreme severity or by its extreme laxity. Absolutely to prohibit all public functionaries from taking presents would be to prohibit a son from contributing to the support of a father, a father from giving a portion with a daughter, a brother from extricating a brother from pecuniary difficulties. No Government would wish to prevent persons intimately connected by blood, by marriage, or by friendship from rendering services to each other; and no tribunals would enforce a law which should make the rendering of such services a crime. Where no such close connexion exists, the receiving of large presents by a public functionary is generally a very suspicious proceeding. But a lime, a wreath of flowers, a slice of betel nut, a drop of atar of roses poured on his handkerchief, are presents which it would, in this country, be held churlish to refuse, and which cannot possibly corrupt the most mercenary of mankind. Other presents of more value than these may, on account of their peculiar nature, be accepted without affording any ground for suspicion. Luxuries socially consumed according to the usages of hospitality are presents of this description. It would be unreasonable to treat a man in office as a criminal for drinking many rupees worth of Champagne in a year at the table of an acquaintance, though if he were to suffer one of his subordinates to accept even a single rupee in specie, he might deserve exemplary punishment.

It appears to us therefore that the taking of presents where a corrupt motive cannot be proved ought not, in general, to be a crime cognizable by the Courts. Whether in any particular case it ought to be punished or not, will depend on innumerable circumstances which it is impossible accurately to define, on the amount of the present, on the nature of the present, on the relation in which the giver and receiver stand to each other. Suppose that a wealthy English agent who is interested in a young civil servant of the Company were to pay the debts of that civil servant. Or suppose that a Resident were to furnish money to enable his invalid Assistant to proceed to the Cape. In these transactions there might be nothing which the most scrupulous could disapprove. But the case would be widely different, if a wealthy native Zemindar were to pay the debts of a Collector of his District, or if any of the Officers at the Residency were to receive money from the Minister of a foreign power. In such a case, though it might be impossible to prove a corrupt motive, we think that the Government would be inexcusable if it suffered the delinquent to remain in the public service.

We have hitherto put only extreme cases, cases in which it is clear that the taking of presents ought not to be punished, or cases in which it is clear that the taking of presents ought to be severely punished. But between the extremes lie an immense variety of cases, some of which call for severe punishment, some for milder punishment, some for censure, some for gentle admonition, while some ought to be tolerated. We have said that if a Collector were to accept a large present of money from a wealthy native Zemindar, he would deserve to be turned out of the service. But if the Collector were to accept such a present from an English Indigo Planter, the case would be different. The Indigo Planter might be his uncle, his brother, his father-in-law, his brother-in-law. In that case there might be no impropriety in the transaction. Again, if a native in the public service were to accept a present from a Zemindar who was connected with him by blood, marriage or friendship, there might be no impropriety in the transaction.

By the act of Parliament to which the malpractices of the first British conquerors of India gave occasion, the servants of the Company were forbidden to receive presents from Asiatics, but were left at liberty to receive presents from Europeans. The legislators of that time appear to have proceeded on the supposition that the servants of the Company would all be Englishmen, and that no Englishman would ever have any such connection with any native as would render the receiving of presents from that native unobjectionable.

Natives are now declared by law to be competent to hold any post in the Company's service. It would evidently be improper to interdict an Asiatic in the service of the Company from receiving pecuniary assistance from his Asiatic father, or from receiving a portion with an Asiatic bride. It seems to us therefore that the rule laid down by Parliament, though it will still be in many cases an excellent rule of evidence, ought not, under the altered circumstances of India, to continue to be a rule of law.

Again: it ought to be remembered that the European and native races are not at present divided from each other by so strong a line of separation, as at the time when the British Parliament laid down the rule which we are considering. The interval is still wide, but it by no means appears to us as it appeared to the legislators of the last generation to be impassable. It is evident therefore that the rule formerly laid down by Parliament is constantly becoming less and less applicable to the state of India. On these grounds we have thought it advisable to leave this matter to the Executive Government, which will doubtless promulgate from time to time such rules as it may deem proper, and will enforce submission to those rules by visiting its disobedient servants with censure, with degradation, or with dismissal from the public service, according to the circumstances of every case.

We have thought it desirable to make one exception. We propose that a Judge who accepts any valuable thing by way of gift from one whom he knows to be a Plaintiff or a Defendant in any cause pending in his Court shall be severely punished. This rule is not to extend to the taking of food in the interchange of ordinary civilities. It appears to us that the objections which we have made to a general law prohibiting the receipt of presents by public functionaries do not apply to this Clause. The rule is clear and definite. The practice against which it is directed is not a practice which ought sometimes to be encouraged, and sometimes to be tolerated. It ought always, and under all circumstances, to be discouraged. It, therefore, appears to unite all the characteristics which mark out a practice as a fit object of penal legislation.

The only other penal provision of this Chapter to which we think it necessary to call the attention of his Lordship in Council is that which is contained in Clause 149.

We are of opinion that the preceding Clauses, and the power which the Government possesses of suspending, degrading, and dismissing public functionaries will be found sufficient to prevent gross abuses. But there will remain a crowd of petty offences with which it is very difficult to deal, offences which separately are too slight to be brought before the criminal Tribunals, which will sometimes be committed by good public servants, and which therefore it would be inexpedient to punish by removal from office, yet which will be very often committed if they can be committed with impunity, and which, if often committed, would impair the efficiency of all departments of the administration, and would produce infinite vexation to the body of the people.

By the existing laws of all the Presidencies a summary judicial power is given in certain cases to certain official superiors for the purpose of restraining their subordinates. We are inclined to believe that this is a wholesome power, and that it has, in the great majority of cases, been honestly employed for the protection of the public. We propose therefore to adopt the principle, and to make the system uniform through all the provinces of the Empire, and through all the departments of the public service. We propose that a public functionary who is guilty of neglect of duty, who treats his superiors with disrespect, or who disobeys the lawful orders given by them for his guidance, shall be liable to a fine not exceeding the official pay which he receives in three months. In default of payment he will be liable (see Clause 54) to seven days' imprisonment.

In the Code of Procedure we think that it will be proper to provide that the power of awarding this penalty shall be given, not to the ordinary tribunals, but to the official superiors of the offender. Thus if a subordinate officer employed in the collection of revenue should incur this penalty it will be imposed by the Collector, and the appeal will probably be to the Board of Revenue. If an officer employed to execute the process of a Zillah Court should neglect his duty, the fine will be imposed by the Zillah Judge, and the appeal will probably be to the Sudder Court. If the offence should be committed by a Tide

Waiter, the Collector of Customs for the port will probably impose the penalty, and the appeal will be to the Board of Customs. These instances we give merely as illustrations of what, at present, appears to us desirable. The details of this part of the law of procedure cannot be arranged without much consideration and enquiry.

One important question still remains to be considered. We are of opinion that we have provided sufficient punishment for the public servant who receives a bribe. But it may be doubted whether we have provided sufficient punishment for the person who offers it. The person who, without any demand express or implied on the part of a public servant, volunteers an offer of a bribe, and induces that public servant to accept it, will be punishable under the general rule contained in Clause 88 as an instigator. But the person who complies with a demand, however signified, on the part of a public servant, cannot be considered as guilty of instigating that public servant to receive a bribe. We do not propose that such a person shall be liable to any punishment, and, as this omission may possibly appear censurable to many persons, we are desirous to explain our reasons.

In all states of society the receiving of a bribe is a bad action, and may properly be made punishable. But whether the giving of a bribe ought or ought not to be punished is a question which does not admit of a short and general answer. There are countries in which the giver of a bribe ought to be more severely punished than the receiver. There are countries, on the other hand, in which the giving of a bribe may be what it is not desirable to visit with any punishment. In a country situated like England, the giver of a bribe is generally far more deserving of punishment than the receiver. The giver is generally the tempter, the receiver is the tempted. The giver is generally rich, powerful, well educated, the receiver needy and ignorant. The giver is under no apprehension of suffering any injury if he refuses to give. It is not by fear, but by ambition that he is generally induced to part with his money. Such a person is a proper subject of punishment. But there are countries where the case is widely different,—where men give bribes to Magistrates from exactly the same feeling which leads them to give their purses to robbers, or to pay ransom to pirates,—where men give bribes because no man can, without a bribe, obtain common justice. In such countries we think that the giving of bribes is not a proper subject of punishment. It would be as absurd, in such a state of society, to reproach the giver of a bribe with corrupting the virtue of public servants, as it would be to say that the traveller who delivers his money when a pistol is held to his breast corrupts the virtue of the highwayman.

We would by no means be understood to say that India, under the British Government, is in a state answering to this last description. Still we fear it is undeniable that corruption does prevail to a great extent among the lower class of public functionaries, that the power which those functionaries possess renders them formidable to the body of the people, that in the great majority of cases the receiver of the bribe is really the tempter, and that the giver of the bribe is really acting in self defence.

Under these circumstances we are strongly of opinion that it would be unjust and cruel to punish the giving of a bribe, in any case in which it could not be proved that the giver had really by his instigations corrupted the virtue of a public servant who, unless temptation had been put in his way, would have acted uprightly.

NOTE F.

ON THE CHAPTER OF CONTEMPTS OF THE LAWFUL AUTHORITY OF PUBLIC SERVANTS.

We were at first disposed to have one Chapter for contempts of the lawful authority of Courts of Justice, another for contempts of the lawful authority of Officers of Revenue, and a third for contempts for the lawful authority of Officers of Police. But we soon found that these three Chapters would be almost the same word for word. It appeared to us also that, in the existing state of the Civil Administration of India, the separation which we were at first inclined to make would produce nothing but perplexity. The functions of Magistrate and Collector are very frequently united in the same person: and that person is perpetually called upon, both as Magistrate and Collector, to perform acts which are judicial in their nature, to try offenders, and to decide litigated questions of civil right.   While the division of labor between the different departments of the public service is so imperfect, it would be idle to make nice distinctions between those departments in the Penal Code.

In order to frame this Chapter we went carefully through the existing Regulations of the three Presidencies, and extracted the numerous penal provisions which are intended to enforce obedience to the lawful authority of different classes of public servants. Having collected these provisions, and discarded a very few which we thought obviously unreasonable, or superfluous, we proceeded to analyse the rest.

It is possible that our analysis may be imperfect; and it is highly probable that the punishments which we propose may require some modification.   It will be seen that we propose the same punishment for all the offences which fall, in our analysis, under the same head.   For example,—one head is the omitting to obey the lawful summons of a public servant.   For this offence we have only one punishment; and this punishment will be applicable alike to the witness who omits to obey the lawful summons of the Court of Sudder Dewanny Adawlut, to the witness who omits to obey the lawful summons of a Moonsiff, to the putwarree who in Bengal omits to obey the lawful summons of the Collector, to the ryot who in the Madras Presidency omits to obey the lawful summons of the Collector, to the trader who in the same Presidency omits to attend a meeting lawfully convened for the distribution of the Vizabuddy.   In the same manner we propose one punishment for the Captain of a ship in the Hoogly who illegally refuses to admit a custom house officer on board, for a landholder who refuses to admit a surveyor lawfully commissioned by the Collector to measure land, for a distiller who refuses to admit the proper officer to examine his distillery.   Again, we propose the same punishment for the person who resists the taking of goods in execution under a decree of a Court of Justice, for the person who resists the taking of property by way of distress for arrears of revenue, for the person who resists the seizure of salt by lawful authority, for the person who resists the seizure of a boat in default of toll by lawful authority, for the person who resists the seizure of smuggled goods by lawful authority.

We are sensible that there may be reasons which have escaped us for making distinctions in punishment between offences which in our classification fall under the same head.   But it is impossible to find in any single person, or in any small body of persons, so extensive and minute a knowledge of every province of India, and of every department of the public service, as would be a security against errors of this description.   We have no doubt that if his Lordship in Council directs the Code to be published for general information, valuable suggestions will be received from servants of the Company in different parts of India, and that those suggestions will enable the Government to modify the provisions which we propose, by introducing proper aggravations and mitigations.

The only provision which appears to us to require any further explanation is that which is contained in Clause 182.

We have, to the best of our ability, framed laws against acts which ought to be repressed at all times and places, or at times and places which it is in our power to define.   But there are acts which at one time and place are perfectly innocent, and which at another time or place are proper subjects for punishment; nor is it always possible for the legislator to say at what time or at what place such acts ought to be punishable.

Thus it may happen that a religious procession which is in itself perfectly legal, and which, while it passes through many quarters of a town is perfectly harmless, cannot, without great risk of tumult and outrage, be suffered to turn down a particular street inhabited by persons who hold the ceremony in abhorrence, and whose passions are excited by being forced to witness it.   Again, there are many Hindoo rites which in Hindoo temples and religious assemblies the law tolerates, but which could not with propriety be exhibited in a place which English gentlemen and ladies were in the habit of frequenting for purposes of exercise.   Again, at a particular season hydrophobia may be common among the dogs at a particular place, and it may be highly advisable that all people at that place should keep their dogs strictly confined.   Again, there may be a particular place in a town which the people are in the habit of using as a receptacle for filth. In general this practice may do no harm, but an unhealthy season may arrive when it may be dangerous to the health of the population, and under such circumstances it is evidently desirable that no person should be allowed to add to the nuisance. It is evident that it is utterly impossible for the legislature to mark out the route of all the religious processions in India, to specify all the public walks frequented by English ladies and gentlemen, to foresee in what months and in what places hydrophobia will be common among dogs, or when a particular dunghill may become dangerous to the health of a town. It is equally evident that it would be unjust to punish a person who cannot be proved to have acted with bad intentions for doing to-day what yesterday was a perfectly innocent act, or for doing in one street what it would be perfectly innocent to do in another street, without giving him some notice.

What we propose, therefore, is to empower the local authorities to forbid acts which these authorities consider as dangerous to the public tranquillity, health, safety, or convenience, and to make it an offence in a person to do any thing which that person knows to be so forbidden, and which may endanger the public tranquillity, health, safety, or convenience. It will be observed that we do not give to the local authorities the power of arbitrarily making any thing an offence. For unless the Court before which the person who disobeys the order is tried shall be of opinion that he has done something tending to endanger the public tranquillity, health, safety, or convenience, he will be liable to no punishment. The effect of the order of the local authority will be merely to deprive the person who knowingly disobeys the order of the plea that he had no bad intentions. He will not be permitted to allege that if he has caused harm, or risk of harm, it was without his knowledge.

Thus, if in a town where no order for the chaining up of dogs has been made, A suffers his dog to run about loose, A will be liable to no punishment for any mischief which the animal may do, unless it can be shewn that A knew the animal to be dangerous. But if an order for confining dogs has been issued, and if A knew of that order, it will be no defence for him to allege, and even to prove, that he believed his dog to be perfectly harmless. If the Court think that A's disobedience has caused harm, or risk of harm, A will be liable to punishment. On the other hand if the Court think that there was no danger, and that the local order was a foolish one, A will not be liable to punishment.

We see some objections to the way in which we have framed this part of the law. But we are unable to frame it better. On the one hand it is, as we have shewn, absolutely necessary to have some local rules which shall not require the sanction of the legislature. On the other hand, we are sensible that there is the greatest reason to apprehend much petty tyranny and vexation from such rules; and this although the framers of those rules may be very excellent and able men. There is scarcely any disposition in a ruler more prejudicial to the happiness of the people than a meddling disposition. Yet experience shews us that it is a disposition which is often found in company with the best intentions, with great activity and energy, and with a sincere regard for the interest of the community. A public servant of more than ordinary zeal and industry, unless he have very much more than ordinary judgment, is the very man who is likely to harass the people under his care with needless restrictions. We have, therefore, thought it necessary to provide that no person shall be punished merely for disobeying a local order, unless it be made to appear that the disobedience has been attended with evil, or risk of evil. Thus no person will be punished for disobeying an idle and vexatious order.

The mode of promulgating these orders belongs to the Code of Procedure, which will of course contain such provisions as may be required for the purpose of enabling the Government to exercise a constant and efficient controul over its local officers.

NOTE G.

ON THE CHAPTER OF OFFENCES RELATING TO PUBLIC JUSTICE.

Many offences which interfere with the administration of justice are sufficiently pro‐vided for in other Chapters, particularly in the Chapter relating to contempts of the lawful authority of public servants. There still remain, however, some offences of that description for which the present Chapter is intended to provide.

The rules which we propose touching the offence of attempting to impose on a Court of Justice by false evidence differ from those of the English law, and of the Codes which we have had an opportunity of consulting.

It appears to us, in the first place, that the offence which we have designated as the fabricating of false evidence is not punished with adequate severity under any of the systems to which we refer. This may perhaps be because the offence, in its aggravated forms, is not one of very frequent occurrence in western countries. It is notorious, how‐ever, that in this country the practice is exceedingly common, and for obvious reasons. The mere assertion of a witness commands far less respect in India than in Europe, or in the United States of America. In countries in which the standard of morality is high, direct evidence is generally considered as the best evidence. In England assuredly it is so considered, and its value as compared with the value of circumstantial evidence is per‐haps overrated by the great majority of the population. But in India we have reason to believe that the case is different. A Judge, after he has heard a transaction related in the same manner by several persons who declare themselves to be eye-witnesses of it, and of whom he knows no harm, often feels a considerable doubt whether the whole from beginning to end be not a fiction, and is glad to meet with some circumstance, however slight, which supports the story, and which is not likely to have been devised for the pur‐pose of supporting the story.

Hence, in England, a person who wishes to impose on a Court of Justice knows that he is likely to succeed best by perjury, or subornation of perjury. But in India, where a Judge is generally on his guard against direct false evidence, a more artful mode of imposition is frequently employed. A lie is often conveyed to a Court, not by means of witnesses, but by means of circumstances, precisely because circumstances are less likely to lie than witnesses. These two modes of imposing on the tribunals appear to us to be equally wicked, and equally mischievous. It will indeed be harder to bring home to an offender the fabricating of false evidence than the giving of false evidence. But where‐ever the former offence is brought home, we would punish it as severely as the latter. If A puts a purse in Z's bag, with the intention of causing Z to be convicted as a thief, we would deal with A as if he had sworn that he saw Z take a purse. If A conceals in Z's house a paper written in imitation of Z's hand, and purporting to be a plan of a treasonable conspiracy, we would deal with A as if he had sworn that he was present at a meeting of conspirators at which Z presided.

The exception in Clause 190 is in strict conformity with this principle. We pro‐pose to treat the giving of false evidence and the fabricating of false evidence in exactly the same way. We have no punishment for false evidence given by a person when on his trial for an offence, though we conceive that such a person ought to be interrogated. The grounds on which this part of the law is founded will shortly be submitted to Go‐vernment in our report on the law of evidence. As we do not propose to punish a prisoner for lying at the bar in order to escape punishment, so we do not propose to punish him for fabricating evidence with the view of escaping punishment, unless he also contemplated some injury to others as likely to be produced by the evidence so fabri‐cated. If A stabs Z, and afterwards on his trial denies that he stabbed Z, we do not propose to punish A as a giver of false evidence. And on the same principle if A, after having stabbed Z, in order to escape detection, disposes of Z's body in such a manner as is likely to lead a jury to think the death accidental, we do not propose to punish A as a fabricator of false evidence.

It appears to us that the offence of attempting to impose on a Court of Justice by false

o

evidence is an offence of which there are numerous grades, some of which may be easily defined. The authors of the French Code have not overlooked these circumstances, though they have not, in our opinion, marked the gradations very successfully. The English law makes no distinction whatever between the man who has attempted to take away his neighbour's life by false swearing, and the man who has strained his conscience to give an undeserved good character to a boy accused of petty theft. The former is punished far too leniently ; the latter perhaps too severely.

The giving of false evidence must always be a grave offence. But few points in penal legislation seem to us clearer than that the law ought to make a distinction between that kind of false evidence which produces great evils and that kind of false evidence which produces comparatively slight evils.

As the ordinary punishment of false evidence, we propose imprisonment for a term of not more than seven years, nor less than one year. If the false evidence is given or fabricated with intent to cause a person to be convicted of a grave offence not capital, we propose that the person who gives or fabricates such evidence may be punished with the punishment of the offence which he has attempted to fix on another. If the false evidence be given or fabricated with the intention of causing death, we propose to punish it in the same manner in which we propose to punish the worst attempts to murder. If such false evidence actually causes death, the person who has given or fabricated it falls under the definition of murder, and is liable to capital punishment. In this last point, the law, as we have framed it, agrees with the old law of England, which, though, in our opinion, just and reasonable, has become obsolete.

We think this the proper place to notice an offence which bears a close affinity to that of giving false evidence, and which we leave, for the present, unpunished, only on account of the defective state of the existing law of procedure. We mean the crime of deliberately and knowingly asserting falsehoods in pleading. Our opinions on this subject may startle persons accustomed to that boundless license which the English law allows to mendacity in suitors. On what principle that license is allowed, we must confess ourselves unable to discover. A lends Z money. Z repays it. A brings an action against Z for the money, and affirms in his declaration that he lent the money, and has never been repaid. On the trial A's receipt is produced. It is not doubted, A himself cannot deny, that he asserted a falsehood in his declaration. Ought A to enjoy impunity ? Again : Z brings an action against A for a debt which is really due. A's plea is a positive averment that he owes Z nothing. The case comes to trial ; and it is proved by overwhelming evidence that the debt is a just debt. A does not even attempt a defence. Ought A in this case to enjoy impunity ? If, in either of the cases which we have stated, A were to suborn witnesses to support the lie which he has put on the pleadings, every one of these witnesses, as well as A himself, would be liable to severe punishment. But false evidence in the vast majority of cases springs out of false pleading, and would be almost entirely banished from the Courts if false pleading could be prevented.

It appears to us that all the marks which indicate that an act is a proper subject for legal punishment meet in the act of false pleading. That false pleading always does some harm is plain. Even when it is not followed up by false evidence it always delays justice. That false pleading produces any compensating good to atone for this harm has never, as far as we know, been even alleged. That false pleading will be more common if it is unpunished than if it is punished appears as certain as that rape, theft, embezzlement, would, if unpunished, be more common than they now are. It is evident also that there will be no more difficulty in trying a charge of false pleading than in trying a charge of false evidence. The fact that a statement has been made in pleading will generally be more clearly proved than the fact that a statement has been made in evidence. The falsehood of a statement made in pleading will be proved in exactly the same manner in which the falsehood of a statement made in evidence is proved. Whether the accused person knew that he was pleading falsely, the Courts will determine on the same evidence on which they now determine whether a witness knew that he was giving false testimony.

We have as yet spoken only of the direct injury produced to honest litigants by false pleading. But this injury appears to us to be only a part, and perhaps not the greatest part, of the evil engendered by the practice. If there be any place where truth ought to be held in peculiar honor, from which falsehood ought to be driven with peculiar severity, in which exaggerations, which elsewhere would be applauded as the innocent sport of the fancy, or pardoned as the natural effect of excited passion, ought to be discouraged, that place is a Court of Justice. We object therefore to the use of legal fictions even when the meaning of those fictions is generally understood, and we have done our best to exclude them from this Code. But that a person should come before a Court, should tell that Court premeditated and circumstantial lies for the purpose of preventing or postponing the settlement of a just demand, and that by so doing he should incur no punishment whatever, seems to us to be a state of things to which nothing but habit could reconcile wise and honest men. Public opinion is vitiated by the vicious state of the law. Men who, in any other circumstances, would shrink from falsehood, have no scruple about setting up false pleas against just demands. There is one place, and only one, where deliberate untruths, told with the intent to injure, are not considered as discreditable; and that place is a Court of Justice. Thus the authority of the tribunals operates to lower the standard of morality, and to diminish the esteem in which veracity is held; and the very place which ought to be kept sacred from misrepresentations such as would elsewhere be venial, becomes the only place where it is considered as idle scrupulosity to shrink from deliberate falsehood.

We consider a law for punishing false pleading as indispensably necessary to the expeditious and satisfactory administration of justice, and we trust that the passing of such a law will speedily follow the appearance of the Code of procedure. We do not, as we have stated, at present propose such a law, because, while the system of pleading remains unaltered in the Courts of this country, and particularly in the Courts established by royal charter, it will be difficult, or to speak more properly, impossible to enforce such a law. We have, therefore, gone no further than to provide a punishment for the frivolous and vexatious instituting of civil suits, a practice which, even while the existing systems of procedure remain unaltered, may, without any inconvenience, be made an offence. The law on the subject of false evidence will, as it appears to us, render unnecessary any law for punishing the frivolous and vexatious preferring of criminal charges.

No other part of this Chapter appears to require comment.

NOTE H.

ON OFFENCES RELATING TO THE REVENUE.

In order to frame this Chapter we took a course similar to that which we took with the Chapter relating to contempts of the lawful authority of public servants. We went carefully through the revenue laws of the three Presidencies, extracted the penal Clauses, analysed them, and reduced them to a small number of general heads.

His Lordship in Council will perceive that we have not thought it proper to insert in the Code any provision for the confiscation of property on the ground of a breach of the revenue laws, and that we leave the existing rules on that subject untouched. We have done so because it does not appear to us that such confiscation is in strictness a punishment. It has indeed much in common with punishment But it appears to us that there is a marked distinction, and that confiscation of the sort which is authorized in many parts of the regulations of the three Presidencies, would, considered in the light of a punishment, be anomalous and indefensible. It is a proceeding directed, not against the person who has broken the law, but against the thing with respect to which the law has been broken. It is not necessary that any misconduct should be proved, that any accusation should be brought, that any particular individual should be in the contemplation of the authority which directs the confiscation. Nay, the revenue laws authorize confiscation, not only in cases where misconduct is not proved, but in cases where it is proved that there has been no misconduct in any quarter; and, where there has been misconduct, those laws authorize the confiscation of the property of a person who is proved to have had no share in the misconduct.

To give a single example; if tobacco be found in the island of Bombay, after the time at which it ought to be exported thence, it is confiscated, together with the receptacles which contain it, the substances in which it is packed, and the carriages and animals which are employed to convey it. This, which is a fair specimen of revenue laws respecting confiscation, is evidently objectionable considered as a penal law. The carriages, the animals, the vessels, the tobacco itself, may all be the property of persons who are not in the least to blame. Indeed we know that, under this law, the boxes of gentlemen have repeatedly been seized because the servants who packed them had concealed tobacco in the baggage. Such a law, put into the form of a penal provision, would be too grotesque to be a subject of serious argument. It would, in the phraseology of our Code, run thus —" If any person places contraband tobacco in the baggage " of any other person, the person in whose baggage such contraband tobacco is placed " shall be punished with the confiscation of such baggage." And the following illustration would make the law, if possible, still more ridiculous. " Contraband tobacco is " hidden in A's baggage, by A's servant, without A's knowledge, and contrary to A's " express command. A has committed the offence defined in this Clause."

It is evident therefore that this law, and many other laws of the same kind, must be defended on principles quite different from those on which penal legislation ought to be conducted. They must be defended, not as being penal laws directed against the guilty, but rather as being sharp and stringent laws of civil procedure which are intended to enable the Government to obtain its due with speed and certainty, at the cost whether of the guilty or of the innocent. Viewing them in this light, and knowing as we know that they are greatly mitigated in practice by the lenity of the Executive Government, we consider them as justifiable. But we are decidedly of opinion that they would be out of place in a penal Code.

NOTE I.

ON THE CHAPTER OF OFFENCES RELATING TO COIN.

Most of the provisions in this Chapter appear sufficiently intelligible, without any explanation.

We have proposed that the Government of India should follow the general practice of Governments in punishing more severely the counterfeiting of its own coin, than the counterfeiting of foreign coin. It appears to us peculiarly advisable, under the present circumstances of India, to make this distinction. It is much to be wished that the Company's currency may supersede the numerous coinages which are issued from a crowd of mints in the dominions of the petty Princes of India. It has appeared to us that this object may be in some degree promoted by the law as we have framed it. That coinage, the purity of which is guarded by the most rigorous penalties, is likely to be the most pure; and that coinage which is likely to be the most pure will be the most readily taken in the course of business.

It is not very probable that any person in this country will employ himself in making counterfeit sovereigns or shillings: but should so improbable an event occur, we think that the King's coin should have the same protection which is given to the coin of the local Government. It may perhaps be thought that in proposing laws for the protection of the King's coin we have departed from the principle which we laid down in our note on the law of offences against the State, and that we should have acted more consistently in leaving the British currency to the care of the British legislature. It appears to us, however, that the offence of coining, though, in an arbitrary classification, it may be called by the technical name of treason, is in substance an offence against property and trade, that it is an offence of very nearly the same kind with the forging of a bank note, and that it would be an offence of exactly the same kind if the bank note, like the notes of the Bank of England formerly, were in all cases legal tender, or if the coin, like the Company's gold mohur at present, were not legal tender. We do not therefore conceive that in proposing a law for punishing the counterfeiting of the King's coin we are proposing a law which can reasonably be said to affect any of the royal prerogatives.

The distinction which we propose to make, (see Clauses 241 and 242,) between two different classes of utterers is marked in the French Code; and it is so obviously agreeable to reason and justice that we are surprised that, having been marked in that Code, it should not have been adopted by Mr. Livingston. We are glad to perceive that the Code of Bombay makes this distinction.

An utterer by profession, an utterer who is the agent employed by the coiner to bring counterfeit coin into circulation, is guilty of a very high offence. Such an utterer stands to the coiner in a relation not very different from that in which a habitual receiver of stolen goods stands to a thief. He makes coining a far less perilous, and a far more lucrative pursuit than it would otherwise be. He passes his life in the systematic violation of the law, and in the systematic practice of fraud in one of its most pernicious forms. He is one of the most mischievous, and is likely to be one of the most depraved of criminals. But a casual utterer, an utterer who is not an agent for bringing counterfeit coin into circulation, but who, having heedlessly received a bad rupee in the course of his business, takes advantage of the heedlessness of the next person with whom he deals to pay that bad rupee away, is an offender of a very different class. He is undoubtedly guilty of a dishonest act, but of one of the most venial of dishonest acts. It is an act which proceeds not from greediness for unlawful gain, but from a wish to avoid. by unlawful means it is true, what to a poor man may be a severe loss. It is an act which has no tendency to facilitate or encourage the operations of the coiner. It is an occasional act, an act which does not imply that the person who commits it is a person of lawless habits. We think, therefore, that the offence of a casual utterer is perhaps the least heinous of all the offences into which fraud enters.

We considered whether it would be advisable to make it an offence in a person to have in his possession at one time a certain number of counterfeit coins, without being able to explain satisfactorily how he came by them. It did not, after much discussion, appear to us advisable to recommend this or any similar provision. We entertain strong objections to the practice of making circumstances which are in truth only evidence of an offence part of the definition of an offence : nor do we see any reason for departing in this case from our general rule.

Whether a person who is possessed of bad money knows the money to be bad, and whether, knowing it to be bad, he intends to put it in circulation, are questions to be decided by the tribunals according to the circumstances of the case, circumstances of which the mere number of the pieces is only one, and may be one of the least important. A few bad rupees which should evidently be fresh from the stamp would be stronger evidence than a greater number of bad rupees which appeared to have been in circulation for years. A few bad rupees, all obviously coined with the same die, would be stronger evidence than a greater number obviously coined with different dies. A few bad rupees placed by themselves, and unmixed with good ones, would be far stronger evidence than a much larger number which might be detected in a large mass of treasure.

NOTE J.

ON THE CHAPTER OF OFFENCES RELATING TO RELIGION AND CASTE.

The principle on which this Chapter has been framed is a principle on which it would be desirable that all Governments should act, but from which the British Government in India cannot depart without risking the dissolution of society. It is this, that every man should be suffered to profess his own religion, and that no man should be suffered to insult the religion of another.

The question whether insults offered to a religion ought to be visited with punishment, does not appear to us at all to depend on the question whether that religion be true, or false. The religion may be false, but the pain which such insults give to the professors of that religion is real. It is often, as the most superficial observation may convince us, as real a pain, and as acute a pain as is caused by almost any offence against the person, against property, or against character. Nor is there any compensating good whatsoever to be set off against this pain. Discussion, indeed, tends to elicit truth. But insults have no such tendency. They can be employed just as easily against the purest faith as against the most monstrous superstition. It is easier to argue against falsehood than against truth. But it is as easy to pull down and defile the temples of truth as those of falsehood. It is as easy to molest with ribaldry and clamour men assembled for purposes of pious and rational worship, as men engaged in the most absurd ceremonies. Such insults, when directed against erroneous opinions, seldom have any other effect than to fix those opinions deeper, and to give a character of peculiar ferocity to theological dissension. Instead of eliciting truth they only inflame fanaticism.

All these considerations apply with peculiar force to India. There is perhaps no country in which the Government has so much to apprehend from religious excitement among the people. The Christians are numerically a very small minority of the population, and in possession of all the highest posts in the Government, in the tribunals, and in the army. Under their rule are placed millions of Mahomedans, of differing sects, but all strongly attached to the fundamental articles of the Mahomedan creed, and tens of millions of Hindoos, strongly attached to doctrines and rites which Christians and Mahomedans join in reprobating. Such a state of things is pregnant with dangers which can only be averted by a firm adherence to the true principles of toleration. On those principles the British Government has hitherto acted with eminent judgment, and with no less eminent success: and on those principles we propose to frame this part of the penal Code.

We have provided a punishment of great severity for the intentional destroying or defiling of places of worship, or of objects held sacred by any class of persons. No offence in the whole Code is so likely to lead to tumult, to sanguinary outrage, and even to armed insurrection. The slaughter of a cow in a sacred place at Benares in 1809 caused violent tumult, attended with considerable loss of life. The pollution of a mosque at Bangalore was attended with consequences still more lamentable and alarming. We have therefore empowered the Courts in cases of this description, to pass a very severe sentence on the offender.

The provisions which we have made for the purpose of protecting assemblies held for religious worship, and of guarding from intentional insult the rites of sepulture and the remains of the dead, do not appear to require any explanation, or defence.

The intentional depriving a Hindoo of his caste by assault or by deception is not at present an offence in any part of India, though it may be a ground for a civil action. It appears to us however that an injury so wanton, an injury which indicates so bad a feeling in the person who causes it, and which gives so much pain and excites so much resentment in the sufferer is as proper a subject for penal legislation as most of the acts which are made punishable by this Code. We have therefore, made it an offence. The rendering the food of a Hindoo useless to him by causing it to be in what he considers as a polluted state is an injury of the same kind, though comparatively venial. We propose to make it an offence, but not to deal with it severely, unless it should be repeatedly committed by the same person.

In framing Clause 282 we had two objects in view. We wish to allow all fair latitude to religious discussion, and at the same time to prevent the professors of any religion from offering, under the pretext of such discussion, intentional insults to what is held sacred by others. We do not conceive that any person can be justified in wounding with deliberate intention the religious feelings of his neighbours by words, gesture, or exhibitions. A warm expression dropped in the heat of controversy, or an argument urged by a person not for the purpose of insulting and annoying the professors of a different creed, but in good faith for the purpose of vindicating his own, will not fall under the definition contained in this Clause.

Clause 283 is intended to prevent such practices as those known among the natives by the names of Dhurna and Traga. Such acts are now punishable by law, and it is unnecessary to adduce any argument for the purpose of shewing that they ought to be so.

NOTE K.

ON THE CHAPTER OF ILLICIT ENTRANCE INTO AND ILLICIT RESIDENCE IN THE TERRITORIES OF THE EAST INDIA COMPANY.

The Indian legislature is required by the Act of Parliament 3 and 4 Wm. IV. Cap. 85 Section LXXXIV, "as soon as conveniently may be, to make laws or regulations pro-" viding for the prevention or punishment of the illicit entrance into or residence in the " said territories of persons not authorized to enter or reside therein."

We have, therefore, thought it our duty to insert in the Penal Code provisions for the purpose of carrying the intentions of Parliament into effect.

NOTE L.

ON OFFENCES RELATING TO THE PRESS.

The penal provisions contained in this Chapter are taken from the Act of the Governor General of India in Council, No. XI. of 1835.

Sufficient provision appears to us to have been made in other parts of the Code, particularly by Clause 195, for the punishment of the offence mentioned in the last Section of the Act to which we have referred.

NOTE M.

ON OFFENCES AGAINST THE BODY.

The first class of offences against the body consists of those offences which affect human life; and highest in this first class stand those offences which fall under the definition of voluntary culpable homicide.

This important part of the law appears to us to require fuller explanation than almost any other.

The first point to which we wish to call the attention of his Lordship in Council is the expression " omits what he is legally bound to do," in the definition of voluntary culpable homicide. These words, or other words tantamount in effect, frequently recur in the Code. We think this the most convenient place for explaining the reason which has led us so often to employ them. For if that reason shall appear to be sufficient in cases in which human life is concerned, it will a fortiori be sufficient in other cases.

Early in the progress of the Code it became necessary for us to consider the following question: When acts are made punishable on the ground that those acts produce, or are intended to produce, or are known to be likely to produce certain evil effects, to what extent ought omissions which produce, which are intended to produce, or which are known to be likely to produce the same evil effects to be made punishable?

Two things we take to be evident; first, that some of these omissions ought to be punished in exactly the same manner in which acts are punished; secondly, that all these omissions ought not to be punished. It will hardly be disputed that a gaoler who voluntarily causes the death of a prisoner by omitting to supply that prisoner with food, or a nurse who voluntarily causes the death of an infant entrusted to her care by omitting to take it out of a tub of water into which it has fallen, ought to be treated as guilty of murder. On the other hand, it will hardly be maintained that a man should be punished as a murderer because he omitted to relieve a beggar, even though there might be the clearest proof that the death of the beggar was the effect of this omission, and that the man who omitted to give the alms knew that the death of the beggar was likely to be the effect of the omission. It will hardly be maintained that a surgeon ought to be treated as a murderer for refusing to go from Calcutta to Meerut to perform an operation, although it should be absolutely certain that this surgeon was the only person in India who could perform it, and that if it were not performed the person who required it would die. It is difficult to say whether a Penal Code which should put no omissions on the same footing with acts, or a Penal Code which should put all omissions on the same footing with acts would produce consequences more absurd and revolting. There is no country in which either of these principles is adopted. Indeed, it is hard to conceive how, if either were adopted, society could be held together.

It is plain, therefore, that a middle course must be taken. But it is not easy to determine what that middle course ought to be. The absurdity of the two extremes is obvious. But there are innumerable intermediate points; and wherever the line of demarcation may be drawn it will, we fear, include some cases which we might wish to exempt, and will exempt some which we might wish to include.

Mr. Livingston's Code provides, that a person shall be considered as guilty of homicide who omits to save life, which he could save " without personal danger, or pecuniary loss." This rule appears to us to be open to serious objection. There may be extreme inconvenience without the smallest personal danger, or the smallest risk of pecuniary loss, as in the case we lately put of a surgeon summoned from Calcutta to Meerut, to perform an operation. He may be offered such a fee that he would be a gainer by going. He may have no ground to apprehend that he should run any greater personal risk by journeying to the Upper Provinces than by continuing to reside in Bengal. But he is about to proceed to Europe immediately, or he expects some members of his family by the next ship, and wishes to be at the presidency to receive them. He, therefore, refuses to go. Surely, he ought not, for so refusing, to be treated as a murderer. It would be somewhat inconsistent to punish one man for not staying three months in India to save the life of another, and to leave wholly unpunished a man who, enjoying ample wealth, should refuse to disburse an anna to save the life of another. Again it appears to us that it may be fit to punish a person as a murderer for causing death by omitting an act which cannot be performed without personal danger, or pecuniary loss. A parent may be unable to procure food for an infant without money. Yet the parent, if he has the means, is bound to furnish the infant with food, and if by omitting to do so he voluntarily causes its death he may with propriety be treated as a murderer. A nurse hired to attend a person suffering from an infectious disease cannot perform her duty without running some risk of infection. Yet if she deserts the sick person, and thus voluntarily causes his death, we should be disposed to treat her as a murderer.

We pronounce with confidence, therefore, that the line ought not to be drawn where Mr. Livingston has drawn it. But it is with great diffidence that we bring forward our own proposition. It is open to objections: cases may be put in which it will operate too severely, and cases in which it will operate too leniently: but we are unable to devise a better.

What we propose is this, that where acts are made punishable on the ground that they have caused, or have been intended to cause, or have been known to be likely to cause a certain evil effect, omissions which have caused, which have been intended to cause, or which have been known to be likely to cause the same effect shall be punishable in the same manner; provided that such omissions were, on other grounds, illegal. An omission is illegal (see Clause 28) if it be an offence, if it be a breach of some direction of law, or if it be such a wrong as would be a good ground for a civil action.

We cannot defend this rule better than by giving a few illustrations of the way in which it will operate. A omits to give Z food, and by that omission voluntarily causes

Z's death. Is this murder? Under our rule it is murder if A was Z's gaoler, directed by the law to furnish Z with food. It is murder if Z was the infant child of A, and had therefore a legal right to sustenance, which right a Civil Court would enforce against A. It is murder if Z was a bedridden invalid, and A a nurse hired to feed Z. It is murder if A was detaining Z in unlawful confinement, and had thus contracted (see Clause 338) a legal obligation to furnish Z, during the continuance of the confinement, with necessaries. It is not murder if Z is a beggar who has no other claim on A than that of humanity.

A omits to tell Z that a river is swollen so high that Z cannot safely attempt to ford it, and by this omission voluntarily causes Z's death. This is murder, if A is a Peon stationed by authority to warn travellers from attempting to ford the river. It is murder if A is a guide who had contracted to conduct Z. It is not murder if A is a person on whom Z has no other claim than that of humanity.

A savage dog fastens on Z. A omits to call off the dog, knowing that if the dog be not called off it is likely that Z will be killed. Z is killed. This is murder in A, if the dog belonged to A, inasmuch as his omission to take proper order with the dog is illegal. (Clause 273.) But if A be a mere passer by it is not murder.

We are sensible that in some of the cases which we have put our rule may appear too lenient. But we do not think that it can be made more severe, without disturbing the whole order of society. It is true that the man who, having abundance of wealth, suffers a fellow creature to die of hunger at his feet, is a bad man,—a worse man, probably, than many of those for whom we have provided very severe punishment. But we are unable to see where, if we make such a man legally punishable, we can draw the line. If the rich man who refuses to save a beggar's life at the cost of a little copper is a murderer, is the poor man just one degree above beggary also to be a murderer if he omits to invite the beggar to partake his hard earned rice? Again: if the rich man is a murderer for refusing to save the beggar's life at the cost of a little copper, is he also to be a murderer if he refuses to save the beggar's life at the cost of a thousand rupees? Suppose A to be fully convinced that nothing can save Z's life, unless Z leave Bengal, and reside a year at the Cape, is A, however wealthy he may be, to be punished as a murderer because he will not, at his own expense, send Z to the Cape? Surely not. Yet it will be difficult to say on what principle we can punish A for not spending an anna to save Z's life, and leave him unpunished for not spending a thousand rupees to save Z's life. The distinction between a legal and an illegal omission is perfectly plain and intelligible. But the distinction between a large and a small sum of money is very far from being so; not to say that a sum which is small to one man is large to another.

The same argument holds good in the case of the ford. It is true that none but a very depraved man would suffer another to be drowned when he might prevent it by a word. But if we punish such a man where are we to stop? How much exertion are we to require? Is a person to be a murderer if he does not go fifty yards through the sun of Bengal at noon in May in order to caution a traveller against a swollen river? Is he to be a murderer if he does not go a hundred yards?—if he does not go a mile?—if he does not go ten? What is the precise amount of trouble and inconvenience which he is to endure? The distinction between the guide who is bound to conduct the traveller as safely as he can, and a mere stranger, is a clear distinction. But the distinction between a stranger who will not give a halloo to save a man's life, and a stranger who will not run a mile to save a man's life is very far from being equally clear.

It is, indeed, most highly desirable that men should not merely abstain from doing harm to their neighbours, but should render active services to their neighbours. In general however the penal law must content itself with keeping men from doing positive harm, and must leave to public opinion, and to the teachers of morality and religion, the office of furnishing men with motives for doing positive good. It is evident that to attempt to punish men by law for not rendering to others all the service which it is their duty to render to others would be preposterous. We must grant impunity to the vast majority of those omissions which a benevolent morality would pronounce reprehensible, and must content ourselves with punishing such omissions only when they are distinguished from the rest by some circumstance which marks them out as peculiarly fit

P

objects of penal legislation. Now, no circumstance appears to us so well fitted to be the mark as the circumstance which we have selected. It will generally be found in the most atrocious cases of omission: it will scarcely ever be found in a venial case of omission: and it is more clear and certain than any other mark that has occurred to us. That there are objections to the line which we propose to draw, we have admitted. But there are objections to every line which can be drawn, and some line must be drawn.

The next point to which we wish to call the attention of his Lordship in Council is the unqualified use of the words " to cause death" in the definition of voluntary culpable homicide.

We long considered whether it would be advisable to except from this definition any description of acts or illegal omissions, on the ground that such acts or illegal omissions do not ordinarily cause death, or that they cause death very remotely. We have determined, however, to leave the Clause in its present simple and comprehensive form.

There is undoubtedly a great difference between acts which cause death immediately, and acts which cause death remotely; between acts which are almost certain to cause death, and acts which cause death only under very extraordinary circumstances. But that difference, we conceive, is a matter to be considered by the tribunals when estimating the effect of the evidence in a particular case, not by the legislature in framing the general law. It will require strong evidence to prove that an act of a kind which very seldom causes death, or an act which has caused death very remotely, has actually caused death in a particular case. It will require still stronger evidence to prove that such an act was contemplated by the person who did it as likely to cause death. But if it be proved by satisfactory evidence that death has been so caused, and has been caused voluntarily, we see no reason for exempting the person who caused it from the punishment of voluntary culpable homicide.

Mr. Livingston, we observe, excepts from the definition of homicide cases in which death is produced by the effect of words on the imagination, or the passions. The reasoning of that distinguished jurist has by no means convinced us that the distinction which he makes is well founded. Indeed there are few parts of his Code which appear to us to have been less happily executed than this. His words are . these—" The " destruction must be by the act of another. Therefore self-destruction is excluded " from the definition. It must be operated by some act. Therefore death, although " produced by the operation of words on the imagination or the passions, is not homi- " cide. But if words are used which are calculated to produce and do produce some " act which is the immediate cause of death it is homicide. A blind man or a stranger " in the dark directed by words only to a precipice where he falls and is killed, a " direction verbally given to take a drug that it is known will prove fatal, and which " has that effect, are instances of this modification of the rule."

This appears to us altogether incoherent. A verbally directs Z to swallow a poisonous drug. Z swallows it and dies. And this, says Mr. Livingston, is homicide in A. It certainly ought to be so considered. But how, on Mr. Livingston's principles, it can be so considered we do not understand. " Homicide," he says, " must be operated by an " act." Where then is the act in this case? Is it the speaking of A. Clearly not, for Mr. Livingston lays down the doctrine that speaking is not an act. Is it the swallowing by Z? Clearly not, for the destruction of life, according to Mr. Livingston, is not homicide unless it be by the act of another, and this swallowing is an act performed by Z himself.

The reasonable course, in our opinion, is to consider speaking as an act, and to treat A as guilty of voluntary culpable homicide, if by speaking he has voluntarily caused Z's death, whether his words operated circuitously by inducing Z to swallow poison or directly by throwing Z into convulsions.

There will indeed be few homicides of this latter sort. It appears to us that a conviction, or even a trial in such a case would be an event of extremely rare occurrence. There would probably not be one such trial in a century. It would be most difficult to prove to the conviction of any Court that death had really been the effect of excitemen produced by words. It would be still more difficult to prove that the person who spok the words anticipated from them an effect which, except under very peculiar circumstances, and on very peculiar constitutions, no words would produce. Still it seems to us that both these points might be made out by overwhelming evidence; and supposing them to be so made out, we are unable to perceive any distinction between the case of him who voluntarily causes death in this manner, and the case of him who voluntarily causes death by means of a pistol, or a sword. Suppose it to be proved to the entire conviction of a Criminal Court that Z, the deceased, was in a very critical state of health, that A, the heir to Z's property, had been informed by Z's physicians that Z's recovery absolutely depended on his being kept quiet in mind, and that the smallest mental excitement would endanger his life, that A immediately broke into Z's sick room, and told him a dreadful piece of intelligence which was a pure invention, that Z went into fits, and died on the spot, that A had afterwards boasted of having cleared the way for himself to a good property by this artifice. These things being fully proved, no judge could doubt that A had voluntarily caused the death of Z; nor do we perceive any reason for not punishing A in the same manner in which he would have been punished if he had mixed arsenic in Z's medicine.

Again, Mr. Livingston excepts from the definition of homicide the case of a person who dies of a slight wound which, from neglect, or from the application of improper remedies, has proved mortal. We see no reason for excepting such cases, from the simple general rule which we propose. It will, indeed, be in general more difficult to prove that death has been caused by a scratch, than by a stab which has reached the heart: and it will in a still greater degree be more difficult to prove that a scratch was intended to cause death, than that a stab was intended to cause death. Yet both these points might be fully established. Suppose such a case as the following. It is proved that A inflicted a slight wound on Z, a child who stood between him and a large property. It is proved that the ignorant and superstitious servants about Z applied the most absurd remedies to the wound. It is proved that under their treatment the wound mortified, and the child died. Letters from A to a confident are produced. In those letters, A congratulates himself on his skill, remarks that he could not have inflicted a more severe wound without exposing himself to be punished as a murderer, relates with exultation the mode of treatment followed by the people who have charge of Z, and boasts that he always foresaw that they would turn the slightest incision into a mortal wound. It appears to us that if such evidence were produced, A ought to be punished as a murderer.

Again, suppose that A makes a deliberate attempt to commit assassination. In the presence of numbers he aims a knife at the heart of Z. But the knife glances aside, and inflicts only a slight wound. This happened in the case of Jean Chatel, of Damien, of Guiscard, and of many other assassins of the most desperate character. In such cases there is no doubt whatever as to the intention. Suppose that the person who received the wound is under the necessity of exposing himself to a moist atmosphere immediately afterwards, and that, in consequence, he is attacked with tetanus, and dies. Here again, however slight the wound may have been, we are unable to perceive any good reason for not punishing A as a murderer.

We will only add that this provision of the Code of Louisiana appears to us peculiarly ill suited to a country in which, we have reason to fear, neglect and bad treatment are far more common than good medical treatment.

The general rule, therefore, which we propose is, that the question whether a person has by an act or illegal omission voluntarily caused death shall be left a question of evidence to be decided by the Courts, according to the circumstances of every case.

We propose that all voluntary culpable homicide shall be designated as murder unless it fall under one of three heads. We are desirous to call the particular attention of his Lordship in Council to the law respecting the three mitigated forms of voluntary culpable homicide; and first to the law of manslaughter.

We agree with the great mass of mankind, and with the majority of jurists, ancient and modern, in thinking that homicide committed in the sudden heat of passion, on great provocation, ought to be punished, but that in general it ought not to be punished so severely as murder. It ought to be punished in order to teach men to entertain a peculiar respect for human life: it ought to be punished in order to give men a motive for accustoming themselves to govern their passions; and in some few cases for which we have made provision we conceive that it ought to be punished with the utmost rigour.

In general, however, we would not visit homicide committed in violent passion which had been suddenly provoked with the highest penalties of the law. We think that to treat a person guilty of such homicide as we should treat a murderer would be a highly inexpedient course. A course which would shock the universal feeling of mankind, and would engage the public sympathy on the side of the delinquent against the law.

His Lordship in Council will remark one important distinction between the law as we have framed it, and some other systems. Neither the English law, nor the French Code extends any indulgence to homicide which is the effect of anger excited by words alone. Mr. Livingston goes still further. " No words whatever," says the Code of Louisiana, " are an adequate cause, no gestures merely shewing derision or contempt, " no assault, or battery so slight as to shew that the intent was not to inflict great " bodily harm."

We greatly doubt whether any good reason can be assigned for this distinction. It is an indisputable fact that gross insults by word or gesture have as great a tendency to move many persons to violent passion, as dangerous or painful bodily injuries. Nor does it appear to us that passion excited by insult is entitled to less indulgence than passion excited by pain. On the contrary the circumstance that a man resents an insult more than a wound is any thing but a proof that he is a man of a peculiarly bad heart. It would be a fortunate thing for mankind if every person felt an outrage which left a stain upon his honor more acutely than an outrage which had fractured one of his limbs. If so, why should we treat an offence produced by the blameable excess of a feeling which all wise legislators desire to encourage, more severely than we treat the blameable excess of feelings certainly not more respectable ?

One outrage which wounds only the honor and the affections is admitted by Mr. Livingston to be an adequate provocation. " A discovery of the wife of the accused, " in the act of adultery with the person killed, is an adequate cause." The law of France, the law of England, and the Mahomedan law are also indulgent to homicide committed under such circumstances. We must own that we can see no reason for making a distinction between this provocation and many other provocations of the same kind. We cannot consent to lay it down as an universal rule that in all cases this provocation shall be considered as an adequate provocation. Circumstances may easily be conceived which would satisfy a Court that a husband had in such a case acted from no feeling of wounded honor or affection, but from mere brutality of nature, or from disappointed cupidity. On the other hand, we conceive that there are many cases in which as much indulgence is due to the excited feelings of a father, or a brother, as to those of a husband. That a worthless, unfaithful, and tyrannical husband should be guilty only of manslaughter for killing the paramour of his wife, and that an affectionate and high spirited brother should be guilty of murder for killing in a paroxysm of rage the seducer of his sister, appears to us inconsistent and unreasonable.

There is another class of provocations which Mr. Livingston does not allow to be adequate in law, but which have been, and, while human nature remains unaltered, will be adequate in fact to produce the most tremendous effects. Suppose a person to take indecent liberties with a modest female in the presence of her father, her brother, her husband, or her lover. Such an assault might have no tendency to cause pain, or danger; yet history tells us what effects have followed from such assaults. Such an assault produced the Sicilian vespers. Such an assault called forth the memorable blow of Wat Tyler. It is difficult to conceive any class of cases in which the intemperance of anger ought to be treated with greater lenity. So far, indeed, should we be from ranking a man who acted like Tyler with murderers, that we conceive that a Judge would exercise a sound discretion in sentencing such a man to the lowest punishment fixed by the law for manslaughter.

We think it right to add that though in our remarks on this part of the law we have used illustrations drawn from the history and manners of Europe, the arguments which we have employed apply as strongly to the state of society in India as to the state of society in any part of the globe. There is perhaps no country in which more cruel suffering is inflicted, and more deadly resentment called forth, by injuries which affect only the mental feelings.

A person who should offer a gross insult to the Mahomedan religion in the presence of a zealous professor of that religion, who should deprive some high-born Rajpoot of his caste, who should rudely thrust his head into the covered palanquin of a woman of rank, would probably move those whom he insulted to more violent anger that if he had caused them some severe bodily hurt. That on these subjects our notions and usages differ from theirs is nothing to the purpose. We are legislating for them, and though we may wish that their opinions and feelings may undergo a considerable change, it is our duty, while their opinions and feelings remain unchanged, to pay as much respect to those opinions and feelings as if we partook of them. We are legislating for a country where many men, and those by no means the worst men, prefer death to the loss of caste, where many women, and those by no means the worst women, would consider themselves as dishonoured by exposure to the gaze of strangers ; and to legislate for such a country as if the loss of caste, or the exposure of a female face were not provocations of the highest order, would, in our opinion, be unjust and unreasonable.

The second mitigated form of voluntary culpable homicide is that to which we have given the name of voluntary culpable homicide by consent. It appears to us that this description of homicide ought to be punished, but that it ought not to be punished so severely as murder. We have elsewhere given our reasons for thinking that this description of homicide ought to be punished.*

Our reasons for not punishing it so severely as murder are these. In the first place the motives which prompt men to the commission of this offence are generally far more respectable than those which prompt men to the commission of murder. Sometimes it is the effect of a strong sense of religious duty, sometimes of a strong sense of honor, not unfrequently of humanity. The soldier who, at the entreaty of a wounded comrade, puts that comrade out of pain, the friend who supplies laudanum to a person suffering the torment of a lingering disease, the freedman who in ancient times held out the sword that his master might fall on it, the high-born native of India who stabs the females of his family at their own entreaty in order to save them from the licentiousness of a band of marauders, would, except in Christian societies, scarcely be thought culpable, and even in Christian societies, would not be regarded by the public, and ought not to be treated by the law as assassins.

Again, this crime is by no means productive of so much evil to the community as murder. One evil ingredient of the utmost importance is altogether wanting to the offence of voluntary culpable homicide by consent. It does not produce general insecurity. It does not spread terror through society. When we punish murder with such signal severity, we have two ends in view. One end is that people may not be murdered. Another end is that people may not live in constant dread of being murdered. This second end is perhaps the more important of the two. For if assassination were left unpunished the number of persons assassinated would probably bear a very small proportion to the whole population. But the life of every human being would be passed in constant anxiety and alarm. This property of the offence of murder is not found in the offence of voluntary culpable homicide by consent. Every man who has not given his consent to be put to death is perfectly certain that this latter offence cannot at present be committed on him, and that it never will be committed, unless he shall first be convinced that it is his interest to consent to it. We know that two or three midnight assassinations are sufficient to keep a city of a million of inhabitants in a state of consternation during several weeks, and to cause every private family to lay in arms and watchmen's rattles. No number of suicides, or of homicides committed with the unextorted consent of the person killed, could possibly produce such alarm among the survivors.

The distinction between murder and voluntary culpable homicide by consent has never, as far as we are aware, been recognized by any Code in the distinct manner in which we propose to recognize it. But it may be traced in the laws of many countries, and often, when neglected by those who have framed the laws, it has had a great effect on the decisions of the tribunals, and particularly on the decisions of tribunals popularly composed. It may be proper to observe that the burning of a Hindoo widow by her own consent, though it is now, as it ought to be, an offence by the regulations of every Presidency, is in no Presidency punished as murder.

* See Note B.

The third mitigated form of voluntary culpable homicide is that which we have designated as voluntary culpable homicide in defence.

We have been forced to leave the law on the subject of private defence, as we have elsewhere said, in an unsatisfactory state ; and, though we hope and believe that it may be greatly improved, we fear that it must always continue to be one of the least precise parts of every system of jurisprudence. That portion of the law of homicide which we are now considering is closely connected with the law of private defence, and must necessarily partake of the imperfections of the law of private defence. But wherever the limits of the right of private defence may be placed, and with whatever degree of accuracy they may be marked, we are inclined to think that it will always be expedient to make a separation between murder and what we have designated as voluntary culpable homicide in defence.

The chief reason for making this separation is that the law itself invites men to the very verge of the crime which we have designated as voluntary culpable homicide in defence. It prohibits such homicide indeed. But it authorizes acts which lie very near to such homicide. And this circumstance we think greatly mitigates the guilt of such homicide.

That a man who deliberately kills another in order to prevent that other from pulling his nose should be allowed to go absolutely unpunished would be most dangerous. The law punishes and ought to punish such killing. But we cannot think that the law ought to punish such killing as murder. For the law itself has encouraged the slayer to inflict on the assailant any harm short of death which may be necessary for the purpose of repelling the outrage,—to give the assailant a cut with a knife across the fingers which may render his right hand useless to him for life, or to hurl him down stairs with such force as to break his leg. And it seems difficult to conceive that circumstances which would be a full justification of any violence short of homicide should not be a mitigation of the guilt of homicide. That a man should be merely exercising a right by fracturing the skull and knocking out the eye of an assailant, and should be guilty of the highest crime in the Code if he kills the same assailant,—that there should be only a single step between perfect innocence and murder, between perfect impunity and liability to capital punishment,—seems unreasonable. In a case in which the law itself empowers an individual to inflict any harm short of death, it ought hardly, we think, to visit him with the highest punishment if he inflicts death.

It is to be considered also that the line between those aggressions which it is lawful to repel by killing, and those which it is not lawful so to repel, is in our Code, and must be in every Code, to a great extent an arbitrary line, and that many individual cases will fall on one side of that line which, if we had framed the law with a view to those cases alone, we should place on the other. Thus we allow a man to kill if he has no other means of preventing an incendiary from burning a house : and we do not allow him to kill for the purpose of preventing the commission of a simple theft. But a house may be a wretched heap of mats and thatch, propped by a few bamboos, and not worth altogether twenty rupees. A simple theft may deprive a man of a pocket-book which contains bills to a great amount, the savings of a long and laborious life, the sole dependence of a large family. That in these cases the man who kills the incendiary should be pronounced guiltless of any offence, and that the man who kills the thief should be sentenced to the gallows, or, if he is treated with the utmost lenity which the Courts can shew, to perpetual transportation or imprisonment, would be generally condemned as a shocking injustice. We are therefore clearly of opinion that the offence which we have designated as voluntary culpable homicide in defence ought to be distinguished from murder in such a manner that the Courts may have it in their power to inflict a slight or a merely nominal punishment on acts which, though not within the letter of the law which authorises killing in self-defence, are yet within the reason of that law.

We have hitherto been considering the law of voluntary culpable homicide. But homicide may be culpable, yet not voluntary. There will probably be little difference of opinion as to the expediency of providing a punishment for the rash and negligent causing of death. But it may be thought that we have dealt too leniently by the offender who while committing a crime causes death which he did not intend to cause or know himself to be likely to cause.

The law as we have framed it differs widely from the English law. " If," says Sir

William Blackstone , " one intends to do another felony, and undesignedly kills a man, this is murder :" and he gives the following illustration of the rule : " If one gives a woman with child a medicine to produce abortion, and it operates so violently as to kill the woman, this is murder in the person who gave it."

Under the provisions of our Code, this case would be very differently dealt with according to circumstances. If A kills Z by administering abortives to her with the knowledge that those abortives are likely to cause her death, he is guilty of voluntary culpable homicide, which will be voluntary culpable homicide by consent if Z agreed to run the risk, and murder if Z did not so agree. If A causes miscarriage to Z, not intending to cause Z's death, nor thinking it likely that he shall cause Z's death, but so rashly or negligently as to cause her death, A is guilty of culpable homicide not voluntary, and will be liable to the punishment provided for the causing of miscarriage, increased by imprisonment for a term not exceeding two years. Lastly, if A took such precautions that there was no reasonable probability that Z's death would be caused, and if the medicine were rendered deadly by some accident which no human sagacity could have foreseen, or by some peculiarity in Z's constitution such as there was no ground whatever to expect, A will be liable to no punishment whatever on account of her death, but will of course be liable to the punishment provided for causing miscarriage.

It may be proper for us to offer some arguments in defence of this part of the Code.

It will be admitted that, when an act is in itself innocent, to punish the person who does it because bad consequences which no human wisdom could have forseen have followed from it would be in the highest degree barbarous and absurd.

A Pilot is navigating the Hooghly with the utmost care and skill : he directs the vessel against a sand bank which has been recently formed, and of which the existence was altogether unknown till this disaster. Several of his passengers are consequently drowned. To hang the Pilot as a murderer on account of this misfortune would be universally allowed to be an act of atrocious injustice. But if the voyage of the Pilot be itself a high offence, ought that circumstance alone to turn his misfortune into a murder ? Suppose that he is engaged in conveying an offender beyond the reach of justice, that he has kidnapped some natives, and is carrying them to a ship which is to convey them to some foreign slave-colony, that he is violating the laws of quarantine at a time when it is of the highest importance that those laws should be strictly observed, that he is carrying supplies, deserters, and intelligence to the enemies of the State. The offence of such a Pilot ought undoubtedly to be severely punished. But to pronounce him guilty of one offence because a misfortune befel him while he was committing another offence, — to pronounce him the murderer of people whose lives he never meant to endanger, whom he was doing his best to carry safe to their destination, and whose death has been purely accidental, — is surely to confound all the boundaries of crime.

Again, A heaps fuel on a fire not in an imprudent manner, but in such a manner that the chance of harm is not worth considering. Unhappily, the flame bursts out more violently than there was reason to expect. At the same moment a sudden puff of wind blows Z's light dress towards the hearth. The dress catches fire, and Z is burned to death. To punish A as a murderer on account of such an unhappy event would be senseless cruelty. But suppose that the fuel which caused the flame to burst forth was a will, which A was fraudulently destroying. Ought this circumstance to make A the murderer of Z ? We think not. For the fraudulent destroying of wills we have provided in other parts of the Code punishments which we think sufficient. If not sufficient they ought to be made so. But we cannot admit that Z's death has in the smallest degree aggravated A's offence, or ought to be considered in apportioning A's punishment.

To punish as a murderer every man who, while committing a heinous offence, causes death by pure misadventure, is a course which evidently adds nothing to the security of human life. No man can so conduct himself as to make it absolutely certain that he shall not be so unfortunate as to cause the death of a fellow creature. The utmost that he can do is to abstain from every thing which is at all likely to cause death. No fear of punishment can make him do more than this : and therefore to punish a man who has done this can add nothing to the security of human life. The only good effect which such punishment can produce will be to deter people from committing any of those offences which turn into murders what are in themselves mere accidents. It is in fact an addition to the punishment of those offences, and it is an addition made in the very worst way. For example, hundreds of persons in some great cities are in the habit of picking pockets. They know that they are guilty of a great offence. But it has never occurred to one of them, nor would it occur to any rational man, that they are guilty of an offence which endangers life. Unhappily one of these hundreds attempts to take the purse of a gentleman who has a loaded pistol in his pocket. The thief touches the trigger: the pistol goes off: the gentleman is shot dead. To treat the case of this pick-pocket differently from that of the numerous pick-pockets who steal under exactly the same circumstances, with exactly the same intentions, with no less risk of causing death, with no greater care to avoid causing death,—to send them to the house of correction as thieves, and him to the gallows as a murderer,—appears to us an unreasonable course. If the punishment for stealing from the person be too light, let it be increased, and let the increase fall alike on all the offenders. Surely the worst mode of increasing the punishment of an offence is to provide that, besides the ordinary punishment, every offender shall run an exceedingly small risk of being hanged. The more nearly the amount of punishment can be reduced to a certainty the better. But if chance is to be admitted there are better ways of admitting it. It would be a less capricious, and therefore a more salutary course, to provide that every fiftieth or every hundredth thief selected by lot should be hanged, than to provide that every thief should be hanged who, while engaged in stealing, should meet with an unforeseen misfortune such as might have befallen the most virtuous man while performing the most virtuous action.

We trust that his Lordship in Council will think that we have judged correctly in proposing that when a person engaged in the commission of an offence causes death by pure accident, he shall suffer only the punishment of his offence without any addition on account of such accidental death.

When a person engaged in the commission of an offence causes death by rashness, or negligence, but without either intending to cause death, or thinking it likely that he shall cause death, we propose that he shall be liable to the punishment of the offence which he was engaged in committing, superadded to the ordinary punishment of involuntary culpable homicide.

The arguments and illustrations which we have employed for the purpose of shewing that the involuntary causing of death without either rashness or negligence ought, under no circumstances, to be punished at all, will, with some modifications which will readily suggest themselves, serve to shew that the involuntary causing of death by rashness or negligence, though always punishable, ought under no circumstances to be punished as murder.

It gives us great pleasure to observe that Mr. Livingston's provisions on this subject, though in details they differ widely from ours, are framed on the principles which we have here defended.

We wish next to call the attention of his Lordship in Council to Clauses 308 and 309.

These Clauses appear to us absolutely necessary to the completeness of the Code. We have provided, under the head of bodily hurt, for cases in which hurt is inflicted in an attempt to murder; under the head of assault, for assaults committed in attempting to murder; under the head of criminal trespass, for some criminal trespasses committed in order to murder. But there will still remain many atrocious and deliberate attempts to murder which are not trespasses, which are not assaults, and which cause no hurt. A, for example, digs a pit in his garden, and conceals the mouth of it, intending that Z may fall in, and perish there. Here, A has committed no trespass, for the ground is his own; and no assault, for he has applied no force to Z. He may not have caused bodily hurt, for Z may have received a timely caution or may not have gone near the pit. But A's crime is evidently one which ought to be punished as severely as if he had laid hands on Z with the intention of cutting his throat.

Again, A sets poisoned food before Z. Here A may have committed no trespass; for the food may be his own; and, if so, he violates no right of property by mixing arsenic with it. H commits no assault, for he means the taking of the food to be Z's voluntary act. If Z does not swallow enough of the poisoned food to disorder him, A causes no bodily hurt. Yet it is plain that A has been guilty of a crime of a most atrocious description.

Similar attempts may be made to commit voluntary culpable homicide in any of the three mitigated forms. A, for example, is excited to violent passion by Z, and fires a pistol intending to kill Z. If the shot proves fatal, A will be guilty of manslaughter; and he surely ought not to be exempted from all punishment if the ball only grazes the intended victim.

It is to meet cases of this description that Clauses 308 and 309 are intended.

With respect to the law on the subject of abortion, we think it necessary to say only that we entertain strong apprehensions that this or any other law on that subject may, in this country, be abused to the vilest purposes. The charge of abortion is one which, even where it is not substantiated, often leaves a stain on the honor of families. The power of bringing a false accusation of this description is, therefore, a formidable engine in the hands of unprincipled men. This part of the law will, unless great care be taken, produce few convictions, but much misery and terror to respectable families, and a large harvest of profit to the vilest pests of society. We trust that it may be in our power in the Code of Procedure to lay down rules which may prevent such an abuse. Should we not be able to do so, we are inclined to think that it would be our duty to advise His Lordship in Council rather to suffer abortion, where the mother is a party to the offence, to remain wholly unpunished, than to repress it by provisions which would occasion more suffering to the innocent, than to the guilty.

Every one of those offences against the human body which remain to be considered falls under some one or more of the following heads: Hurt, Restraint, Assault, Kidnapping, Rape, Unnatural Crimes.

Many of the offences which fall under the head of Hurt will also fall under the head of Assault. A stab, a blow which fractures a limb, the flinging of boiling water over a person, are assaults, and are also acts which cause bodily hurt. But bodily hurt may be caused by many acts which are not assaults. A person, for example, who mixes a deleterious potion, and places it on the table of another; a person who conceals a scythe in the grass on which another is in the habit of walking; a person who digs a pit in a public path, intending that another may fall into it, may cause serious hurt, and may be justly punished for causing such hurt. But they cannot, without extreme violence to language, be said to have committed assaults. We propose to designate all pain, disease, and infirmity, by the name of hurt.

We have found it very difficult to draw a line between those bodily hurts which are serious, and those which are slight. To draw such a line with perfect accuracy is, indeed, absolutely impossible: but it is far better that such a line should be drawn, though rudely, than that offences some of which approach in enormity to murder, while others are little more than frolics which a good natured man would hardly resent, should be classed together.

We have, therefore, designated certain kinds of hurt as *grievous*.

We have given this name to emasculation,—to the loss of the sight of either eye,— to the loss of the hearing of either ear,—to the loss of any member or joint,—to the permanent loss of the perfect use of any member or joint,—to the permanent disfiguration of the head, or face,—to the fracture, and to the dislocation of bones. Thus far we proceed on sure ground. But a more difficult task remains. Some hurts which are not, like those kinds of hurt which we have just mentioned, distinguished by a broad and obvious line from slight hurts, may nevertheless be most serious. A wound, for example, which neither emasculates the sufferer, nor blinds him, nor destroys his hearing, nor deprives him of a member or a joint, nor permanently deprives him of the use of a member or a joint, nor disfigures his countenance, nor breaks his bones, nor dislocates them, may yet cause intense pain, prolonged disease, lasting injury to the constitution. It is evidently desirable that the law should make a distinction between such a wound, and a scratch which is healed with a little sticking plaster. A beating, again, which does not maim the sufferer, or break his bones, may be so cruel as to bring him to the point of death. Such a beating, it is clear, ought not to be confounded with a bruise which requires only to be bathed with vinegar, and of which the traces disappear in a day.

After long consideration we have determined to give the name of grievous bodily hurt to all hurt which causes the sufferer to be in pain, diseased, or unable to pursue his ordinary avocations, during the space of twenty days.

This provision was suggested to us by Article 309 of the French Penal Code. That

Article runs thus : " Sera puni de la peine de la réclusion, tout individu qui aura fait
" des blessures ou porté des coups, s'il est resulté de ces actes de violence une maladie
" ou incapacité de travail personnel pendent plus de vingt jours." *Réclusion*, it is to
be observed, signifies imprisonment and hard labour for a term of not less than five,
nor more than ten years.

This law appears from the *procès verbal* of Napoleon's Council of State to have been
adopted without calling forth a single* observation. But it has since been severely
criticised by French jurists, and has been mitigated by the French legislature. Indeed,
it ought to have been completely recast. For it is undoubtedly one of the most excep-
tionable laws in the Code.

A man who means only to inflict a slight hurt may, without intending or expecting
to do so, cause a hurt which is exceedingly serious. A push which to a man in health
is a trifle may, if it happens to be directed against a diseased part of an infirm person,
occasion consequences which the offender never contemplated as possible. A blow
designed to inflict only the pain of a moment may cause the person struck to lose his
footing, to fall from a considerable height, and to break a limb. In such cases to
punish the assailant with five years of strict imprisonment would be in the highest
degree unjust and cruel. It is said, and we can easily believe it,† that, in such cases,
the French juries have frequently refused, in spite of the clearest evidence, to pronounce a decision which would have subjected the accused to a punishment so obviously
disproportioned to his offence.

We have attempted to preserve and to extend what is good in this article of the
French Code, and to avoid the evils which we have noticed. It appears to us that the
length of time during which a sufferer is in pain, diseased, or incapacitated from pur-
suing his ordinary avocations, though a defective criterion of the severity of a hurt,
is still the best criterion that has ever been devised. It is a criterion which may, we
think, with propriety be employed not merely in cases where violence has been used,
but in cases where hurt has been caused without any assault, as by the administration
of drugs, the setting of traps, the digging of pit-falls, the placing of ropes across a
road. But though we have borrowed from the French Code this test of the severity of
bodily injuries, we have framed our penal provisions on a principle quite different from
that by which the authors of the French Code appear to have been guided. In apportioning the punishment, we take into consideration both the extent of the hurt, and the
intention of the offender.

What we propose is that the voluntary infliction of simple bodily hurt shall be
punished with imprisonment of either description which may extend to one year or fine
or both; the voluntary infliction of grievous bodily hurt with imprisonment of either
description for a term which may extend to ten years and must not be less than six
months, to which fine may be added.

These are the ordinary punishments. But there are certain aggravating and mitigating circumstances which make a considerable difference.

Where bodily hurt is voluntarily inflicted in an attempt to murder the person hurt,
we propose to punish the offender with transportation for life, or with imprisonment for
a term which may extend to life, and cannot be less than seven years. It does not
appear to us that, where the murderous intention is made out, the severity of the hurt
inflicted is a circumstance which ought to be considered in apportioning the punishment.
It is undoubtedly a circumstance which will be important as evidence. A Court will
generally be more easily satisfied of the murderous intention of an assailant who has
fractured a man's skull, than of one who has only caused a slight contusion. But the
proof might be complete. To take examples which are universally known ;—Harley
was laid up more than twenty days by the wound which he received from Guiscard ;
the scratch which Damien gave to Louis the Fifteenth was so slight that it was followed
by no feverish symptoms. Yet it will be allowed that it would be absurd to make a
distinction between the two assassins on this ground.

We propose that when bodily hurt is inflicted by way of torture the punishment shall
be very severe. In England, happily, such a provision would be unnecessary. But

---

* Locré Legislation de France. Vol. 30, page 362.
† Pajllet Manuel de droit Français. Note on Clause 309 of the Penal Code.

the execrable cruelties which are committed by robbers in this country for the purpose of extorting property, or information relating to property, render it absolutely necessary here. We propose that in such cases, if the hurt inflicted be what we have designated as *grievous*, the offender shall be punished with transportation for life, or with imprisonment for a term which may extend to life, and which shall not be less than seven years. Where the hurt is not grievous, we propose that the imprisonment shall be for a term of not more than fourteen years, nor less than one year.

Bodily hurt may be inflicted by means the use of which generally indicates great malignity. A blow with the fist may cause as much pain, and produce as lasting injury, as laceration with a knife, or branding with a hot iron. But it will scarcely be disputed that, in the vast majority of cases, the offender who has used a knife, or a hot iron, for the purpose of wreaking his hatred, is a far worse and more dangerous member of society than he who has only used his fist. It appears to us that many hurts which would not, according to our classification, be designated as grievous, ought yet, on account of the mode in which they are inflicted, to be punished more severely than many grievous hurts. We propose, therefore, that where bodily hurt is voluntarily caused by means of any sharp instrument, of fire, of any heated substance, of any corrosive substance, of any explosive substance, of any poison internal or external, or of any animal, the maximum of imprisonment may be increased, in cases of grievous bodily hurt to fourteen years, in other cases to three years.

In cases where bodily hurt is voluntarily caused on grave and sudden provocation, we propose to mitigate the punishment. This mitigation is common to cases of hurt, and of grievous hurt. But the voluntary causing of grievous hurt on great and sudden provocation will still be punishable more severely than the voluntary causing of hurt not grievous, on grave and sudden provocation. The provisions which we propose on this subject are framed on the same principles on which we have framed the law of manslaughter, and may be defended by the same arguments by which the law of manslaughter is defended.

Hitherto we have been considering cases in which hurt has been caused voluntarily. But hurt may be caused involuntarily, yet culpably. There may have been no design to cause hurt, no expectation that hurt would be caused. Yet there may have been a want of due care not to cause hurt. For these cases of the involuntary yet culpable infliction of bodily hurt, we have provided rules which bear a close analogy to those which we have provided for cases of involuntary culpable homicide.

The provision contained in Clause 329 bears, it will be seen, a close analogy to those contained in Clauses 308 and 309. We have provided under the head of assault for cases in which an assault is committed in an attempt to cause grievous bodily hurt. But there may be most malignant and atrocious attempts to cause grievous bodily hurt without any assault. For example, Z is directed to use a lotion for his eyes. A substitutes for that lotion a corrosive substance intending that it may destroy Z's eyesight. Again : A makes up a letter addressed to Z, and sends it to the post office, having placed a strongly explosive substance under the seal, intending that the explosion may seriously injure Z. These are not assaults. Yet they are evidently acts which deserve severe punishment, and that punishment is provided by Clause 329.

By wrongful restraint we mean the keeping a man out of a place where he wishes to be and has a right to be. Wrongful confinement, which is a form of wrongful restraint, is the keeping a man within limits out of which he wishes to go, and has a right to go.

The offence of wrongful restraint, when it does not amount to wrongful confinement, and when it is not accompanied with violence, or with the causing of bodily hurt, is seldom a serious offence, and we propose, therefore, to visit it with a light punishment.

The offence of wrongful confinement may be also a slight offence. But, when attended by aggravating circumstances, it may be one of the most serious that can be committed.

One aggravating circumstance is the duration of the confinement. Confinement for a quarter of an hour may sometimes be a mere frolic, which would deserve only a nominal punishment, which, indeed, might be so harmless as not to amount to an offence. (See Clause 73.) But wrongful confinement continued during many days will always be a most serious offence. We have attempted to frame the law on this subject in such a manner as to give the offender a strong motive for abridging the detention of his prisoner. Another aggravating circumstance is the circumstance that the offender persists in wrongfully confining a person notwithstanding an order issued by a competent authority for the liberation, or production of that person. The mode in which these orders are to be issued will be set forth in the Code of Procedure. A third aggravating circumstance is the circumstance that the offender uses criminal confinement for purposes of extortion. For all these aggravated forms of wrongful confinement we have provided severe punishments.

We have also provided a separate punishment for a person, who, while detaining another in wrongful confinement, omits to supply his prisoner with every thing necessary to health, ease, and comfort. The effect of this provision is that a person who wrongfully confines another will be answerable for any bodily hurt which he may cause by wrongfully omitting so to supply his prisoner.

We have found great difficulty in giving a definition of assault, and are by no means satisfied with that which we now offer. As, however, it at present appears to us to include all that we mean to include, and to exclude all that we mean to exclude, we have adopted it in spite of the objections which we feel to its harsh and quaint phraseology. We have adopted it with the less scruple, because we trust that the illustrations will render every part of it intelligible to an attentive reader.

A large proportion of the acts which we have designated as assaults will be offences falling under the heads of hurt and restraint. Thus, a stab with a knife is an offence falling under the head of hurt, and it is also an assault. The seizing a man by the collar, and thus preventing him from proceeding on his way, is unlawful restraint, and is also an assault. But there will be many assaults, which it is absolutely necessary to punish, yet which cause neither bodily hurt, nor unlawful restraint. A man who impertinently puts his arm round a lady's waist, who aims a severe stroke at a person with a horsewhip, who maliciously throws a stone at a person, squirts dirty water over a person, or sets a dog at a person, may cause no hurt and no restraint, yet it is evident that such acts ought to be prevented.

The ordinary punishment which we propose for assault is slight. But we propose to punish assaults which are committed in attempting murder with transportation for life, or with imprisonment for a term which may extend to life, and which cannot be less than seven years. We have also provided severe punishments for assault, when it is committed in an attempt to commit any grave offence against the person, when it is committed with the intention of dishonouring the sufferer, or when it is an outrage offered to female modesty.

The offence of kidnapping is sometimes committed by means of assault, and is sometimes attended with restraint. But this will not always be the case. A child, for example, who is decoyed from its guardians, who soon forgets its home, and who consents to remain with the kidnapper cannot be said to have been assaulted, or restrained. A labourer who has been induced to embark on board of a ship by false assurances that he shall be taken to a country where he shall have good wages, but whom the captain of the ship intends to sell for a slave, has not as yet been either assaulted, or restrained.

The crime of kidnapping consists, according to our definition of it, in conveying a person without his consent, or the consent of some person legally authorized to consent on his behalf, or with such consent obtained by deception, out of the protection of the law, or of those whom the law has appointed his guardians.

This offence may be committed on a child by removing that child out of the keeping of its lawful guardian or guardians. On a grown man it can only be committed by conveying him beyond the limits of the Company's territories, or by receiving him on board of a ship for that purpose.

The carrying of a grown up person by force from one place within the Company's territories to another, and the enslaving him within the Company's territories, are offences sufficiently provided for under the heads of restraint and confinement.

The enticing a grown up person by false promises to go from one place in the Company's territories to another place also within those territories may be a subject for a civil action, and, under certain circumstances, for a criminal prosecution ; but it does not appear to us to come properly under the head of kidnapping.

We propose to make the punishment of kidnapping peculiarly severe, when it is committed with murderous intentions, as in the case of those subjects of the Company who were lately carried into the Jynteah country for purposes of human sacrifice.

We also propose to enhance the punishment of kidnapping in cases in which it is committed with the intention of inflicting grievous bodily harm on the person kidnapped, or of reducing that person to slavery, and when it is committed for purposes of rape, or of unnatural lust.

We have placed under this head a provision for punishing persons who export labourers by sea from the Company's territories, in contravention of the Act recently passed by Government on that subject.

The provisions which we propose on the subject of rape do not appear to require any remark.

Clauses 361 and 362 relate to an odious class of offences respecting which it is desirable that as little as possible should be said. We leave without comment to the judgment of His Lordship in Council the two Clauses which we have provided for these offences. We are unwilling to insert, either in the text, or in the notes, any thing which could give rise to public discussion on this revolting subject; as we are decidedly of opinion that the injury which would be done to the morals of the community by such discussion would far more than compensate for any benefits which might be derived from legislative measures framed with the greatest precision.

NOTE N.

ON THE CHAPTER OF OFFENCES AGAINST PROPERTY.

There is such a mutual relation between the different parts of the law that those parts must all attain perfection together. That portion, be it what it may, which is selected to be first put into the form of a Code, with whatever clearness and precision it may be expressed and arranged, must necessarily partake to a considerable extent of the uncertainty and obscurity in which other portions are still left.

This observation applies with peculiar force to that important portion of the Penal Code which we now propose to consider. The offences defined in this Chapter are made punishable on the ground that they are violations of the right of property. But the right of property is itself the creature of the law. It is evident, therefore, that if the substantive civil law touching this right be imperfect or obscure, the penal law which is auxiliary to that substantive law, and of which the object is to add a sanction to that substantive law, must partake of the imperfection or obscurity. It is impossible for us to be certain that we have made proper penal provisions for violations of civil rights till we have a complete knowledge of all civil rights ; and this we cannot have while the law respecting those rights is either obscure or unsettled. As the present state of the civil law causes perplexity to the legislator in framing the Penal Code, so it will occasionally cause perplexity to the Judges in administering that Code. If it be matter of doubt what things are the subjects of a certain right, in whom that right resides, and to what that right extends, it must also be matter of doubt whether that right has, or has not been violated.

For example, A, without Z's permission, shoots snipes on Z's ground, and carries them away : here, if the law of civil rights grants the property in such birds to any person who can catch them, A has not, by killing them and carrying them away, invaded Z's right of property. If, on the other hand, the law of civil right declares such birds the property of the person on whose lands they are, A has invaded Z's right of property. If it be matter of doubt what the state of the civil law on the subject actually is, it must also be matter of doubt whether A has wronged Z, or not.

By the English law* pigeons, while they frequent a dove-cote, are the property of the owner of the dove-cote. By the Roman law† they were not so. By the French law‡ they are his property at one time of the year, and not his property at another. Here it is evident that the taking of such a pigeon, which would in England be a violation of the right of property, would be none in a country governed by the Roman law, and that, in France, it would depend on the time of the year whether it were so, or not.

A lends a horse to B. B sells the horse to Z, who buys it believing in good faith that B has a right to sell it. A sees the horse feeding. He mounts it, and rides away with it. Here, if the law of civil rights provides that a thing sold by one who has no right to sell it shall nevertheless be the property of a *bona fide* purchaser, A has invaded Z's right of property. If, on the other hand, A's right is not affected by what has passed between B and Z, A does not commit an infraction of Z's right of property. If it be doubtful whether the right to the horse be in A or in Z, it must also be doubtful whether A has or has not committed an infraction of Z's right.

A path running across a field which belongs to Z has, during three years, been used as a public way. A, in spite of a prohibition from Z, uses it as such. Here, if, by the civil law, an usage of three years is sufficient to create a right of way, A has committed no infraction of Z's right. But if a prescription of more than three years, or an express grant, be necessary to create a right of way, A has committed an infraction of Z's right of property.

A discovers a mine on land occupied by him. Here, if the civil law assigns all minerals to the occupier of the land, A violates no right of property by appropriating the minerals. But if the civil law assigns all minerals to the Government, A violates the right of property by such appropriation.

The sea recedes, and leaves dry land in the immediate neighbourhood of Z's property. Z cultivates the land. A turns cattle on the land, and destroys Z's crops. Here, if the civil law assigns alluvial additions to the occupier of the nearest land, A is a wrongdoer. If it declares alluvial additions common, A is not a wrongdoer. If it assigns alluvial additions to the Government, both A and Z are wrongdoers. If it be uncertain to whom the law assigns alluvial additions, it must be also uncertain who is the wrongdoer, and whether there be any wrongdoer.

The substantive civil law, in the instances which we have given, is different in different countries, and in the same country at different times. As the substantive civil law varies, the penal law, which is added as a guard to the substantive civil law, must vary also. And while many important questions of substantive civil right are undetermined, the Courts must occasionally feel doubtful whether the provisions of the Penal Code do or do not apply to a particular case.

It would, evidently, be impossible for us to determine in the Penal Code all the momentous questions of civil right which, in the unsettled state of Indian jurisprudence, will admit of dispute. We have, indeed, ventured to take for granted in our illustrations many things which properly belong to the domain of the civil law, because, without doing so, it would have been impossible for us to explain our meaning. But we have, to the best of our judgment, avoided questions respecting which, even in the present state of Indian jurisprudence, much doubt could exist. And in the text of the law we have, as closely as was possible, confined ourselves to what is in strictness the duty of persons engaged in framing a Penal Code. We have provided punishments for the infraction of rights, without determining in whom those rights vest, or to what those rights extend. We are inclined to hope that, even if the Penal Code should come into operation before the Code of civil rights has been framed, the number of cases in which the want of a Code of civil rights would occasion perplexity to the criminal tribunals will bear but a very small proportion to those in which no such perplexity will exist.

All the violations of the rights of property which we propose to make punishable, by this chapter, fall under one or more of the following heads:

1. Theft.
2. Extortion.
3. Robbery.

* Blackstone, Book II. Chap. 25.
† Columbarum fera natura est, nec ad rem pertinet, quod ex consuetudine evolare et revolare solent. Inst. Lib. II. Tit. 1.
‡ Paillet Manuel de Droit Francais.

4. The criminal misappropriation of property not in possession.
5. Criminal breach of trust.
6. The receiving of stolen property.
7. Cheating.
8. Fraudulent bankruptcy.
9. Mischief.
10. Criminal trespass.

All these offences resemble each other in this, that they cause, or have some tendency, directly or indirectly, to cause some party not to have such a dominion over property as that party is entitled by law to have.

The first great line which divides these offences may be easily traced. Some of them merely prevent, or disturb the enjoyment of property by one who has a right to it. Others transfer property to one who has no right to it. Some merely cause injury to the sufferer. Others, by means of wrongful loss to the sufferer, cause wrongful gain to some other party. The latter class of offences are designated in this Code as fraudulent. (See Clause 16.)

Every offence against property may be fraudulently committed. But theft, extortion, robbery, the criminal misappropriation of property not in possession, criminal breach of trust, the receiving of stolen property, fraudulent bankruptcy, and cheating, must be in all cases fraudulently committed. Fraud enters into the definition of every one of these offences. But fraud does not enter into the definition of mischief, or of criminal trespass.

Theft, the criminal misappropriation of property not in possession, and criminal breach of trust, are in the great majority of cases easily distinguishable. But the distinction becomes fainter and fainter as we approach the line of demarcation, and at length the offences fade imperceptibly into each other. This indistinctness may be greatly increased by unskilful legislation. But it has its origin in the nature of things, and in the imperfection of language, and must still remain in spite of all that legislation can effect.

We believe it to be impossible to mark with precision, by any words, the circumstances which constitute possession. It is easy to put cases about which no doubt whatever exists, and about which the language of lawyers and of the multitude would be the same. It will hardly be doubted, for example, that a gentleman's watch lying on a table in his room is in his possession, though it is not in his hand, and though he may not know whether it is on his writing table, or on his dressing table. As little will it be doubted that a watch which a gentleman lost a year ago on a journey, and which he has never heard of since, is not in his possession. It will not be doubted that when a person gives a dinner, his silver forks, while in the hands of his guests, are still in his possession; and it will be as little doubted that his silver forks are not in his possession when he has deposited them with a pawnbroker as a pledge. But between these extreme cases lie many cases in which it is difficult to pronounce, with confidence, either that property is, or that it is not in a person's possession.

This difficulty, sufficiently great in itself, would, we conceive, be increased by laws which should pronounce that in a set of cases arbitrarily selected from the mass property is in the possession of some party in whose possession according to the understanding of all mankind it is not. The rule of English law respecting what is called breaking bulk is an instance of what we mean. A person who has entrusted a hamper of wine to another to carry to a great distance is not in possession of that hamper of wine. But if the person in trust opens the hamper and takes out a bottle, the possession, according to the English law books, forthwith flies back to the distant owner. Mr. Livingston has laid down a rule of a similar kind, the effect of which, if we understand it rightly, is to annul the whole law of theft as he has framed it, and indeed to render it impossible that theft can be committed in Louisiana. Theft is defined by him to be " the fraudulently " taking of corporal personal property having some assignable value, and belonging to " another, from his possession and without his assent." But in a subsequent clause he says that " neither the ownership nor the legal possession of property is changed by " theft alone, without the circumstances required in such case by the Civil Code, in " order to produce a change of property; therefore, stolen goods, if fraudulently taken " from the thief, are stolen from the original proprietor." But, if stolen by the second thief from the original proprietor, they must, according to Mr. Livingston's definition of theft, be taken by the second thief out of the possession of the original proprietor. Therefore the first thief has left them in the possession of the original proprietor. That is to say, the first thief has not committed theft.

It will not be imagined that we refer to this inconsistency in the Code of Louisiana, for the purpose of throwing any censure on the distinguished author of that Code. To do so would be unjust, and in us especially most ungrateful, and also most imprudent. For we are by no means confident that inconsistencies quite as remarkable will not be detected in the Code which we now submit to Government. We note this error of Mr. Livingston for the purpose of shewing how dangerous it is for a legislator to attempt to escape from a difficulty by giving a technical sense to an expression which he nevertheless continues to use in a popular sense.

For the purpose of preventing any difference of opinion from arising in cases likely to occur very often, we have laid down a few rules (see Clauses 17, 18, 19) which we believe to be in accordance with the general sense of mankind as to what shall be held to constitute possession. But, in general, we leave it to the tribunals, without any direction, to determine whether particular property is at a particular time in the possession of a particular person, or not.

Much uncertainty will still remain. This we cannot prevent. But we can, as it appears to us, prevent the uncertainty from producing any practical evil. The provision contained in Clause 61 will, we think, obviate all the inconveniences which might arise from doubts as to the exact limits which separate theft from misappropriation, and from breach of trust.

The effect of that Clause will be to prevent the Judges from wasting their time and ingenuity in devising nice distinctions. If a case which is plainly theft comes before them the offender will be punished as a thief. If a case which is plainly breach of trust comes before them the offender will be punished as guilty of breach of trust. If they have to try a case which lies on the frontier, one of those thefts which are hardly distinguishable from breaches of trust, or one of those breaches of trust which are hardly distinguishable from theft, they will not trouble themselves with subtle distinctions, but, leaving it undetermined by which name the offence should be called, will proceed to determine what is infinitely of greater importance, what shall be the punishment.

In theft, as we have defined it, the object of the offender always is to take property which is in the possession of a person out of that person's possession. Nor have we admitted a single exception to this rule. In the great majority of cases our classification will coincide with the popular classification. But there are a few aggravated cases of what we designate as misappropriation and breach of trust, which bear such an affinity to theft that it may seem idle to distinguish them from thefts. And it certainly would be idle to distinguish such cases from thefts, if the distinction were made with a view to those cases alone. But, as we have a line of distinction which we think it desirable to maintain in the great majority of cases, we think it desirable also to maintain that line in the few cases in which it may separate things which are of a very similar description.

One offence which it may be thought that we ought to have placed among thefts is the pillaging of property during the interval which elapses between the time when the possessor of the property dies, and the time when it comes into the possession of some person authorized to take charge of it. This crime, in our classification, falls under the head, not of theft, but of misappropriation of property not in possession.

The ancient Roman jurists viewed it in the same light. The property taken under such circumstances, they argued, being in no person's possession, could not be taken out of any person's possession. The taking therefore was not *furtum*, but belonged to a separate head called the *crimen expilatæ hæreditatis*.* The French lawyers, however, long ago found out a legal fiction by means of which this offence was treated as theft in those parts of France where the Roman law was in force.† Mr. Livingston's definition of theft appears to us to exclude this species of offence, nor indeed do we think that it could be reached by any provision of his Code. That it ought to be punished with severity under some name or other is indisputable. By what name it should be designated may admit of some dispute. If we call it theft, we speak the popular language.

---

* Justinian Dig. Lib. XLVII. Tit. 19.   † Domat. Sup. III.

If we call it misappropriation of property not in possession, we avoid an anomaly, and maintain a line which in the great majority of cases is reasonable and convenient. On the whole we are inclined to maintain this line.

Again, a carrier who opens a letter entrusted to his charge, and takes thence a bank note, would be commonly called a thief. It is certain that his offence is not morally distinguishable from theft. Here, however, as before, we think it expedient to maintain our general rule; and we therefore designate the offence of the carrier not as theft, but as criminal breach of trust.

The illustrations which we have appended to the provisions respecting theft, the misappropriation of property not in possession, and breach of trust, will, we hope, sufficiently explain to his Lordship in Council the reasons for most of those provisions.

It may possibly be remarked that we have not, like Mr. Livingston, made it part of our definition of theft, that the property should be of some assignable value. We would therefore observe that we have not done so only because we conceive that the law, as framed by us, obtains the same end by a different road. By one of the general exceptions which we have proposed (Clause 73) it is provided that nothing shall be an offence by reason of any harm which it may cause, or be intended to cause, or be known to be likely to cause, if the whole of that harm is so slight that no person of ordinary sense and temper would complain of such harm. This provision will prevent the law of theft from being abused for the purpose of punishing those venial violations of the right of property which the common sense of mankind readily distinguishes from crimes, such as the act of a traveller who tears a twig from a hedge, of a boy who takes stones from another person's ground to throw at birds, of a servant who dips his pen in his master's ink. It does not appear to us that any further rule on this subject is necessary.

The offence of extortion is distinguished from the three offences which we have been considering by this obvious circumstance, that it is committed by the wrongful obtaining of a consent. In one single class of cases theft and extortion are in practice confounded together so inextricably, that no Judge however sagacious could discriminate between them. This class of cases therefore has, in all systems of jurisprudence with which we are acquainted, been treated as a perfectly distinct class; and we think that this arrangement, though somewhat anomalous, is strongly recommended by convenience. We have therefore made robbery a separate crime.

There can be no case of robbery which does not fall within the definition either of theft, or of extortion. But in practice it will perpetually be matter of doubt whether a particular act of robbery was a theft, or an extortion. A large proportion of robberies will be half theft, half extortion. A seizes Z, threatens to murder him, unless he delivers all his property, and begins to pull off Z's ornaments. Z in terror begs that A will take all he has, and spare his life, assists in taking off his ornaments, and delivers them to A. Here, such ornaments as A took without Z's consent are taken by theft. Those which Z delivered up from fear of death are acquired by extortion. It is by no means improbable that Z's right arm bracelet may have been obtained by theft, and left arm bracelet by extortion, that the rupees in Z's girdle may have been obtained by theft, and those in his turban by extortion. Probably in nine-tenths of the robberies which are committed something like this actually takes place, and it is probable that a few minutes later neither the robber nor the person robbed would be able to recollect in what proportions theft and extortion were mixed in the crime; nor is it at all necessary for the ends of justice that this should be ascertained. For though in general the consent of a sufferer is a circumstance which very materially modifies the character of the offence, and which ought therefore to be made known to the Courts, yet the consent which a person gives to the taking of his property by a ruffian who holds a pistol to his breast is a circumstance altogether immaterial.

His Lordship in Council will perceive that we have provided punishment of exemplary severity for that atrocious crime, which is designated in the Regulations of Bengal and Madras by the name of Dacoity. This name we have thought it convenient to retain for the purpose of denoting, not only actual gang-robbery, but the attempting to rob when such an attempt is made or aided by a gang.

The law relating to the offence of receiving stolen goods appears to require no comment.

The offence of cheating must, like that of extortion, be committed by the wrongful obtaining of a consent. The difference is that the extortioner obtains the consent by intimidation, and the cheat by deception. There is no offence in the Code with which we have found it so difficult to deal as that of cheating. It is evident that the practising of intentional deceit for purposes of gain ought sometimes to be punished. It is equally evident that it ought not always to be punished. It will hardly be disputed that a person who defrauds a banker by presenting a forged cheque, or who sells ornaments of paste as diamonds, may with propriety be made liable to severe penalties. On the other hand to punish every defendant who obtains pecuniary favours by false professions of attachment to a patron, every legacy hunter who obtains a bequest by cajoling a rich testator, every debtor who moves the compassion of his creditors by overcharged pictures of his misery, every petitioner who, in his appeals to the charitable, represents his distresses as wholly unmerited, when he knows that he has brought them on himself by intemperance and profusion, would be highly inexpedient. In fact if all the misrepresentations and exaggerations, in which men indulge for the purpose of gaining at the expense of others, were made crimes, not a day would pass in which many thousands of buyers and sellers would not incur the penalties of the law. It happens hourly that an article which is worth ten rupees is affirmed by the seller to be cheap at twelve rupees, and by the buyer to be dear at eight rupees. The seller comes down to eleven rupees, and declares that to be his last word. The buyer rises to nine, and says that he will go no higher. The seller falsely pretends that the article is unusually good of its kind, the buyer that it is unusually bad of its kind; the seller that the price is likely soon to rise, the buyer that it is likely soon to fall. Here we have deceptions practised for the sake of gain, yet no judicious legislator would punish these deceptions. A very large part of the ordinary business of life is conducted all over the world, and no where more than in India, by means of a conflict of skill, in the course of which deception to a certain extent perpetually takes place. The moralist may regret this: but the legislator sees that the result of the attempts of the buyer and seller to gain an unfair advantage over each other is that, in the vast majority of cases, articles are sold for the prices which it is desirable that they should fetch; and therefore he does not think it necessary to interfere. It is enough for him to know that all this great mass of falsehood practically produces the same effect which would be produced by truth; and that any law directed against such falsehood would in all probability be a dead letter, and would, if carried into rigorous execution, do more mischief in a month than all the lies which are told in the making of bargains throughout all the bazars of India produce in a century.

If then it be admitted that many deceptions committed for the sake of gain ought to be punished, and that many such deceptions ought not to be punished, where ought the line to run?

It appears to us that the line which we have drawn is correct in theory, that it is not more inconvenient in practice than any other line must be which can be drawn while the civil law of India remains in its present state, and that it will be unexceptionable whenever the civil law of India shall be ascertained, digested and corrected.

We propose to make it cheating to obtain property by deception in all cases where the property is fraudulently obtained, that is to say, in all cases where the intention of the person who has by deceit obtained the property was to cause a distribution of property which the law pronounces to be a wrongful distribution, and in no other case whatever. However immoral a deception may be, we do not consider it as an offence against the rights of property, if its object is only to cause a distribution of property which the law recognizes as rightful. A few examples will shew the way in which this principle will operate.

A intentionally deceives Z into a belief that he is strongly attached to Z. A thus induces Z to make a will, by which a large legacy is left to A. Here A's conduct is immoral and scandalous. But still A has a legal right on Z's death to receive the legacy. Even if the clearest proofs of A's insincerity are laid before a tribunal, even if A in open Court avows his insincerity, the will cannot, on that account, be set aside. The gain, therefore, which A obtains under Z's will is not, in the legal sense of the expression, wrongful gain. He has practised deception. He has thus caused gain to himself, and loss to others. But that gain is a gain to which the civil law declares him entitled, and which the civil law will assist him to recover if it be withheld from him. That loss is a loss with which the civil law declares that the losers must put up. A therefore has not committed the offence of cheating under our definition.

But suppose that the civil law should contain, as we think that it ought to contain, a provision declaring null a will made in favor of strangers by a testator, who erroneously believed his children to be dead. And suppose that A intentionally deceives Z into a belief that Z's only son has been lost at sea, and by this deception induces Z to make a will by which every thing is left to A. Here, the case will be different. The will being null, any property which A could obtain under that will would be property which he had no legal right so to obtain, and to which another person had a legal right. The object of A has therefore been wrongful gain to himself, attended with wrongful loss to another party. A has therefore, under our definition, been guilty of cheating.

Again, take the case which we before put of a buyer and a seller. They have told each other many untruths, but none of those untruths was such as, after the article had been delivered, and the price paid, would be held by a Civil Court to be a ground for pronouncing that either of them possessed what he had no right to possess. Though the buyer has falsely depreciated the article, yet when he takes it, and pays for it, the legal right to it is transferred to him, as well as the possession. Though the seller has falsely extolled the article, yet when he receives the price, and delivers the article, the legal right to the price passes with the possession. However censurable, in a moral point of view, the deceptions practised by both may have been, yet those deceptions were intended to produce a distribution of property strictly legal. Neither the buyer nor the seller, therefore, has been guilty of cheating. But if the seller has produced a sample of the article, and has falsely assured the buyer that the article corresponds to that sample, the case is different. If the article does not correspond to the sample, the buyer is entitled to have the purchase money back. The seller has taken and kept the purchase money without having a legal right to take or keep it, and it may be recovered from him by a legal proceeding. His gain is therefore wrongful, and is attended with wrongful loss to the buyer. He is therefore guilty of cheating under the definition.

So if the seller passes off ornaments of paste on the buyer for diamonds, the price which the seller receives is a price to which he has no right, and which the buyer may recover from him by an action. Here therefore the object of the seller has been wrongful gain attended with wrongful loss to the buyer. The seller is therefore guilty of cheating.

So if the buyer, intending to acquire possession of the goods without paying for them, induces the seller by deception to take a note which the buyer knows will be dishonoured, the buyer is guilty of cheating. His object is to retain in his own possession money which he is legally bound to pay to the seller. The gain which he makes by retaining the money is wrongful gain, and is attended with wrongful loss to the seller. He is, therefore, within the definition.

Whether the principle on which this part of the law is framed be a sound principle, is a question which will be best determined by examining, first, whether our definition excludes any thing that ought to be included, and, secondly, whether it includes any thing that ought to be excluded.

It can scarcely, we think, be contended that our definition excludes any thing that ought to be included. For surely it would be unreasonable to punish, as an offence against the right of property, an act which has caused, and was intended to cause a distribution of property which the law declares to be right, and refuses to disturb. If such an act be an offence, it must be an offence on some ground distinct from the effect which it produces on the state of property. Thus if a person to whom a debt is due, thinking that he shall obtain payment more easily if he assumes the appearance of being in the public service, wears a badge of office which he has no right to wear when he goes to make his demand, he is guilty of the offence defined in Clause 150: but if he gains only what he has a legal right to possess, if he deprives the debtor only of that which the debtor has no legal right to retain, he is not a wrongdoer as respects property, inasmuch as he has only rectified a wrong distribution of property.

Indeed, it appears to us that there is the strongest objection to punishing a man for a deception, and yet allowing him to retain what he has gained by that deception. What the civil law ought to say may be doubtful. But there can be no doubt that the civil and criminal law ought to say the same thing; that the one ought not to invite, while the other repels; that the Code ought not to be divided against itself. To send a person to prison for obtaining a sum of money, and yet to suffer him to keep that sum of money, is to hold out at once motives to deter and motives to incite. Humanity requires that punishment should be the last resource, a resource only employed when no other means can be found of producing the desired effect. Penal laws clearly ought not to be made for the preventing of deception, if deception could be prevented by means of the civil Code. To tempt men, therefore, to deceive by means of the civil Code, and then to punish them for deceiving, is contrary to every sound principle.

We are, therefore, not apprehensive that we shall be thought to have granted impunity to any deception which ought to be punished as cheating.

But it is possible that our definition may be thought to include much that ought to be excluded. It certainly includes many acts which are not punishable by the law of England, or of France. We propose to punish as guilty of cheating a man who, by false representations, obtains a loan of money, not meaning to repay it; a man who, by false representations, obtains an advance of money, not meaning to perform the service, or to deliver the article for which the advance is given; a man who, by falsely pretending to have performed work for which he was hired, obtains pay to which he is not entitled.

In all these cases there is deception. In all the deceiver's object is fraudulent. He intends in all these cases to acquire or retain wrongful possession of that to which some other person has a better claim, and which that other person is entitled to recover by law. In all these cases, therefore, the object has been wrongful gain, attended with wrongful loss. In all, therefore, there has, according to our definition, been cheating. We cannot see why such acts as these should be treated as mere civil injuries,— why they should be classed with the mere non-payment of a debt, and the mere non-performance of a contract. They are infractions of a legal right effected by deliberate dishonesty. They are more pernicious than most of the acts which will be punishable under our Code. They indicate more depravity, more want of principle, more want of shame than most of the acts which will be punishable under our Code. We punish the man who gives another an angry push. We punish the man who locks another up for a morning. We punish the man who makes a sarcastic epigram on another. We punish the man who merely threatens another with outrage. And surely the man who, by premeditated deceit, enriches himself to the wrongful loss, perhaps to the utter ruin of another, is not less deserving of punishment.

That some deceptions of this sort ought to be punished, is admitted. But almost every argument which can be urged for punishing any is an argument for punishing all. The line between wilful fraudulent deception and good faith is a plain line. If there is any difficulty in applying it, that difficulty will arise, not from any defect in the line, but from the want of evidence in particular cases. But we are unable to find any reason for distinguishing one sort of fraudulent deception from another sort. The French Courts apply a test which appears to us to be very objectionable. They have decided that it is not *escroquerie* to cheat by false promises, or by exciting chimerical hopes, unless the sufferer had reasons of weight for believing that the promises were sincere, and the hopes well grounded.* This rule seems to us to be a license for deception granted to cunning against simplicity. A weak and credulous person is more easily imposed on, than a judicious and discerning person. And just so an infant is poisoned with a dose of laudanum which would hardly put a grown person to sleep; yet the poisoner is a murderer: a pregnant woman is grievously hurt by a blow which would make no impression on a boxer; yet the person who gives such a blow is punished with exemplary severity. The law in such cases enquires only whether the harm has been voluntarily caused, or no. And why should the violation by deceit of the right of property be treated differently? The deceiver proportions his artifices to the mental strength of those whom he has to deal with, just as the poisoner proportions his drugs to their bodily strength. And we see no more reason for exempting the deceiver from punishment, because he has effected his purpose by a gross fiction which could have duped only a weak person, than for exempting the poisoner from punishment because he

---

* Paillet Manuel de Droit Francois. Note on Clause 408 of the Penal Code.

has effected his purpose with a few drops of laudanum, which could have been fatal only to a young child.

Some persons may be startled at our proposing to punish, as a cheat, every man who obtains a loan by making promises of payment which he does not mean to keep. But let it be considered that a debtor, though he may have contracted his debts honestly, though it may be from absolute inability that he does not pay them, though his misfortunes may be the effect of no want of industry, or caution, on his part, is now actually liable to imprisonment. Surely it is unreasonable to detain in prison the man who, by mere misfortune, has involuntarily violated the rights of property, and to leave unpunished the man who has voluntarily, and by wilful deceit, attacked those rights, if only he is lucky enough to have money to satisfy the demands on him.

For example, A and B both borrow money from Z. A obtains it by boasting falsely of his great means, of the large remittances which he looks for from England, of his expectations from rich relations, of the promises of preferment which he has received from the Government. Having obtained it, he secretly embarks on board of a ship, intending to abscond without repaying what he has borrowed. B, on the other hand, has obtained a loan without the smallest misrepresentation, and fully purposes to repay it. The failure of an agency-house in which all his funds were placed renders it impossible for him to meet his engagements. Can it be doubted which of these two debtors ought rather to be sent to prison ? Can it be doubted that A is a proper subject of punishment, and that B is not so ? Yet at present A, if he is arrested before the ship sails, and lays down the money, enjoys entire impunity, while B may pass years in a jail. It would be improper for us here to discuss at length the question of imprisonment for debt. But it seems clear that whether it be or be not proper that a debtor, as such, should be imprisoned, a distinction ought to be made between the honest and dishonest debtor. We are inclined to believe that the indiscriminate imprisonment of all debtors would be found to be unnecessary if this distinction were made. But while they are all put on the same footing the law must be formed upon a rough calculation of the chances of dishonesty. All must be treated worse than honest debtors ought to be treated, because none are treated so severely as dishonest debtors ought to be treated. A respectable man must be imprisoned for a storm, a bad season, or a fire, because his dishonest neighbour is not liable to criminal proceedings for cheating. We are satisfied that the only way to get rid of imprisonment for debt, as debt, is to extend the penal law on the subject of cheating in a manner similar to that in which we propose to extend it.

The provisions which we have framed on the subject of fraudulent bankruptcy are necessarily imperfect, and must remain so, until the whole of that important part of the law has undergone an entire revision.

The provisions which we propose on the subject of mischief do not appear to us to require any explanation.

We have given the name of trespass to every usurpation, however slight, of dominion over property. We do not propose to make trespass, as such, an offence, except when it is committed in order to the commission of some offence injurious to some person interested in the property on which the trespass is committed, or for the purpose of causing annoyance to such a person. Even then, we propose to visit it with a light punishment, unless it be attended with aggravating circumstances.

These aggravating circumstances are of two sorts. Criminal trespass may be aggravated by the way in which it is committed. It may also be aggravated by the end for which it is committed.

There is no sort of property which it is so desirable to guard against unlawful intrusion, as the habitations in which men reside, and the buildings in which they keep their goods. The offence of trespassing on these places we designate as house-trespass, and we treat it as an aggravated form of criminal trespass.

House-trespass again may be aggravated by being committed in a surreptitious, or in a violent manner. The former aggravated form of house-trespass we designate as lurking house-trespass; the latter we designate as housebreaking. Again; house-trespass in every form may be aggravated by the time at which it is committed. Trespass of this sort has, for obvious reasons, always been considered as a more serious offence, when committed by night, than when committed by day. Thus we have four aggravated forms of that sort of criminal trespass which we designate as house-trespass, lurking house-trespass, housebreaking, lurking house-trespass by night, and house-breaking by night.

These are aggravations arising from the way in which the criminal trespass is committed. But criminal trespass may also be aggravated by the end for which it is committed. It may be committed for a frolic. It may be committed in order to a murder. It may also often happen that a criminal trespass which is venial, as respects the mode, may be of the greatest enormity as respects the end ; and that a criminal trespass committed in the most reprehensible mode, may be committed for an end of no great atrocity. Thus A may commit housebreaking by night, for the purpose of playing some idle trick on the inmates of a dwelling. B may commit simple criminal trespass by merely entering another's field for the purpose of murder, or gang robbery. Here, A commits trespass in the worse way. B commits trespass with the worse object. In our provisions we have endeavoured to combine the aggravating circumstances in such a way that each may have its due effect in settling the punishment.

NOTE O.

ON THE CHAPTER OF THE ILLEGAL PURSUIT OF LEGAL RIGHTS.

This Chapter is intended to prevent the enforcing of just claims by means which are so liable to be abused that, even when used for an honest end, they ought not to be tolerated. A creditor, for example, who has repeatedly in vain urged his debtor to pay him, finds that he has no chance of recovering his money without a troublesome and expensive law suit. He accordingly seizes on property belonging to the debtor, sells it, keeps only just as much as will satisfy the debt, and sends back the surplus to the debtor. This act is distinguished from theft by one of the broadest lines of demarcation which can be found in the Code. It is not a fraudulent act. It is intended to correct a wrongful distribution of property, to do what the Courts of law, if recourse were had to them, would order to be done. Public feeling would be shocked if such a creditor were called by the ignominious name of a thief.

At the same time it cannot be doubted that it would be most dangerous to allow men to pronounce judgment, however honestly, in their own favour, and to proceed to take property in execution, for the purpose of satisfying that judgment. A specific thing, indeed, which a man has a right to possess, it is no offence in him to take wherever he finds it. He may commit other offences in order to take it. But the mere taking is no crime at all. If Z has borrowed A's horse, and illegally refuses to return it, it is no offence at all in A to take the horse if he sees it feeding by the roadside. If A enters Z's stables in order to take it, he may commit house-trespass but he commits no theft. If A knocks Z down in order to take it, he may be guilty of assault, or of voluntarily causing bodily hurt, but he commits no robbery. This license, as it appears to us, must be confined to cases in which specific things are taken. In such cases the chance of abuse is very small. But where one thing is due, and another is taken, where a man seizes on another's furniture in satisfaction of a promissory note, or drives away another's cattle by way of paying himself for a suit of clothes, the case is very different. Honest men so often think themselves entitled to more than a court of justice would award to them, that it will be difficult to say, in cases in which the taker really has a plausible claim, and in which the value of what has been taken is not out of all proportion to the value of what is claimed, that the taker has acted dishonestly. In such cases, therefore, we think it absolutely necessary to provide a punishment for the illegal pursuit of legal rights. We observe that the French Courts have decided that the taking of property by a creditor, in good faith, for the purpose of paying himself, is not theft: and this decision seems to us, as we have said, to be well grounded. But it does not appear to us that such an act is punishable under any Clause of the French Code: and this we consider as a serious omission.

NOTE P.

ON THE CHAPTER OF THE CRIMINAL BREACH OF CONTRACTS OF SERVICE.

We agree with the great body of jurists in thinking that, in general, a mere breach of contract ought not to be an offence, but only to be the subject of a civil action.

To this general rule there are however some exceptions. Some breaches of contract are very likely to cause evil such as no damages, or only very high damages, can repair, and are also very likely to be committed by persons from whom it is exceedingly improbable that any damages can be obtained. Such breaches of contract are, we conceive, proper subjects for penal legislation.

In England it would be unnecessary to provide a punishment for a stage coachman who should, however maliciously or dishonestly, drive on, leaving behind a passenger whom he is bound to carry. The evil inflicted is seldom very serious. The country is every where well inhabited. The roads are secure. The means of conveyance can easily be obtained, and damages sufficient to compensate for any inconvenience or expense which may have been suffered can easily be recovered from the coach-proprietors. But the mode of performing journeys and the state of society in this country are widely different. It is often necessary for travellers of the upper classes, even for English ladies, ignorant perhaps of the native languages, and with young children at their breasts, to perform journeys of many miles, over uninhabited wastes, and through jungles in which it is dangerous to linger for a moment, in palanquins borne by persons of the lowest class. If, as sometimes happens, these persons should, in a solitary place, set down the palanquin and run away, it is difficult to conceive a more distressing situation than that in which their employer would be left. None but very high damages would be any reparation for such a wrong. But the class of people by whom alone such wrong is at all likely to be committed can pay no damages. The whole property of all the delinquents would probably not cover the expense of prosecuting them civilly. It therefore appears to us that breaches of contract of this description may, with strict propriety, be treated as crimes.

The law which we have framed on this subject applies, it will be perceived, only to cases in which the contract with the bearers is lawful. The traveller therefore who resorts to the highly culpable, though, we fear, too common practice of unlawfully compelling persons against their will to carry his palanquin or his baggage will not be protected by it. If they quit him, it is what they have a legal right to do, nor will they be punishable, whatever may be the consequence of their desertion.

Another species of contract which ought, we conceive, to be guarded by a penal sanction is that by which seamen are bound to their employers. The insubordination of seamen during a voyage often produces fatal consequences. Their desertion in port may cause evils, such as very large damages only could repair. But they are utterly unable to pay any damages for which it would be worth while to sue. If a ship in the Hooghly, at a critical time of the year, is compelled by the desertion of some of the crew to put off its voyage for a fortnight, it would be mere mockery to tell the owners that they may sue the runaways for damages in the Supreme Court.

We also think that persons who contract to take care of infants, of the sick, and of the helpless, lay themselves under an obligation of a very peculiar kind, and may with propriety be punished if they omit to discharge their duty. The misery and distress which their neglect may cause is such as the largest pecuniary payment would not repair. They generally come from the lower ranks of life, and would be unable to pay any thing. We therefore propose to add to this class of contracts the sanction of the penal law.

Here we are inclined to stop. We have indeed been urged to go further, and to punish as a criminal every menial servant who, before the expiration of the term for which he is hired, quits his employer. But it does not appear to us that, in the existing state of the market for that description of labour in India, good masters are in much danger of being voluntarily deserted by their menial servants, or that the loss or inconvenience occasioned by the sudden departure of a cook, a groom, a hurkaru, or a khidmutgar, would often be of a very serious description. We are greatly apprehensive that by making these petty breaches of contracts offences we should give, not protection to good masters, but means of oppression to bad ones.

NOTE Q.

ON THE CHAPTER OF OFFENCES RELATING TO MARRIAGE.

As this is a part of the law in which the English inhabitants of India are peculiarly interested, and which we have framed on principles widely different from those in which the English law on the same subject is framed, we think it necessary to offer some explanations.

The act which in the English law is designated as bigamy is always an immoral act. But it may be one of the most serious crimes that can be committed. It may be attended with circumstances which may excuse though they cannot justify it.

The married man who, by passing himself off as unmarried, induces a modest woman to become, as she thinks, his wife, but in reality his concubine, and the mother of an illegitimate issue, is guilty of one of the most cruel frauds that can be conceived. Such a man we would punish with exemplary severity.

But suppose that a person arrives from England, and pays attentions to one of his countrywomen at Calcutta. She refuses to listen to him on any other terms than those of marriage. He candidly owns that he is already married. She still presses him to go through the ceremony with her. She represents to him that if they live together without being married she shall be an outcast from society, that nobody in India knows that he has a wife, that he may very likely never fall in with his wife again, and that she is ready to take the risk. The lover accordingly agrees to go through the forms of marriage.

It cannot be disputed that there is an immense difference between these two cases. Indeed, in the second case the man can hardly be said to have injured any individual in such a manner as calls for legal punishment. For what individual has he injured? His second wife? He has acted by her consent, and at her solicitation. His first wife? He has certainly been unfaithful to his first wife. But we have no punishment for mere conjugal infidelity. He will often have injured his first wife no more than he would have done by keeping a mistress, calling that mistress by his own name, introducing her into every society as his wife, and procuring for her the consideration of a wife from all his acquaintance. The legal rights of the first wife and of her children remain unaltered. She is the wife; the second is the concubine. But suppose that the first wife has herself left her husband, and is living in adultery with another man. No individual can then be said to be injured by this second invalid marriage. The only party injured is society, which has undoubtedly a deep interest in the sacredness of the matrimonial contract, and which may therefore be justified in punishing those who go through the forms of that contract for the purpose of imposing on the public.

The law of England on the subject of bigamy appears to us to be in some cases too severe, and in others too lenient. It seems to bear a close analogy to the law of perjury. The English law on these two subjects has been framed less for the purpose of preventing people from injuring each other, than for the purpose of preventing the profanation of a religious ceremony. It therefore makes no distinction between perjury which is intended to destroy the life of the innocent, and perjury which is intended to save the innocent; between bigamy which produces the most frightful suffering to individuals, and bigamy which produces no suffering to individuals at all. We have proceeded on a different principle. While we admit that the profanation of a ceremony so important to society as that of marriage is a great evil, we cannot but think that evil immensely aggravated when the profanation is made the means of tricking an innocent woman into the most miserable of all situations. We have therefore proposed that a man who deceives a woman into believing herself his lawful wife when he knows that she is not so, and induces her, under that persuasion, to cohabit with him should be punished with great severity.

There are reasons similar, but not exactly the same, for punishing a woman who deceives a man into contracting with her a marriage which she knows to be invalid. For this offence we propose a punishment which, for reasons too obvious to require explanation, is much less severe than that which we have provided for a similar deception practised by a man on a woman.

We also propose to punish every person who, with what we have defined as a fraudulent intention, goes through the forms of a marriage which he knows to be invalid.

We do not at present propose any law for punishing a person who, without practising any deception, or intending any fraud, goes through the forms of a marriage which he knows to be invalid. The difficulty of framing such a law in this country is great. To make all classes subject to one law would, evidently, be impossible. If the law be made dependent on the race, birth-place, or religion of the offender endless perplexity would arise. Races are mixed; religion may be changed or dissembled. An East Indian, half English half Asiatic by blood, may call himself a Mahomedan, or a Hindoo; and there exists no test by which he can be convicted of deception. We by no means intend to express an opinion that these difficulties may not be got over. But we are satisfied that this part of the penal law cannot be brought to perfection till the law of marriage and divorce has been thoroughly revised.

We leave it to his Lordship in Council to consider whether, during the interval which must elapse before the necessary inquiry can be made, it might not be, on the whole, better to retain the existing law applicable to Christians in India, objectionable as that law is, than to allow absolute impunity to bigamy.

We consider whether it would be advisable to provide a punishment for adultery, and in order to enable ourselves to come to a right conclusion on this subject we collected facts and opinions from all the three Presidencies. The opinions differ widely. But as to the facts there is a remarkable agreement.

The following positions we consider as fully established: first, that the existing laws for the punishment of adultery are altogether inefficacious for the purpose of preventing injured husbands of the higher classes from taking the law into their own hands; secondly, that scarcely any native of the higher classes ever has recourse to the Courts of law in a case of adultery for redress against either his wife, or her gallant; thirdly, that the husbands who have recourse in cases of adultery to the Courts of law are generally poor men whose wives have run away, that these husbands seldom have any delicate feelings about the intrigue, but think themselves injured by the elopement, that they consider their wives as useful members of their small households, that they generally complain not of the wound given to their affections, not of the stain on their honour, but of the loss of a menial whom they cannot easily replace, and that generally their principal object is that the woman may be sent back. The fiction by which seduction is made the subject of an action in the English Courts is, it seems, the real gist of most proceedings for adultery in the Mofussil. The essence of the injury is considered by the sufferer as lying in the " per quod servitium amisit." Where the complainant does not ask to have his wife again, he generally demands to be reimbursed for the expenses of his marriage.

These things being established it seems to us that no advantage is to be expected from providing a punishment for adultery. The population seems to be divided into two classes—those whom neither the existing punishment nor any punishment which we should feel ourselves justified in proposing will satisfy, and those who consider the injury produced by adultery as one for which a pecuniary compensation will sufficiently atone. Those whose feelings of honor are painfully affected by the infidelity of their wives will not apply to the tribunals at all. Those whose feelings are less delicate will be satisfied by a payment of money. Under such circumstances we think it best to treat adultery merely as a civil injury.

Some who admit that the penal law now existing on this subject is in practice of little or no use, yet think that the Code ought to contain a provision against adultery. They think that such a provision, though inefficacious for the repressing of vice, would be creditable to the Indian Government, and that by omitting such a provision we should give a sanction to immorality. They say, and we believe with truth, that the higher class of natives consider the existing penal law on the subject as far too lenient, and are unable to understand on what principle adultery is treated with more tenderness than forgery or perjury.

These arguments have not satisfied us that adultery ought to be made punishable by law. We cannot admit that a Penal Code is by any means to be considered as a body of ethics, that the legislature ought to punish acts merely because those acts are immoral, or that because an act is not punished at all it follows that the legislature considers that act as innocent. Many things which are not punishable are morally worse than many things which are punishable. The man who treats a generous benefactor with gross ingratitude and insolence, deserves more severe reprehension than the man who aims a blow in a passion, or breaks a window in a frolic. Yet we have punishments for assault and mischief, and none for ingratitude. The rich man who refuses a mouthful of rice to save a fellow creature from death may be a far worse man than the starving wretch who snatches and devours the rice. Yet we punish the latter for theft, and we do not punish the former for hard-heartedness.

That some classes of the natives of India disapprove of the lenity with which adultery is now punished we fully believe, but this in our opinion is a strong argument against punishing adultery at all. There are only two courses which in our opinion can properly be followed with respect to this and other great immoralities. They ought to be punished very severely, or they ought not to be punished at all. The circumstance that they are left altogether unpunished does not prove that the Legislature does not regard them with disapprobation. But when they are made punishable the degree of severity of the punishment will always be considered as indicating the degree of disapprobation with which the Legislature regards them. We have no doubt that the natives would be far less shocked by the total silence of the penal law touching adultery than by seeing an adulterer sent to prison for a few months while a coiner is imprisoned for fourteen years.

An example will illustrate our meaning. We have determined not to make it penal in a wealthy man to let a fellow creature whose life he could save by disbursing a few pice, die at his feet of hunger. No rational person, we are convinced, will suppose because we have framed the law thus that we do not hold such inhumanity in detestation. But if we had proposed to punish such inhumanity with a fine not exceeding fifty rupees we should have offered a gross outrage to the feelings of mankind. That we do not think a certain act a proper subject for penal legislation does not prove that we do not think that act a great crime. But that thinking it a proper subject for penal legislation we propose to visit it with a slight penalty does seem to indicate that we do not think it a great crime.

No body proposes that adultery should be punished with a severity at all proportioned to the misery which it produces in cases where there is strong affection and a quick sensibility to family honour. We apprehend that among the higher classes in this country nothing short of death would be considered as an expiation for such a wrong. In such a state of society we think it far better that the law should inflict no punishment than that it should inflict a punishment which would be regarded as absurdly and immorally lenient.

There is yet another consideration which we cannot wholly leave out of sight. Though we well know that the dearest interests of the human race are closely connected with the chastity of women, and the sacredness of the nuptial contract, we cannot but feel that there are some peculiarities in the state of society in this country which may well lead a humane man to pause before he determines to punish the infidelity of wives. The condition of the women of this country is unhappily very different from that of the women of England and France. They are married while still children. They are often neglected for other wives while still young. They share the attentions of a husband with several rivals. To make laws for punishing the inconstancy of the wife while the law admits the privilege of the husband to fill his zenana with women, is a course which we are most reluctant to adopt. We are not so visionary as to think of attacking by law an evil so deeply rooted in the manners of the people of this country as polygamy. We leave it to the slow, but we trust the certain operation of education and of time. But while it exists, while it continues to produce its never failing effects on the happiness and respectability of women, we are not inclined to throw into a scale already too much depressed the additional weight of the penal law. We have given the reasons which lead us to believe that any enactment on this subject would be nugatory. And we are inclined to think that if not nugatory it would be oppressive. It would strengthen hands already too strong. It would weaken a class already too weak. It will be time enough to guard the matrimonial contract by penal sanctions when that contract becomes just, reasonable, and mutually beneficial.

NOTE R.

ON THE CHAPTER OF DEFAMATION.

The essence of the offence of defamation consists in its tendency to cause that description of pain which is felt by a person who knows himself to be the object of the unfavorable sentiments of his fellow creatures, and those inconveniences to which a person who is the object of such unfavorable sentiments is exposed.

According to the theory of the criminal law of England, the essence of the crime of private libel consists in its tendency to provoke breach of the peace: and, though this doctrine has not, in practice, been followed out to all the startling consequences to which it would legitimately lead, it has not failed to produce considerable inconvenience.

It appears to us evident that between the offence of defaming, and the offence of provoking to a breach of the peace, there is a distinction as broad as that which separates theft and murder. Defamatory imputations of the worst kind may have no tendency to cause acts of violence. Words which convey no discreditable imputation whatever may have that tendency in the highest degree. Even in cases where defamation has a tendency to cause acts of violence, the heinousness of the defamation considered as defamation is by no means proportioned to its tendency to cause such acts : nay, circumstances which are great aggravations of the offence, considered as defamation, may be great mitigations of the same offence, considered as a provocation to a breach of the peace. A scurrilous satire against a friendless woman, published by a person who carefully conceals his name, would be defamation in one of its most odious forms. But it would be only by a legal fiction that the satirist could be said to provoke a breach of the peace. On the other hand, an imputation on the courage of an officer, contained in a private letter, meant to be seen only by that officer and two or three other persons, might, considered as defamation, be a very venial offence. But such an imputation would have an obvious tendency to cause a serious breach of the peace.

On these grounds we have determined to propose that defamation shall be made an offence, without any reference to its tendency to cause acts of illegal violence.

We considered whether it would be advisable to make a distinction between the different modes in which defamatory imputations may be conveyed : and we came to the conclusion that it would not be advisable to make any such distinction.

By the English law, defamation is a crime only when it is committed by writing, printing, engraving, or some similar process. Spoken works reflecting on private character, however atrocious may be the imputations which those words convey, however numerous may be the assembly before which such words are uttered, furnish ground only for a civil action. Herein the English law is scarcely consistent with itself. For if defamation be punished on account of its tendency to cause breach of the peace, spoken defamation ought to be punished even more severely than written defamation, as having that tendency in a higher degree. A person who reads in a pamphlet a calumnious reflection on himself, or on some one for whom he is interested, is less likely to take a violent revenge than a person who hears the same calumnious reflection uttered. Public men who have, by long habit, become callous to slander and abuse in a printed form, often shew acute sensibility to imputations thrown on them to their faces. Indeed defamatory words spoken in the presence of the person who is the object of them, necessarily have more of the character of a personal affront, and are therefore more likely to cause breach of the peace, than any printed libel.

The distinction which the English criminal law makes between written and spoken defamation is generally defended on the ground that written defamation is likely to be more widely spread and to be more permanent than spoken defamation. These considerations do not appear to us to be entitled to much weight. In the first place it is by no means necessarily the fact that written defamation is more extensively circulated than spoken defamation. Written defamation may be contained in a letter intended for a single eye. Spoken defamation may be heard by an assembly of many thousands. It seems to us most unreasonable that it should be penal to say in a private letter that a man is dissipated, and not penal to stand up at the town-hall, and there, before the whole society of Calcutta, falsely to accuse him of poisoning his father.

In the second place it is not necessarily the fact that the harm caused by defamation is proportioned to the extent to which the defamation is circulated. Some slanders,— and those slanders of a most malignant kind,—can produce harm only while confident to a very small circle, and would be at once refuted if they were published. A malignant whisper addressed to a single hearer, and meant to go no further, may indicate greater depravity, may cause more intense misery, and may deserve more severe punishment than a satire which has run through twenty editions. A person, for example, who, in private conversation, should infuse into the mind of a husband suspicions of the fidelity of a virtuous wife, might be a defamer of a far worse description than one who should insert the lady's name in a printed lampoon.

It must be allowed that, in general, a printed story is likely to live longer than a story which is only circulated in conversation. But on the other hand it is far easier for a calumniated person to clear his character, either by argument, or by legal proceedings, from a charge fixed in a printed form, than from a shifting rumour which nobody repeats exactly as he heard it. In general, we believe, a man would rather see in a newspaper a story discreditable to him which he had the means of refuting than know that such a story, though not published, was current in society.

On the whole we are so far from being able to discover any reason for exempting any mode of defamation from all punishment, that we have not even thought it right to provide different degrees of punishment for different modes of defamation. We do not conceive that on this subject any general rule can, with propriety, be laid down. We have therefore thought it best to leave to the Courts the business of apportioning punishment with due regard to the circumstances of every case.

We have thought it necessary, under the peculiar circumstances of this country, to lay down for the guidance of the Courts a rule which, if we were legislating for a population among whom there was an uniform standard of morality, and honor, might appear superfluous. India is inhabited by races which differ widely from each other in manners, tastes, and religious opinions. Practices which are regarded as innocent by one large portion of society, excite the horror of another large portion. A Hindoo would be driven to despair if he knew that he was believed by persons of his own race to have done something, which a Christian or a Mussulman would consider as indifferent or as laudable. Where such diversities of opinion exist, that part of the law which is intended to prevent pain arising from opinion ought to be sufficiently flexible to suit those diversities. We have, therefore, directed the Judge not to decide the question whether an imputation be or be not defamatory, by reference to any particular standard, however correct, of honor, of morality, or of taste; but to extend an impartial protection to opinions which he regards as erroneous, and to feelings with which he has no sympathy.

There are nine excepted cases, (see Clauses from 470 to 478 inclusive,) in which we propose to tolerate imputations prejudicial to character.

The exception which stands first in order will probably be thought by many persons objectionable. It is opposed to the rules of the English criminal law. It goes, we fear, beyond what even the boldest reformers of English law have proposed. It is at variance with the provisions of the French Code, and with the sentiments of the most distinguished French jurists. It is at variance also with the provisions of the Code of Louisiana. It is, therefore, with some diffidence that we venture to lay before the Governor General in Council the results of a long and anxious consideration of this question.

The question is whether the truth of an imputation prejudicial to character should, in all cases, exempt the author of that imputation from punishment as a defamer. We conceive that it ought to exempt him.

It will hardly be disputed, even by those who dissent from us on this point, that there is a marked distinction between true and false imputations, as respects both the degree of malignity which they indicate, and the degree of mischief which they produce. The accusing a man of what he has not done implies, in a vast majority of cases, greater depravity than the accusing him of what he has done. The pain which a false imputation gives to the person who is the object of it, is clear, uncompensated evil. There is no set-off whatever. The pain which a true imputation gives to the person who is the object of it is in itself an evil, and, therefore, ought not to be wantonly inflicted. But there is often some counterbalancing good. A true imputation may produce a wholesome effect on the person who has, by his misconduct, exposed himself to it. It may deter others from imitating his example. It may set them on their guard against his bad designs.

Not only do true imputations generally produce some good to counterbalance the evil caused by them, but in many cases this counterbalancing good appears to us greatly to preponderate. However skilfully penal laws may be framed, however vigorously they may be carried into execution, many bad practices will always be out of reach of the tribunals. The state of society would be deplorable, if public opinion did not repress much that legislators are compelled to tolerate. The wisest legislators have felt this, and have assigned it as a reason for not visiting certain acts with legal punishment that those acts will be sufficiently punished by general disapprobation. It seems inconsistent and unwise to rely on the public opinion in certain cases as a valuable auxiliary to the law, and at the same time to treat the expression of that opinion in those very cases as a crime.

It is easy to put cases about which there could scarcely be any difference of opinion. A person who has been guilty of gross acts of swindling, at the Cape, comes to Calcutta, and proposes to set up a house of agency. A person who has been forced to fly from England, on account of his infamous vices, repairs to India, opens a school, and exerts himself to obtain pupils. A captain of a ship induces natives to emigrate, by promising to convey them to a country where they will have large wages, and little work. He takes them to a foreign colony where they are treated like slaves, and returns to India to hold out similar temptations to others. A man introduces a common prostitute, as his wife, into the society of all the most respectable ladies of the Presidency. A person in a high station is in the habit of encouraging ruinous play among young servants of the Company. In all these cases, and in many others which might be named, we conceive that a writer who publishes the truth renders a great service to the public, and cannot, without a violation of every sound principle, be treated as a criminal.

There are undoubtedly many cases in which the spreading of true reports prejudicial to the character of an individual would hurt the feelings of that individual, without producing compensating advantage in any other quarter. The proclaiming to the world that a man keeps a mistress, that he is too much addicted to wine, that he is penurious in his house-keeping, that he is slovenly in his person, the raking up of ridiculous and degrading stories about the youthful indiscretions of a man who has long lived irreproachably as a husband and a father, and who has attained some post which requires gravity, and even sanctity of character, can seldom or never produce any good to the public sufficient to compensate for the pain given to the person attacked, and to those who are connected with him. Yet we greatly doubt whether, where the imputations are true, it be advisable to inflict on the propagators of such miserable scandal any legal punishment in addition to that general aversion and contempt with which their calling and their persons are every where regarded. Even in such cases the question whether the imputation be true or false is not an unimportant question. Those who would not allow truth to be, in such cases, a justification, would admit that it ought generally to be a mitigating circumstance. Indeed, we find it impossible to imagine any case in which we should punish a man who told no more than the truth respecting another, as severely as if what he told had been a lie invented to blast the reputation of that other.

These two propositions then we consider as established;—first, that in some cases of prosecution for defamation the truth of the imputations alleged to be defamatory ought to be a justification;—secondly, that in the vast majority of such cases, if not in all, truth, if it be not a justification, ought to be a mitigation.

From these two propositions a third proposition necessarily follows;—that in all cases of prosecution for defamation, if the defendant avers that the imputations complained of as defamatory are true, the Court ought to go into the question of the truth of those imputations.

This ought to be done, not only in justice to the public, and to the defendant, but in justice to the innocent complainant. It must not be forgotten that one of the most important ends which a person proposes to himself in prosecuting a slanderer is the refuting of the slander. He generally considers the punishment of the offender as a secondary object; and, when there is no circumstance of peculiar aggravation in the case, is often willing to stay proceedings after obtaining a retraction and apology. To clear his fame is his first object. It is, we conceive, an object for the attaining of which he is entitled to the assistance of the law. But it is an object which cannot be attained unless the Courts go into the question of truth.

The effect of a rule excluding evidence of the truth is to put on a par descriptions of persons between whom it is desirable to make the widest distinction. The public spirited man who warns the mercantile community against a notorious cheat, or advises families not to admit into their intimacy a practised seducer of innocence, is placed on the same footing with the slanderer who invents the most infamous falsehoods against persons of the purest character. On the other hand, a man who has, without the slightest reason, been held up to the world as a seducer or a swindler, is placed in exactly the same situation with one who well deserves those disgraceful names. So defective is the investigation that it leaves a suspicion lying on the most innocent, and no more than a suspicion lying on the most guilty.

We therefore think that in all cases of prosecution for defamation the Courts ought to allow the question of truth to be gone into. But if in all cases the Courts allow the question of truth to be gone into, we are satisfied that no respectable person will venture to institute a prosecution for defamation in a case in which he knows that the truth of the defamatory matter is likely to be proved. He will feel that by prosecuting he should injure his own character far more deeply than any libeller can do. However disagreeable it may be to his feelings that a discreditable story concerning him should be repeated in society, and should furnish paragraphs for the newspapers, it must be much more disagreeable that such a story should be proved, in open Court, by legal evidence. By prosecuting he turns what was at most a strong suspicion into an absolute certainty. While he forbears to prosecute, many people will probably disbelieve the scandalous report: many will doubt about its truth. The mere circumstance that he abstans from prosecuting is no proof of guilt. It is notorious that slanders are often passed by with silent contempt by those who are the objects of them. Indeed, in a country where the press is free, a man whose station exposes him to remark would have nothing to do but to prosecute, if he should institute legal proceedings every time that he might be calumniated.

It seems to us therefore certain that a man on whose character imputations have been thrown which can be proved to be true will, if he possess ordinary prudence, and ordinary sensibility, abstain from having recourse to a Court of Law, which will fully investigate the truth of those imputations. By having recourse to a Court of law he would show that he belonged to a class of persons who are the last that a legislator would wish to favor, to that class of persons in whom the sense of shame is weak, and the malicious passions strong, and who are content to incur dishonour for the chance of obtaining revenge.

Being therefore of opinion that, in all cases of prosecution for defamation, evidence of the truth of the imputations alleged to be defamatory ought to be received, and being of opinion that practically there is no difference between receiving evidence of truth and allowing truth to be a justification, we have thought it advisable to provide, expressly, that truth shall always be a justification. By framing the law thus we have not in the smallest degree diminished the real security of private character, or the real risk of detraction. We have merely made the language of the Code correspond with its virtual operation.

As we are satisfied that no practical mischief will be produced by the rule which we have proposed, we think that its perfect simplicity and certainty are strong reasons for adopting it.

If it be not adopted it will be necessary to take one of two courses; either to provide that truth shall in no case be a justification, or to provide that truth shall be a justification in some cases, and not in others. To the former course we feel, for reasons which we have already assigned, insurmountable objections. The effect of such a state of the law would be that eminent public services would often be treated as crimes. If the latter course be taken, we are convinced that it would be found impossible to draw any line approaching to accuracy. We are convinced that it would be necessary to leave to the Judges an almost boundless discretion, a discretion which no two Judges would exercise in the same manner.

It has been suggested to us, from quarters entitled to great respect, that it would be a preferable course to admit in every case the truth of matter alleged to be defamatory to be given in evidence, for the purpose of proving that the accused person had not acted maliciously ; but not to allow the proof of the truth to be a justification if it should appear that reputation had been maliciously assailed.

If a provision of this kind were adopted it would, for the reasons which we have already given; be in practice nugatory. For no respectable person would prosecute the author of an imputation which could be proved to be true. And we take it for granted that the law of procedure will not be framed in so cruel and unreasonable a manner as to permit a prosecution for defamation to be instituted in opposition to the wishes of the person defamed. Such a power of prosecution would scarcely ever be used by a friend of the person defamed: it would never be used by a judicious friend : and it would be a most formidable weapon in the hands of a malignant enemy.

But if the provision which we are considering were not certain to be in practice nugatory, we should think it a highly objectionable provision. When an act is of such a description that it would be better that it should not be done, it is quite proper to look at the motives and intentions of the doer for the purpose of deciding whether he shall be punished or not. But when an act which is really useful to society,—an act of a sort which it is desirable to encourage, has been done, it is absurd to inquire into the motives of the doer for the purpose of punishing him if it shall appear that his motives were bad.

If A kills Z it is proper to inquire whether the killing was malicious: for killing is *prima facie* a bad act. But if A saves Z's life no tribunal inquires whether A did so from good feeling or from malice to some person who was bound to pay Z an annuity. For it is better that human life should be saved from malice than not at all. If A sets on fire a quantity of cotton belonging to Z, it is proper to inquire whether A acted maliciously. For the destruction of valuable property by fire is *prima facie* a bad act. But if Z's cotton is burning, and A puts it out, no tribunal inquires whether A did so from good feeling, or from malice to some other dealer in cotton who, if Z's stock had been destroyed, would have been a great gainer. For the saving of valuable property from destruction is an act which it is desirable to encourage ; and it is better that such property should be saved from bad motives than that it should be suffered to perish. Since then no act ought to be made punishable on account of malicious intention, unless it be in itself an act of a kind which it is desirable to prevent, it follows that malice is not a test which can with propriety be used for the purpose of determining what true imputations on character ought to be punished, and what true imputations on character ought not to be punished. For the throwing of true imputations on character is not *prima facie* a pernicious act. It may indeed be a very pernicious act. But we are not prepared to say that in the majority of instances it is so. We are sure that it is often a great public service; and we are sure that it may be very pernicious when it is not done from malice, and that it may be a great public service when it is done from malice. It is perfectly conceivable that a person might, from no malicious feeling, but from an honest though austere and injudicious zeal for what he might consider as the interests of religion and morality, drag before the public frailties which it would be far better to leave in obscurity. It is also perfectly conceivable that a person who has been concerned in some odious league of villainy and has quarrelled with his accomplices, may, from vindictive feelings, publish the history of their proceedings, and may by doing so render a great service to society. Suppose that a knot of sharpers lives by seducing young men to the gaming table and pillaging them to their last rupee. Suppose that one of these knaves, thinking himself ill-used in the division of the plunder, should revenge himself by printing an account of the transactions in which he has been concerned. He is prosecuted by the rest of the gang for defamation. He proves that every word in his account is true. But it is admitted that his only motives for publishing it were rancorous hatred and disappointed rapacity. It would surely be most unreasonable in the Court to say—" You " have told the public a truth which it greatly concerned the public to know. You have " been the saving of many promising youths. You have been the means of ridding " society of a dreadful pest. You have done in short what it was most desirable that you " should do. But as you have done this, not from public spirit, but from dislike of your " old associates, we pronounce you guilty of an offence, and condemn you to fine and " imprisonment."

It is evident that society cannot spare any portion of the services which it receives. Far from scrutinizing the motives which lead people to render such services, and punishing such services when they proceed from bad motives, all societies are in the habit of offering motives addressed to the selfish passions of bad men for the purpose of inducing those men to do what is beneficial to the mass. We offer pardons and pecuniary rewards to the worst members of the community for the purpose of inducing them to betray their accomplices in guilt. That the quarrels of rogues are the security of honest men·is an important truth which has passed into a proverb; and of that security we should to a certain extent deprive honest men if we were to make it an offence in one rogue to speak the truth about another rogue under the influence of passions excited in the course of a quarrel.

We have hitherto argued this point on the supposition that by malice is meant real malice, and not a fictitious, a constructive malice. We have the strongest objections to introducing into the Code such a kind of malice—a malice of which a person may be acquitted when it is clear that he has acted from the most deadly personal rancour, and found guilty when those who find him guilty are satisfied that he has acted only from the best feelings,—a malice which may be only the technical name for benevolence.

On these grounds, we recommend to the Governor General in Council that the first exception, as we have drawn it, be suffered to stand part of the Code.

The remaining exceptions will not require so long a defence. By Clause 471 we allow the public conduct of public functionaries to be discussed, provided that such discussion be conducted in good faith. That the advantages arising from such discussion far more than compensate for the pain which it occasionally gives, will hardly be disputed by any English statesman.

But there are public men who are not public functionaries. Persons who hold no office may yet, in this country, take a very active part in urging or opposing the adoption of measures in which the community is deeply interested. It appears clear to us that every person ought to be allowed to comment, in good faith, on the proceedings of these volunteer servants of the public, with the same freedom with which we allow him to comment on the proceedings of the official servants of the public. We have provided for this by Clause 472.

By Clause 473 we have allowed all persons freely to discuss in good faith the proceedings of Courts of law, and the characters of parties, agents, and witnesses, as connected with those proceedings. It is almost universally acknowledged that the Courts of law ought to be thrown open to the public. But the advantage of throwing them open to the public will be small indeed, if the few who are able to press their way into a Court are forbidden to report what has passed there to the vast numbers who were absent, or if those who are allowed to know what has passed are not allowed to comment on what has passed. The only reason that the whole community is not admitted to hear every trial that takes place is that it is physically impossible that they should find room; and by Clause 473 we do our best to counteract the effect of this physical impossibility.

Whether public writers ought to be allowed to publish comments on trials, while those trials are still pending, is a question which, in the present state of India, it is hardly worth while to discuss. We have not thought it necessary to insert any provision on that subject in the Chapter of offences against public justice; and such a provision, even if it were necessary, would evidently not belong to the head of defamation, for the harm done by such comments, as respects public justice, is exactly the same when the comments are laudatory as when they are abusive.

By Clause 474 we allow every person to criticise, in good faith, published books, works of art which are publicly exhibited, and other similar performances.

By Clause 475 we allow a person under whose authority others have been placed either by their own consent, or by the law, to censure, in good faith, those who are so placed under his authority, as far as regards matter to which that authority relates.

By Clause 476 we allow a person to prefer an accusation against another, in good faith, to any person who has lawful authority to restrain or punish the accused.

By Clause 477 we have excepted from the definition of defamation private communications which a person makes, in good faith, for the protection of his own interests; and by Clause 478 we have excepted private communications which a person makes in good faith for the benefit of others.

It will be observed that in the eight last exceptions we do not require that an imputation should be true. We require only that it should be made in good faith. For to require in these cases that the imputation should be true, would be to render these exceptions mere nullities. Whether a public functionary is or is not fit for his situation;—whether a person who has bestirred himself to get up a petition in favour of a public measure ought to be considered as an enlightened and public spirited citizen, or as a foolish meddler;—whether a person who has been tried for an offence was, or was not guilty;—which of two witnesses who contradicted each other on a trial ought to be believed;—whether a portrait is like;—whether a song has been well sung;—whether a book is well written;—these are questions about which honest and discerning men may hold opinions diametrically opposite: and to require a man to prove to the satisfaction of a Court of law that the opinion which he has expressed on such a question is a right opinion, is to prohibit all discussion on such questions. The same may be said of those private communications which we propose to allow. It is plainly desirable that a merchant should disclose to his partners his unfavourable opinion of the honesty of a person with whom the firm has dealings. It is desirable that a father should caution his son against marrying a woman of bad character. But if the merchant is permitted to say to his partners, if the father is permitted to say to his son, only what can be legally proved before a Court, it is evident that the permission is worth nothing.

Whether an imputation be or be not made in good faith is a question for the Courts of law. The burden of the proof will lie sometimes on the person who has made the imputation, and sometimes on the person on whom the imputation has been thrown. No general rule can be laid down. Yet scarcely any case could arise respecting which a sensible and impartial judge would feel any doubt. If, for example, a public functionary were to prosecute for defamation a writer who had described him in general terms as incapable, the Court would probably require the prosecutor to give some proof of bad faith. If the prosecutor had no such proof to offer, the defendant would be acquitted. If the prosecutor were to prove that the defendant had applied to him for money, had promised to write in his praise if the money were advanced, and had threatened to abuse him if the money were withheld, the Court would probably be of opinion that the defendant had not written in good faith, and would convict him.

On the other hand if the imputation were an imputation of some particular fact, or an imputation which, though general in form, yet implied the truth of some particular fact which, if true, might be proved, the Court would probably hold that the burden of proving good faith lay on the defendant. Thus if a person were to publish that a Collector was in the habit of receiving bribes from the zemindars of his district, and were unable to specify a single case, or to give any authority for his assertion, the Courts would probably be of opinion that the imputation had not been made in good faith.

Again: if a critic described a writer as a plagiarist, the Courts would not consider this as defamation without very strong proof of bad faith. But if it were proved that the critic had, like Lauder, interpolated passages in old books in order to bear out the charge of plagiarism, the Court would doubtless be of opinion that he had not criticised in good faith, and would convict him of defamation.

It will be necessary to provide in the Code of Procedure rules for pleading in cases of defamation, which may give to an innocent man who has been calumniated the means of clearing his character. It will be proper to provide that a defendant who is accused of defamation, and who rests his defence on the truth of the imputation alleged to be defamatory, shall be held strictly to the proof of the substance of the imputation if the imputation be particular, and shall be compelled to descend to particulars in his plea, if the imputation be general. It will not be expected that we should here go into any details respecting the law of criminal pleading. It is sufficient here to say that the importance of framing that part of the law in such a manner as to give full protection to persons whose character has been unjustly aspersed has not escaped our attention.

We may here observe that an imputation which is not defamatory may, under certain circumstances, be punishable on other grounds. Such an imputation may be intended to excite disaffection. If so, though not punishable as defamation, it will be punishable as sedition. An attack made, in good faith, on the public administration of the Governor of a Presidency will in no case be a defamation. But if the author of it designed to inflame the people against the Government, he will be liable to punishment under Clause 113.

Again, an imputation which is not defamatory may be intended to excite a mob to violence against an individual. If so the author of the imputation is punishable under Clause 94.

Again, an imputation which is not defamatory may be uttered in the hearing of the person who is the object of it for the purpose of wantonly and maliciously annoying that person. If so, it is punishable under Clause 485. There are many cases in which it is fit that unpleasant truth should be told respecting an individual. But there is no case in which it is desirable that such truth should be told in such a way that the telling of it is a gross personal outrage. A person who has detected, or thinks that he has detected a dishonest misrepresentation in a book has a right to expose it publicly. But he cannot be allowed to intrude into the presence of the author of the book, and to tell him to his face that he is a liar. A person who knows the mistress of a female school to be a woman of infamous character deserves well of society if he states what he knows. But he cannot be allowed to follow her through the streets calling her by opprobrious names, though he may be able to prove that all those names were merited. A person who brings to notice the malversation of a public functionary deserves applause. But a person who hangs a public functionary in effigy at that functionary's door, with an opprobrious label, does what cannot be permitted even though every word on the label, and every imputation which the exhibition was meant to convey, may be perfectly true.

We do not apprehend that the Clauses relating to the printers and publishers of defamatory matter require any explanation or defence.

THE END.